REGNUM STUDIES IN MISSION

Strategy Coordinator

Changing the Course of Southern Baptist Missions

REGNUM STUDIES IN MISSION

Series Preface

Regnum Studies in Mission are born from the lived experience of Christians and Christian communities in mission, especially but not solely in the fast growing churches among the poor of the world. These churches have more to tell than stories of growth. They are making significant impacts on their cultures in the cause of Christ. They are producing 'cultural products' which express the reality of Christian faith, hope and love in their societies.

Regnum Studies in Mission are the fruit often of rigorous research to the highest international standards and always of authentic Christian engagement in the transformation of people and societies. And these are for the world. The formation of Christian theology, missiology and practice in the twenty-first century will depend to a great extent on the active participation of growing churches contributing biblical and culturally appropriate expressions of Christian practice to inform World Christianity.

Series Editors

Julie C. Ma	Oxford Centre for Mission Studies, Oxford, UK
Wonsuk Ma	Oxford Centre for Mission Studies, Oxford, UK
Doug Petersen	Vanguard University, Costa Mesa, CA, USA
Terence Ranger	University of Oxford, Oxford, UK
C.B. Samuel	Emmanuel Hospital Association, Delhi, India
Chris Sugden	Anglican Mainstream, Oxford, UK

REGNUM STUDIES IN MISSION

Strategy Coordinator

Changing the Course of Southern Baptist Missions

R. Bruce Carlton

Forward by E. Coye Still, III

Copyright © R. Bruce Carlton 2010

First published 2010 by Regnum Books International

Regnum is an imprint of the Oxford Centre for Mission Studies
St. Philip and St. James Church
Woodstock Road
Oxford OX2 6HR, UK
www.ocms.ac.uk/regnum

09 08 07 06 05 04 03   8 7 6 5 4 3 2 1

The right of R. Bruce Carlton to be identified as the Author of this Work has been asserted by him in accordance with the Copyright, Designs and Patents Act 1988.

All rights reserved. No part of this publication may be reproduced, stored in a retrieval system, or transmitted, in any form or by any means, electronic, mechanical, photocopying, recording or otherwise, without the prior permission of the publisher or a license permitting restricted copying. In the UK such licenses are issued by the Copyright Licensing Agency, 90 Tottenham Court Road, London W1P 9HE.

British Library Cataloguing in Publication Data
A catalogue record for this book is available from the British Library

ISBN 978-1-506477-16-9

Typeset by RBI,

Distributed by 1517 Media in the US and Canada

Dedicated to Gloria, who has been my wife and best friend for the past 32 years

Contents

FOREWORD

I have enjoyed friendship and partnership in the gospel with Bruce Carlton in different capacities. When I served as the Strategy Coordinator for a South Asian city Bruce was my supervisor. He helped me understand what I was trying to do and how I should be doing it. Since my return to pastoral ministry in America, Bruce has been a missiological dialogue partner. In both capacities Bruce has been a "flame stoker"—fanning the flames of commitment to "make disciples of all nations."

I'm glad that Bruce has taken on the task of explaining and evaluating the development of the Non-residential Missionary (NRM) and Strategy Coordinator (SC) paradigms. He writes from three important perspectives.

Bruce writes as an insider. In Cambodia Bruce was a practitioner of what has developed into the SC approach. His work was at the wellspring of hundreds of reproducing churches. After leaving Cambodia, Bruce taught and mentored many men and women in methodologies for planting reproducing churches. Bruce has lived through the development of these paradigms as an effective practitioner.

Bruce writes as an insightful researcher. He asks important questions about the NRM, SC, and Church Planting Movement paradigms and searches for honest answers.

Finally, Bruce writes as a respecter of the relational character of missions. On the front lines of gospel advance the Spirit mediates the word through people. Grand strategies and paradigms also develop within relational contexts.

From these three perspectives Bruce helps us understand why the paradigms have developed as they have and equips us to ask key questions as we look forward.

E. Coye Still, III, Ph.D.
Senior Pastor
University Hills Baptist Church
Charlotte, North Carolina

PREFACE

Having served with the International Mission Board (IMB) since 1986, I have witnessed a variety of changes in the Board's Missiology. However, no change has dramatically altered the way Southern Baptists do missions like the Non-residential Missionary/Strategy Coordinator (NRM/SC) paradigm. In my encounters with many Southern Baptists churches and individuals, I discovered a general lack of knowledge regarding the history of this missiological paradigm. Thus, I have sought to inform Southern Baptists as well as offer an analysis of this paradigm's impact on my denomination's global missionary efforts. Having served as a strategy coordinator and a trainer of strategy coordinators, I have helped to shape the direction of this emergent paradigm. Although I bring to this analysis an insider's perspective; nonetheless, through painstaking research of a wealth of archive information and personal communications with several of the key shapers of this paradigm, I have sought to provide an objective analysis of this paradigm's impact on the IMB.

I want to extend my heartfelt thanks to Dr. Willem Saayman, my promoter at UNISA, for his patient guidance and thoughtful insights. While Dr. Saayman and I admittedly differ on various issues in missiology, I am grateful for the freedom he gave as I developed this thesis. At no time, did I feel pressured to take a specific position or pursue any specific missiological agendum. At the same time, Dr. Saayman exposed me to a wealth of missiological literature that has broadened my perspective and stimulated a hunger for lifelong learning in the field of missiological studies. My only regret is that I did not have the opportunity to learn from this scholar until now.

I also want to thank God for my wife Gloria who has been my ministry partner and strongest advocate during our thirty years of marriage. It was Gloria who persistently encouraged me to pursue this research and who lovingly assumed additional ministry and family responsibilities to enable me to complete this research.

I believe wholeheartedly in the vision of the IMB and Southern Baptists to take the good news of Jesus Christ to every tongue, tribe and nation. I dedicate the following pages to the multitude of strategy coordinators and their co-labourers around the world who share this vision and who daily pour out their lives for the sake of sharing the good news of Jesus Christ with those who have never had the opportunity to hear and respond. May we always been found faithful, and may Southern Baptists never lose their passion and vision for joining God in His great missionary effort. As God reminds us, He is not willing that any perish, but wants all to be reconciled to Him. If God is not willing that people perish, than neither should we.

This research was initially submitted as my doctoral thesis in Missiology (D.Th.) through the University of South Africa (UNISA). I have made some changes and sought to adapt the material for publication.

List of Tables

Abbreviations

CPM	Church-Planting Movement
CSI	Cooperative Services International
FEBC	Far East Broadcasting Corporation
FMB	Foreign Mission Board
GCC	Great Commission Christian
GSG	Global Strategy Group
IFMA	International Foreign Mission Association
IMB	International Mission Board
ISC	International Service Corps
NRM	Non-residential Missionary
ODI	Open Doors International
SBC	Southern Baptist Convention
SC	Strategy Coordinator
TWR	Trans World Radio
UPG	Unreached People Group
WEC	World Evangelization Crusade

Introduction

> I am convinced that we have been called into the Kingdom for such an hour as this. I believe that the richness of our heritage will enable our future to be richer still. I am persuaded that our eyes have not yet seen nor our minds yet thought the tremendous, exciting and thrilling things that God has in store for us. It is my prayer that our hearts will be opened wide enough and our spirits adventuresome enough and our wills bold enough that we will not hinder what God is trying to do through us in his world in our generation. I am confident that we will allow him to work his will among us.[1]

The Southern Baptist Convention (SBC) in 1976 adopted its Bold New Thrusts in Foreign Missions with its overarching goal of taking the gospel to all the peoples of the earth.[2] Nearly four years later, trustees elected R. Keith Parks as the Executive Director of the Foreign Mission Board (FMB) of the Convention.[3] Parks' consuming passion, throughout his tenure, was leading the board and its missionaries to have a vision and strategy for reaching the entire world with the message of Jesus Christ. The Convention's Bold New Thrusts energized this global vision and inspired the efforts in designing a global strategy.

Parks' vision led Southern Baptists to move beyond the precincts of earlier missiological paradigms, challenging Southern Baptists to be audacious and resolute in taking the gospel message to the ends of the earth. Parks believed that if Southern Baptists were going to have a genuine global strategy, such a

---

[1] R. Keith Parks, *Report to the Board* (Richmond: Southern Baptist Foreign Mission Board Accession Number 736, January 7, 1980).

[2] Baker J. Cauthen and Frank K. Means, *Advance to Bold Mission Thrust: A History of Southern Baptist Foreign Missions, 1845-1980* (Richmond: Foreign Mission Board, 1981), 319-20. These Bold New Thrusts were popularly known among Southern Baptists as Bold Mission Thrust. See Appendix B.

[3] See "Board of Trustees Minutes," (Little Rock: Southern Baptist International Mission Board, Accession Number 2530, April 7, 1997). From 1845 until 1997, the name Foreign Mission Board was used. In 1997, the organization officially became known as the International Mission Board. Throughout this paper, the term Foreign Mission Board will be used in reference to events and persons prior to June 1997 and the term International Mission Board will be used in reference to events and persons after June 1997. For explanation regarding the rationale behind the change see Rankin's article, "What's In a Name?" *The Commission* (June, 1997), 53; and "Board of Trustees Minutes" (Richmond: Southern Baptist Foreign Mission Board, Accession Number 2464, October 6, 1996).

strategy must include developing plans and methodologies for penetrating places and peoples where a traditional missionary approach was not possible.[4] Parks alluded to the possibility of a new paradigm during his first year of leadership when he expressed to the trustees, "Whatever plans we develop must give attention to all the peoples of the world – whether or not we have career missionaries residing in their countries."[5]

Concerted efforts by leaders of the FMB to transform this global evangelization vision into reality spawned a new missionary paradigm. The formation of Cooperative Services International (CSI) in 1985 and the assigning of the first non-residential missionary (NRM) in 1987 were the key Southern Baptist initiatives in this emerging paradigm. [6] CSI was the Board's initiative to reach into countries (geographical entities) that restricted access by traditional missionaries. Although China was the early focus of CSI, its mandate extended to other restricted countries as well.[7] The NRM role was the Board's initiative for evangelizing the neglected ethno-linguistic people groups of the world who were heretofore inaccessible to traditional missionaries.

At the same time, events and persons within the wider evangelical missions community profoundly influenced Southern Baptists as they embarked on developing methods to penetrate the restricted countries and neglected people groups of the world with the gospel.[8] Southern Baptist missiologists within the Board, who were the major contributors toward the development of the NRM role,[9] did not conceive this new paradigm within a historical vacuum. In fact,

---

[4] R. Keith Parks, *Report to the Board,* (Richmond,: Southern Baptist Foreign Mission Board, Accession Number 751, October 13, 1980); R. Keith Parks, *God-Given Visions Transform,* (Richmond: Southern Baptist Foreign Mission Board, Accession Number 588, September 8, 1986).

[5] Parks, *Report to the Board,* October 13, 1980.

[6] "Board of Trustee Minutes," (Nashville: Southern Baptist Foreign Mission board, Accession Number 589, April 15, 1985). At this meeting, the board of trustees set up Cooperative Services International as an "additional administrative entity" within the Foreign Mission Board. William Smith, "Additional Document," Electronic Mail Letter to Bruce Carlton, (November 26, 2004) and "Board of Trustee Minutes," (Glorieta: Southern Baptist Foreign Mission Board, Accession Number 573, August 8, 1987). There is no official record of trustee action on the approval of Smith for this position, although at the August 1987 board meeting in Glorieta, NM, Parks introduced Smith as someone working on a strategy to reach neglected peoples in a country in Asia. Smith states that he was given permission to launch his effort as a pilot project in August 1987.

[7] "Board of Trustee Minutes," April 15, 1985.

[8] See Appendix A for a chronology of significant events that influenced the creation and development of the non-residential missionary role.

[9] "Global Strategy Group Minutes," (Richmond: Southern Baptist Foreign Mission Board, Accession Number 395, November 24, 1987). Initially, the term non-residential missionary was utilized for internal purposes.

Southern Baptists cannot make sole claim to the paradigm's conception. The concern, which Parks and other leaders at the Board had for completing world evangelization and reaching the unreached peoples of our world, was also a concern shared and influenced by a number of other evangelical missiologists and leaders.

The NRM role was the most prominent influence in the shaping of this new missionary paradigm. The NRM role ushered in one of the most notable eras of Southern Baptist mission outreach since the formation of the convention and its FMB in 1845. The NRM role also significantly influenced the missiology of other evangelical mission agencies. The role of the NRM gradually evolved into the strategy coordinator (SC) role.[10] The SC paradigm has been so remarkably successful over the past two decades that, in 2003, the Board affirmed the SC role as one of the primary emphases of the International Mission Board (IMB) as it entered the twenty-first century.[11] At the same time, Southern Baptist leaders and trainers have been instrumental in exposing numerous other evangelical missionaries and mission agencies to this missiological paradigm.

Because of its significant impact on Southern Baptist missiology, I will describe and analyze the NRM/SC paradigm. I will seek to provide a detailed description and analysis of the recent historical development of this paradigm within the IMB. Further, I will describe and analyze the significant components of the paradigm itself as it has evolved over the past twenty years. The overall objective is to seek to answer the primary research question, "What is the extent of the impact and influence of the non-residential missionary/strategy coordinator paradigm on Southern Baptist missiology over the past twenty years?"

While the primary research question limits the scope of the research to the impact of the paradigm on Southern Baptist missiology, the research may serve as a valuable resource for those within the wider evangelical community that have also adopted or who have been influenced by this unique missiological paradigm. The NRM/SC paradigm, although influenced in its development by various concepts and individuals within the evangelical missions community, has developed its own unique ethos over the past twenty years both within and

---

[10] Smith, "Additional Document," November 26, 2004. There is no official record of the name change from non-residential missionary to strategy coordinator. According to Smith, the name change occurred simultaneously with the decision, in 1992, to elevate the status of Cooperative Services International (CSI) to become the fifth strategic region within the board's structure. See "Board of Trustees Minutes," (El Paso: Southern Baptist Foreign Mission Board, Accession Number 1033, June 22, 1992).

[11] "Board of Trustee Minutes," (Lexington: Southern Baptist International Mission Board, Accession Number 2788, November 10, 2003). At the same meeting in Lexington, the board also affirmed the people group focus as another key emphasis; an emphasis championed by the non-residential missionary and strategy coordinator roles.

outside of Southern Baptists. Further, the paradigm, as it has evolved, has led the IMB and other evangelical agencies to make some fundamental shifts in their mission strategy. The NRM/SC paradigm has left an indelible imprint on the missiology of the IMB as well as that of the wider evangelical community. However, researchers have delineated neither a historical development of NRM/SC paradigm nor an analysis of its impact.[12]

Various persons have written about the FMB and IMB from a historical perspective and some of the specific personalities who have provided leadership to the Board.[13] Others have sought to analyze and evaluate some of the strategic directions of the IMB resulting from the influence of this paradigm.[14] This study is not duplicative of other academic inquiries, since previous efforts have not focused on the NRM/SC paradigm itself, but have focused more on a few specific issues that have emerged in Southern Baptist missiology resulting from the influence of this paradigm.

The specific focus of this study necessitates placing the non-residential missionary/strategy coordinator role within its historical context. Chapter 1 will focus on the historical antecedents within the evangelical mission movement of the twentieth century. Southern Baptists may have refined the NRM/SC role, but it would be deceptive to assert that this is an exclusive Southern Baptist paradigm. To the contrary, Parks and other Board leaders were products of the evangelical mission movement of the twentieth century. Key evangelical

---

[12] A database search of dissertation abstracts on the topic of non-residential missionary and strategy coordinator yielded no results.

[13] For example see Jesse C. Fletcher, *Baker James Cauthen: A Man for All* Nations (Nashville: Broadman Press, 1977); Baker J. Cauthen and Frank K. Means, *Advance to Bold Mission Thrust: A History of Southern Baptist Foreign Missions, 1945-1980* (Richmond: Foreign Mission Board, 1981); Winston Crawley, *Global Mission A Story to Tell: An Interpretation of Southern Baptist Foreign* Missions (Nashville: Broadman Press, 1985); Charles D. Grant, Jr., "James Winston Crawley's Contribution to the Strategy of the Foreign Mission Board of the Southern Baptist Convention from 1968 to 1987" (Ph.D. dissertation, New Orleans, LA: New Orleans Baptist Theological Seminary, 1993); Richard Edward Bray, "An Examination of the Life and Ministry of M. Theron Rankin" (Ph.D. dissertation, New Orleans: New Orleans Baptist Theological Seminary, 1994); and Gary Baldridge *Keith Parks: Breaking Barriers & Opening Frontiers* (Macon: Smyth & Helwys Publishing, Inc., 1999).

[14] For example see Jon D. Sherrill, "Jerry Rankin: Ideology of a Postmodern Paradigm," *Faith and Mission* 16, No. 1 (Fall, 1998): 25-43; Keith E. Eitel, *Paradigm Wars: The Southern Baptist International Mission Board Faces the Third Millennium* (Waynesboro: Paternoster Publishing, 2000); Robin Hadaway, "Balancing the Biblical Perspectives: A Missiological Analysis," *Journal of Evangelism and Missions* 2 (Spring 2003): 103-14; and Jon Edward Smith, "A Comparative Analysis of Factors Affecting Southern Baptist Church-planting Grids in the East Asia, Middle America and East Africa Regions" (Ph.D. dissertation, Wake Forest: Southeastern Baptist Theological Seminary, 2004);

missiologists and major events influenced the Board. Trends such as the internationalization of missions, the ecumenical movement and the call by many evangelicals to a return to frontier missions did impact the FMB as it sought to find its role in fulfilling the Great Commission. The scope of the investigation is limited to those persons, events and concepts that influenced the FMB leadership in the creation and development of this new missionary paradigm.

The non-residential missionary role was a unique, yet unproven, concept of missions for the FMB. Parks' global vision and global strategy were the sparks that ignited the board's efforts to move beyond traditional fields and traditional missionary methods, yet there were several other men who contributed significantly to the naissance of this new paradigm. Key contributors within the Board, besides Parks, to this revolutionary concept included David Barrett, Winston Crawley, David Garrison, Lewis Myers and Bill Smith. The non-residential missionaries explored new frontiers in mission for Southern Baptists and, at times, faced opposition from missionary colleagues. Chapter 2 will explore the birth and early years of development of the NRM paradigm, focusing on the personalities who gave shape to this paradigm as well as the primary features of the paradigm. The analysis of primary and secondary documents will demonstrate the unique contributions of each man and how their thinking converged, resulting in the birth and maturation of the NRM role within Southern Baptist missions.

By 1992, the NRM role had established itself as a permanent fixture within the ranks of FMB missionary personnel. The merging of the CSI –China office and the NRM program into one administrative area, equal in stature with the other geographical areas of the Board, was a clear indication that this new paradigm was gaining considerable influence within the FMB. With the merging of the two programs, the NRM title changed to strategy coordinator (SC), and it became the foundational role within the restructured CSI.

Chapter 3 will probe the years between 1992 and 1997, years of accelerated growth of CSI and the strategy coordinator paradigm under the visionary leadership of Mike Stroope. Mike Stroope assumed the leadership of CSI in 1992, and a year later Jerry Rankin replaced Keith Parks as the leader of the FMB.[15] Rankin had previously served as the Area Director for Southeast Asia and had been one of the sharpest critics of CSI. Chapter 3 also will detail some of the controversy surrounding the work of CSI, which eventually led to the demise of CSI as an administrative area within the Board. The final section of Chapter 3 will seek to compare the SC paradigm with Bosch's postmodern

---

[15] "Board of Trustees Minutes," (Richmond: Southern Baptist Foreign Mission Board, Accession Number 1113, August 17, 1992) and "New FMB President: Jerry A. Rankin," *The Commission*, (August 1993), 6.

paradigm, highlighting several areas of convergence while illustrating significant points of departure.

Although CSI would not survive as an administrative area beyond 1997, the influence of the SC paradigm gradually permeated the entire Board. New Directions, launched in 1997, was Rankin's and the Board's attempt to reconfigure the FMB in order to position itself for the twenty-first century. New Directions sought to introduce parts of the SC paradigm throughout the entire organization. The reconfiguration further sought to establish CSI-like entities within each geographical region of the Board. However, except in a few cases, this did not come to fruition within every region as projected. Chapter 4 will explore the details of the demise of CSI by New Directions and the gradual impact of the SC paradigm throughout the regions of the Board.

While the FMB was undergoing a structural change and a name change in 1997, the SC role also was experiencing a monumental paradigm shift. Previous non-residential missionaries/strategy coordinators serving in Asia experienced rapid, multiplicative growth in church planting among several unreached people groups. This growth became known as a church-planting movement (CPM). Chapter 5 will demonstrate how the paradigm shift within the SC role, in turn, influenced the overall strategy of the IMB to the present day.

Finally, this chapter will seek to expound on some of the major implications of the strategy coordinator role and the accompanying CPM paradigm for Southern Baptist missiology in the twenty-first century. There are crucial theological, ecclesiological and practical issues that have emerged because of the NRM/SC role. Chapter 5 will explore possible implications on Southern Baptist missiology in the twenty-first century.

The emphasis of this study is an examination and analysis of a Southern Baptist missiological paradigm that has developed within the past twenty years. There are various personalities involved with and various stages of progression in the development of this paradigm. Therefore, a major portion of this research is a qualitative, historical analysis of primary records such as Board meeting minutes, personal writings of significant individuals, and direct correspondence with key personalities. These primary records serve to document the convictions, beliefs, attitudes and actions of the Board as a whole and various leaders during various stages of the paradigm development. These primary sources also serve to document key events within their proper historical setting.

Secondary resources provide interpretation of events and concepts related to the research topic. Such perspectives enhance understanding of the significant events and issues arising from this missiological paradigm. Finally, tertiary resources are necessary in placing this Southern Baptist missiological paradigm within the broader evangelical mission context and provide informative background information important in the researcher's critical analysis of this historical period and the specific paradigm examined.

This research effort is also phenomenological as it seeks to describe and analyze the phenomenon of the NRM/SC role as it has evolved within the IMB. Further, this study will describe and analyze the phenomenon of church-planting movements, which are now a core component of the SC paradigm and the global strategy of the IMB.

Today, the SC paradigm forms a major part of the core training for IMB missionaries deployed around the world. Therefore, Southern Baptists are in need of a critical analysis and evaluation of this emergent missionary paradigm. Although an ardent supporter of the SC paradigm, it is my desire to undertake a critical analysis of this paradigm's impact, believing that it will hone and refine Southern Baptist missiology in this present generation and beyond.

CHAPTER 1

Antecedents and Influences

Introduction

The history of Southern Baptist missions is one integral part of the history of the wider evangelical and ecumenical movements of the twentieth century. Therefore, it is imperative that one examines the multiple developments in what Barrett calls the Global Mission and Multidimensional Era[1] if one is to understand the development of the non-residential missionary/strategy coordinator (NRM/SC) paradigm within Southern Baptist circles. The global evangelization strategy of the Foreign Mission Board (FMB) in the mid-1980s, which spawned the non-residential missionary paradigm, was an eclectic strategy with its various components influenced by events and persons outside of Southern Baptist life.[2]

Although Southern Baptists, for the most part, shied away from active and direct participation in these movements, the FMB was neither immune to nor insulated from the developments in the wider Christian community. According to Garrison, the first director of the NRM program at the Board, it was not until the tenure of Parks that the FMB began to become more amenable to the possibilities expounded by these twentieth-century movements.[3] He adds, "By the mid-1980s a convergence of events made the NRM paradigm possible, if not inevitable."[4] This chapter will focus on those key events, persons and

---

[1] David B. Barrett, "Five Statistical Eras of Global Mission," *Missiology*, 12, No. 1 (January 1984): 31.

[2] Winston Crawley, *Global Mission A Story to Tell: An Interpretation of Southern Baptist Foreign Missions* (Nashville: Broadman Press, 1985), 275. In his book, Crawley states that the Foreign Mission Board has never been associated with a specific school of mission strategy and thought. Rather, the Board has been open to incorporating "insights, concepts, or approaches derived from many different sources, if we feel they can be useful and are harmonious with our basic understanding of our mission and with the main thrust of our work."

[3] V. David Garrison, "Response to Bruce," Electronic Mail Letter to Bruce Carlton, December 21, 2004.

[4] Garrison, "Response to Bruce."

concepts that directly and indirectly influenced the leadership of the FMB in the development and implementation of this unique missionary paradigm.

The Milieu: Global Conferences on Global Evangelization

Edinburgh 1910

In 1806, William Carey brought forth the idea of a meeting for missionaries in the Cape of Good Hope in 1810, for discussing together a plan aimed at the completion of world evangelization.[5] A century later, Carey's proposal came to fruition when global delegates from mission agencies met in Edinburgh with the specific intent to focus on what they called the "unoccupied" fields.[6] Edinburgh was a precursor to the modern day ecumenical movement among Protestants.[7] At the same time, Edinburgh "set the stage for a series of significant world missionary conferences which followed" and "projected a great forward look and paved the way for the innovations of the future conferences."[8] Even more noteworthy is the fact that Edinburgh was the first global missionary conference that convened around the issue of the "unoccupied" fields,[9] a concern the delegates expressed as follows:

> The unoccupied fields of the world have a claim of peculiar weight and urgency upon the attention and missionary effort of the Church. In this twentieth century of Christian history there should be no unoccupied fields. The Church is bound to remedy this lamentable condition with the least possible delay....It is the neglected opportunities that are the reproach of the church.[10]

According to Winter, there were two prominent limitations of the conference. First, the conference defined the "unoccupied" fields geographically rather than in ethno-linguistic terms.[11] This limitation most likely was the result of ignorance on the part of the participants who, for the most part, interpreted the world with the simplistic colonial categorizations of "us" and "them." It is, therefore, inconceivable that participants would have thought

---

[5] Ralph Winter, *Thy Kingdom Come: The Story of a Movement* (Pasadena: US Center for World Mission, May 1995); available from http://dawnministries.org/resources/downloads/download_files/thy_kingdom_come.pdf; Internet, 1.

[6] Winter, *Thy Kingdom Come,* 1. According to Winter, Edinburgh was the first global conference whose participants consisted solely of delegates from Mission agencies and societies.

[7] "Findings of the Commission Edinburgh 1910," in *Classics of Christian Missions,* ed., Francis M. DuBose (Nashville: Broadman Press, 1979), 329.

[8] "Findings of the Commission Edinburgh 1910," 329-30.

[9] Winter, *Thy Kingdom Come,* 2.

[10] "Findings of the Commission Edinburgh 1910," 334.

[11] Winter, *Thy Kingdom Come,* 1.

in ethno-linguistic categories. Nonetheless, this was a significant limitation to strategic mission planning. Second, the conference delegates projected the attitude that the source and solution for completing the task of evangelizing the "unoccupied" fields lay in the hands of the Western missionary agencies and societies.[12] At this particular time in history, however, it was not a major problem or concern that the primary base of missions was the West and that the sending of missionaries was unidirectional.[13] Despite its limitations, the Edinburgh conference did launch a genuine concern by Protestant, evangelical mission agencies for completing the task of global evangelization, a concern that has yet to subside, indeed, and a concern that has grown with intensity in the twentieth century and into the twenty-first.

According to Bosch, "Edinburgh represented the all-time high-water mark in Western missionary enthusiasm, the zenith of the optimistic and pragmatist approach to mission."[14] Hundreds of mission agencies throughout the twentieth century adopted the optimistic spirit that Bosch credits Edinburgh for creating. Barrett and Reapsome documented this wave of optimism when they revealed the hundreds of various global plans for evangelization developed in the twentieth century.[15] Bold Mission Thrust, launched in 1976, was evidence that Southern Baptists shared the same optimism.

The Edinburgh conference may not have directly influenced the development of the NRM/SC paradigm within the FMB; however, from the Edinburgh conference flowed two distinct streams of global conferences. One such tributary developed into the modern day ecumenical movement championed by the World Council of Churches in Geneva. The other tributary was a line of conferences focusing on the task of global evangelization eventually championed by the Lausanne Committee on World Evangelization.[16]

---

[12] Brian Stanley, "Twentieth-Century World Christianity: A Perspective from the History of Missions," in *Christianity Reborn: The Global Expansion of Evangelicalism in the Twentieth Century,* Donald M. Lewis, ed. Studies in the History of Christian Missions, eds. R.E. Frykenberg and Brian Stanley (Grand Rapids: William B. Eerdmans, 2004), 71.

[13] David J. Bosch, *Transforming Mission: Paradigm Shifts in Theology of Mission,* American Society of Missiology Series, No. 16. (Maryknoll: Orbis Books, 1991), 338.

[14] Bosch, *Transforming Mission,* 338.

[15] See David B. Barrett and James W. Reapsome, *Seven Hundred Plans to Evangelize the World: The Rise of a Global Evangelization Movement,* AD2000 Series. (Birmingham: New Hope, 1988).

[16] See Willem A. Saayman, *Unity and Mission: A study of the concept of unity in ecumenical discussions since 1961 and its influence on the world mission of the church.* (Pretoria: University of South Africa, 1984). Saayman describes the effect of unity on global mission from the 1910 Edinburgh conference until the present. He addresses the relationship between unity and mission within the global mission community. Bosch in *Transforming Mission,* 461, acknowledges the two tributaries, citing the New Delhi

The Edinburgh conference was a precursor for a variety of global conferences, each one uniquely different and each one focusing on a specific issue or concern expressed in missions.[17] Issues that arose in some of these conferences had varying degrees of influence on the strategy developing at the FMB under the leadership of Keith Parks. Several of these conferences laid the groundwork for the 1974 International Congress on World Evangelism held in Lausanne, a conference that left an ineffaceable impression on the FMB and its subsequent decision to develop the NRM concept.

Chicago 1960

Fifty years after Edinburgh, the International Foreign Mission Association (IFMA) brought together several thousand missionaries, pastors and lay people in Chicago.[18] The Chicago conference, in similar fashion to the Edinburgh 1910 conference, issued a call to young people in churches to rise up and respond to the need to occupy the fields (geographical) that remained unevangelized.[19] The Chicago conference shared a similar emphasis on mobilizing young people for global evangelization as the Urbana conferences, which began on the campus of the University of Toronto in 1946.[20]

This emphasis on calling out young people to fulfil global evangelization seems to have influenced the FMB. In July 1964, the Board approved a two-year missionary program for single young people called the Missionary

conference when the International Missionary Council (IMC) integrated into the World Council of Churches (WCC) as the primary cause for many evangelical denominations opting out of the ecumenical movement. Bosch adds that, in essence, there arose an evangelical ecumenical movement. In this movement, they defined unity more in terms of its spiritual dimensions and less pragmatically. See "Board of Trustees Minutes," (Richmond: Southern Baptist International Mission Board, Accession Number 531, February 13, 1989). William O'Brien, the FMB Executive Vice-President, expressed how the Board viewed this evangelical ecumenical movement. He saw cooperation with other evangelicals arising from a sense of obedience to the Great Commission, achieved, according to O'Brien, not in union with each another, but out of submission of corporate giftedness to Christ alongside the giftedness of others. O'Brien would assert that, in this way, Southern Baptist autonomy and uniqueness could be preserved while, at the same time, offering our talents, services, and gifts to others.

[17] See Bosch, *Transforming Mission,* 369-72, for a brief discussion about the contributions of various global missionary conferences, Protestant and Catholic, regarding the relationship between mission and church. Bosch's discussion follows a line of conferences arising out of Edinburgh that focused more on ecumenical and ecclesiological issues.

[18] Winter, *Thy Kingdom Come,* 2.

[19] Winter, *Thy Kingdom Come,* 2.

[20] *The Urbana Heritage: A Brief History of Urbana Conventions* (Urbana: Intervarsity, n.d.); available from http://www.urbana.org/_articles.cfm?RecordId=60; Internet.

Journeyman program.[21] By 1990, the Journeyman program merged with the Board's Mission Service Corps (volunteer program) to become the International Service Corps (ISC), still a program for appointing short-term missionaries.[22] As the NRM/SC paradigm developed, these short-term ISC personnel and the Journeyman program were valuable assets to the success of the Board's work among unreached people groups.[23]

Board strategists, who developed the Journeyman program in the early 1960s, were unaware of the NRM/SC concept, thus it is improbable that they could have foreseen how the Journeyman program would become an instrumental part of the NRM/SC paradigm. Nonetheless, the Board strategists did have the foresight to see that mobilizing young people and students for short-term missions was rapidly gaining popularity in evangelical circles and becoming a major trend of latter twentieth-century American missions. The NRM/SC paradigm simply discovered how to effectively integrate these short-term missionaries into various strategies aimed at the evangelization of unreached people groups.[24]

Mexico 1963 and Berlin 1966

The Commission on World Missions and Evangelism of the World Council of Churches convened a conference in Mexico City in 1963 with the theme "Mission in Six Continents."[25]The Mexico conference, following in the tradition of the Willingen conference of 1952 where the concept of *missio Dei* initially emerged within ecumenical theology, "dealt intensively with witness in a world understood as the place where God was active, inviting churches to join in *missio Dei.*"[26] The conference also brought to the forefront the concept of

---

[21] "Board of Trustees Minutes," (Richmond: Southern Baptist Foreign Mission Board, Accession Number 1659, July 16, 1964).

[22] William R. Estep, *Whole Gospel Whole World: The Foreign Mission Board of the Southern Baptist Convention 1845-1995* (Nashville: Broadman, 1994), 357.

[23] See Glossary for a definition of an unreached people group.

[24] William Smith, "Thoughts for Bruce," Electronic Letter to Bruce Carlton, November 28, 2004. Smith highlights the effective use of short-term personnel as a key component of the NRM/SC paradigm, and one that has affected the Board's missiology significantly. Chapter 3 will explore this idea in more depth.

[25] Crawley, *Global Mission,* 233.

[26] *Mission and Evangelism – History* (Geneva: World Council of Churches, n.d.); available from http://www.wcc-coe.org/wcc/what/mission/hist-e.html; Internet. See Bosch, *Transforming Mission,* 389-93, for a brief explanation on this theological paradigm that significantly has influenced missionary and missiological thinking over the last half of the twentieth century. Bosch credits Karl Barth with birthing this theological and missiological concept that defines mission as God moving toward the world and the church understood to be an instrument for God's mission. Also, see George F. Vicedom *The Mission of God* (translated from *Missio Dei: Einfulhrung in*

the internationalization of missions, reflected in the conference's call for increasing partnership among Christians from all continents in global mission.[27]

The concept of *missio Dei* eventually permeated the NRM/SC paradigm as espoused by key FMB leaders. FMB leaders interpreted the Board's mission as essentially God's mission. God is already at work in the world seeking to bring all peoples to a saving faith in Jesus Christ; therefore, the missionary task is to join with God in what He is doing in the world.[28] Lewis Myers, in addressing the Board about the NRM program, stated that God "has not left Himself without witness in any place in any culture, and our task it to try to get in rhythm with that point of reference, of witness that He has left in the countries of the world or in the people groups of the World."[29] In his report to Board in October 1995, Mike Stroope, Area Director for Cooperative Services International (CSI), reported that the role of CSI was to evangelize the unreached peoples of the world, thereby demonstrating that Southern Baptists were participants with God in His mission.[30]

In 1996, the FMB provided expenses for H. Franklin Paschall, president of the SBC, and various missionaries of the Board to attend the World Congress on Evangelism held in Berlin.[31] Coordinated by the editor of *Christianity Today* Carl F.H. Henry on the tenth anniversary of the magazine, this congress pulled together 1100 worldwide delegates and observers.[32] World-renowned evangelist Billy Graham served as the honorary chairperson, and the aim was a:

---

eine Theologie der Mission, 1958). Vicedom traces the development of this missiological concept and expounds on its meaning and application.

[27] Crawley, *Global Mission,* 233.

[28] Michael W. Stroope, *Report to the Board: Cooperative Services International* (Richmond: Southern Baptist Foreign Mission Board, Accession Number 1395, December 08, 1993). Also see Jon D. Sherrill, "Jerry Rankin: Ideology of a Postmodern Paradigm," *Faith and Mission,* 16, No. 1 (Fall 1998): 25-43. Sherrill seeks to show how postmodern concepts like *missio Dei* have become an integral part of IMB strategy under Jerry Rankin, successor to Keith Parks. Henry Blackaby and Claude King in *Experiencing God* (Nashville: Lifeway Christian Resources, 1990) popularized the concept –seeing where God was at work and joining Him – among Southern Baptists in the US.

[29] Lewis I. Myers, Jr. *Report to the Board: Cooperative Services International* (Glorieta: Southern Baptist Foreign Mission Board, Accession Number 530, July 16, 1988).

[30] Michael W. Stroope, *One Day...Is Today!* (Richmond: Southern Baptist Foreign Mission Board, Accession Number 1961, October 10, 1995)

[31] "Board of Trustee Minutes," (Richmond: Southern Baptist Foreign Mission Board, Accession Number 1835, April 12, 1966); "Board of Trustee Minutes," (Richmond: Southern Baptist Foreign Mission Board, Accession Number 1502, September 08, 1966).

[32] *Records of World Congress on Evangelism Collection 14* (Wheaton: Billy Graham Center Archives, 2004); available from http://www.wheaton.edu/bgc/archives/GUIDES/014.htm; Internet.

> ...desire to provide a forum for the growing Evangelical Christian movement worldwide....It was intended as a spiritual successor of the 1910 World Missionary Conference in Edinburgh, Scotland. The congress helped to illustrate the shift of Evangelicalism's centre of gravity to Africa, Asia and Latin America and laid the groundwork for the 1974 International Congress on World Evangelization in Lausanne, Switzerland.[33]

Winter notes that Berlin was a worldwide congress on evangelism rather than a congress focusing on world evangelization, thus there was little emphasis placed on completing the task of global evangelization.[34] Nonetheless, there was evidence of the urgency of global evangelization present at the congress as "a 'population clock' kept ticking all through the meeting, emphasizing the fearfully fast growth of world population."[35]

Just as the sense of optimism toward global evangelization emerging from the Edinburgh 1910 conference may have indirectly served as a stimulus for the SBC's adoption of its Bold Missions Thrust in 1976, so the sense of urgency emerging from the Berlin conference may have stimulated the Board's resulting push for a global strategy during the 1980s under Parks' leadership. Parks and other Board leaders were aware of the trends arising within the wider evangelical community.[36]

Further, the fact that Berlin drew delegates from around the world and illustrated the shift of gravity within the evangelical community from the West to the South and the East influenced FMB strategists. This trend in the internationalization of missions was similar to the trend reflected in the earlier ecumenical conference in Mexico City. It is clear that events taking place within both the ecumenical and evangelical movements were influencing the Board.

As the FMB was engaged in developing its global strategy under Park's leadership, Board strategists acknowledged this trend towards the internationalization of missions and affirmed it in the call for Southern Baptists

---

[33] *Records of World Congress on Evangelism Collection 14.*

[34] Winter, *Thy Kingdom Come,* 3.

[35] Winter, *Thy Kingdom Come,* 3.

[36] Winston Crawley's *Global Mission A Story to Tell,* 61-63 presents evidence that FMB strategists were aware of such trends within the greater evangelical community. Crawley exerted a significant influence on FMB strategy from 1968 to 1987. See also Charles D. Grant's dissertation "James Winston Crawley's Contribution to the Strategy of the Foreign Mission Board of the Southern Baptist Convention 1968-1987" for a more thorough discussion of Crawley's impact, which demonstrates Crawley's awareness of trends in evangelical missions. R. Keith Parks *World in View*, AD 2000 Series (Birmingham: New Hope, 1987) also demonstrates awareness of the board to the various trends emerging in the wider evangelical community. Further, many of Parks' reports to the FMB Trustees during the 1980s reflect his awareness of such trends.

to link with Baptist partners and like-minded Christian groups from around the world.[37] Parks expressed the following benefits gained by linking with Baptist partners:

> The distinctive gifts and decision making of each group remain unchanged. But the mutual strengthening and joint planning cause the impact of the total witness to be much greater than could possibly happen if each group continued unilaterally to plan its own work.
>
> As Baptists of varied bodies work as equal partners under Christ committed to the same task, a gospel witness will come more quickly to more people than would happen otherwise.[38]

From its inception, recognition of the internationalization of missions and the resulting concept of working in partnership with Great Commission Christians (GCC)[39] became one of the cornerstones of the NRM/SC paradigm. In his report to the board in October 1988, Myers pointed out that the ministry of the NRM was "indirect, enabling, stimulative, coordinative, cooperative …not…competitive, redundant or 'lone ranger.'"[40] Myers went on to describe one aspect of the NRM paradigm in terms of developing and nurturing networks that would embrace GCC groups and individuals for the overarching purpose of evangelizing the targeted population segment.[41]

As the NRM paradigm developed, Southern Baptists did envision partnership with GCC groups as an essential element. However, the FMB did not travel the road of ecumenism or what Bosch calls "mission as common witness."[42] Bosch, referring to the birth of the ecumenical movement out of the Edinburgh 1910 conference, states, "It was gradually beginning to dawn on Christians that authentic mission was impossible without authentic unity; likewise, it was inconceivable to divorce the church's obligation to take the Gospel to the whole world from its obligation to draw all Christ's people

---

[37] See Charles W. Bryan, *Report to the Board – Office of Overseas Operations* (Richmond: Southern Baptist Foreign Mission Board, Accession Number 1335, February 08, 1983); R. Keith Parks, *Foreign Missions – The Next Thrust* (Indianapolis: Southern Baptist Foreign Mission Board, Accession Number 871, April 11, 1983) and R. Keith Parks, *Report to the Board* (Biloxi: Southern Baptist Foreign Mission Board, Accession Number 597, April 9, 1984).

[38] Parks, *World in View,* 36.

[39] See Glossary for definitions of "people group" and "Great Commission Christians."

[40] Lewis I. Myers, Jr. *The World of Gaps* (Richmond: Southern Baptist Foreign Mission Board, Accession Number 528, October 10, 1988).

[41] Myers, *The World of Gaps.*

[42] Bosch, *Transforming Mission,* 457-67.

together."[43] Within the NRM paradigm, cooperation and partnership with GCC groups and unity in mission were not the same.

The Lausanne Movement: 1974 and Beyond

Of all the movements that emerged in the twentieth century among conservative evangelicals, perhaps none exerted as much influence on the FMB and the NRM paradigm as the Lausanne Movement. This movement materialized from the International Congress on World Evangelism that met in Lausanne, Switzerland in 1974. The influence of the Lausanne meeting on conservative evangelicals was as substantial as the Edinburgh 1910 conference on the ecumenical movement of the twentieth century. According to Winter:

> …the most important achievement of the conference was the great emphasis on looking at the world as *peoples* rather than *countries.* Strategically, Lausanne also changed one key word from Berlin: the World Congress on *Evangelism* of 1996 became the International Congress on World *Evangelization* in 1974 – the word *evangelism* being a never-ending activity, and *evangelization* being intended to be a project to be completed. Here, in embryo, was the concept of closure.[44]

This idea of closure to global evangelization fanned the flames of the theme ignited by the Edinburgh conference, the theme of taking the gospel message to the entire world. This theme eventually became the overarching purpose put forth by the FMB in the early 1980s, the strategy out which the NRM role eventually emerged.[45]

While the Lausanne meeting emphasis of looking at the world through ethno-linguistic lenses was important, even more important was the emergence of the concept of unreached peoples defined "by the presence of less than a certain *percentage of Christians.*"[46] The Lausanne meeting announced that research had identified 16,750 unreached people groups.[47] McGavran brought to the attention of the participants the reality of over two billion people in the world who had no knowledge of Christ, the majority of whom lived in Latin

---

[43] David J. Bosch, "Mission in the 1990s: Three Views," *International Bulletin,* 14, No. 4 (October 1990): 150.

[44] Winter, *Thy Kingdom Come,* 5.

[45] "Board of Trustees Minutes," (Richmond: Southern Baptist Foreign Mission Board, Accession Number 679, September 14, 1982).

[46] "Board of Trustees Minutes," September 14, 1982. See Glossary for a definition of unreached people groups.

[47] Harley C. Shreck and David B. Barrett, eds. *Unreached Peoples: Clarifying the Task,* Lausanne Unreached People Series, eds. Edward R. Dayton and Samuel Wilson (Monrovia: MARC, 1987), 55.

America, Africa and Asia.[48] Winter added that these "hidden" peoples, those without access to the gospel, necessitated an increasing emphasis by the church on E-3 evangelism.[49]

In a era when some were calling for a moratorium on missionaries from the West and when many mission agencies were moving away from pioneer missions in favour of providing inter-church assistance to the so-called younger churches in the non-Western world, Winter's appeal was somewhat radical. At Lausanne, Winter chastised the Western church for sending expatriate missionaries to carry out ministries that the existing Christians in the existing Churches could easily perform. In other words, missionaries were "doing evangelism on an E-3 basis, at an E-3 distance from people, when there are local Christians who are effectively winning the same people as part of their E-1 sphere."[50] The greatest need in missions, according to Winter, was for the Western church to rediscover the "hidden" peoples because the existing younger churches could not easily incorporate these people into their churches due to a variety of barriers.[51] Until every people group had a church among it, able to reach its own people (E-1 evangelism), there would still be a need for pioneer, cross-cultural missionaries (E-2 and E-3 evangelism).[52]

Lausanne 1974 spawned other conferences in subsequent years, each of which focused on global evangelization. Two such conferences of note took place in Pattaya, Thailand (June 1980) and Edinburgh (November 1980). The FMB, as it developed its global strategy under Parks' leadership, felt the impact of these conferences. The FMB sent representatives to both conferences.[53] In his report to the Board after having attended both conferences, Crawley reported the following about the Pattaya meeting:

---

[48] Donald A. McGavran, "The Dimensions of World Evangelization," in *Let the Earth Hear His Voice: International Congress on World Evangelization Lausanne, Switzerland,* ed., J.D. Douglas (Minneapolis: World Wide Publications, 1975), 99.

[49] Ralph D. Winter, "The Highest Priority: Cross-Cultural Evangelism," in *Let the Earth Hear His Voice: International Congress on World Evangelization Lausanne, Switzerland,* ed., J.D. Douglas (Minneapolis: World Wide Publications, 1975), 227. E-3 evangelism, as defined by Winter, refers to evangelism among people of a different culture, customs and language (cross-cultural) or what some often refer to as pioneer evangelism. Winter compared E-3 evangelism with E-2 (near cultural) and E-1 (same culture).

[50] Winter, "The Highest Priority," 220.

[51] Ralph D. Winter, "Penetrating the New Frontiers," in *Unreached Peoples '79,* eds., C. Peter Wagner and Edward R. Dayton (Elgin: David C. Cook Publishing, 1979), 47.

[52] Winter, "The Highest Priority," 220.

[53] Winston Crawley, *Report to the Board: Vice-President for Planning* (Richmond: Southern Baptist Foreign Mission Board, Accession Number 1368, February 10, 1981).

> This conference was called "Consultation on World Evangelization" and that describes its nature exactly. Its focus was on evangelizing the entire world. The theme of the conference was "How Shall They Hear!" The theme at Lausanne had been "Let the Earth Hear His Voice." The emphasis at Lausanne had been on the challenge of world evangelization, on inspiration for world evangelization. At Pattaya, the emphasis moved on to strategy, to the practical question how the peoples of the world can hear the gospel.[54]

In the same report, Crawley shares his insights from the Edinburgh conference:

> That third conference was a "World Consultation on Frontier Missions." The idea is to identify places in missions where we are still having to cross significant frontiers with the gospel. The theme of the conference was "A Church for Every People by the Year 2000." The concept of a people and of peoples had been in the background of the Pattaya conference. It came into the forefront at Edinburgh.[55]

As Crawley reported to Board in 1981 he further talked about the concept of "hidden" peoples put forth by Winter, and he emphasized that the FMB would need to give attention to the "hidden" peoples of the world as it developed its strategy.[56] In his follow-up report to the Board a month later, Crawley indicated that the FMB would be identifying some of these "hidden" peoples and countries closed to traditional missionaries with the intent of deploying personnel to work among them.[57] Besides the "hidden" peoples and the restricted-access or closed countries, Crawley also reported to the Board that it must begin confronting major blocs of unevangelized peoples such as Muslims, Hindus and Chinese.[58]

Eighteen months later, Crawley presented a position paper on FMB strategy to the Board, which highlighted all three of these concerns.[59] Crawley's reports to the Board are a clear indication that the FMB was grappling with how to integrate these concepts, emerging within the wider evangelical community, into the Board's global strategy. It would take several more years for the rhetoric to become reality.

However, although the Board was beginning to seriously confront the challenge of unreached peoples, restricted-access countries and major unevangelized blocs of people, McGavran and the Church Growth movement exerted strong influence over the Board's strategy. This influence revealed

---

[54] Crawley, *Report to the Board,* February 10, 1981.
[55] Crawley, *Report to the Board,* February 10, 1981.
[56] Crawley, *Report to the Board,* February 10, 1981.
[57] Winston Crawley, *Report to the Board: Vice-President for Planning* (Richmond: Southern Baptist Foreign Mission Board, Accession Number 1314, March 10, 1981).
[58] Crawley, *Report to the Board*, March 10, 1981.
[59] "Board of Trustees Minutes," September 14, 1982.

itself as the Board indicated a need to continue to concentrate on so-called "responsive" areas while probing into some of the neglected peoples and areas.[60] Over twenty years later, primarily because of the success of the NRM/SC paradigm that emerged from this 1980s strategy, the Board finally and intentionally began to concentrate more of its resources on the unreached peoples and even began to re-deploy personnel away from traditional mission fields into unreached peoples and countries.

Three Key Men: Their Influence and Contribution

Ralph D. Winter

As noted above, beginning at the Lausanne 1974 conference, Winter began appealing to the evangelical Christian community to address the "hidden" peoples of the world. Winter pointed out to the evangelical community that there were large numbers of people groups, in both open and closed countries, that mission organizations and agencies had neglected. This appeal affected the strategic thinking of the FMB in the development of a global strategy under Parks' leadership. In addition to the influence of Winter as already noted above, a few more aspects of his influence on the NRM paradigm warrant mentioning.

Bill Smith, the first NRM assigned by the FMB, notes that one of Winter's rationales behind his appeal was that the work of most mission agencies focused on the majority populations in most countries, thus causing them to overlook the hidden minority peoples.[61] Crawley, in a report to the board in 1981, admitted that this was often the case with the FMB, noting:

> …in the countries we entered, we did tend to focus on particular ethnic, linguistic or social groups. It took place spontaneously, unthinkingly….Our work has usually been with a segment of the majority population. One reason for this is that most of the lost people in that country were in that majority population.[62]

Winter called on evangelical mission agencies to re-evaluate their mission strategies.[63] Many denominations and mission agencies had grown complacent, thinking that a single missions strategy would suffice in any cross-cultural environment and with any people group.[64] The FMB was listening to Winter, and began to evaluate seriously its strategy in the early 1980s. Responding to the reality of 16,750 "hidden" peoples who constituted nearly half of the

---

[60]"Board of Trustees Minutes," September 14, 1982; Crawley, *Report to the Board,* March 10, 1981.

[61] Smith, "Thoughts for Bruce."

[62] Crawley, *Report to the Board,* March 10, 1981.

[63] Winter, "Penetrating the New Frontiers," 51.

[64] Smith, "Thoughts for Bruce."

world's overall population, Crawley stated the attitude of the FMB, "The concern for hidden peoples will be a growing part of our ongoing concern."[65]

Winter called for new pioneer mission approaches, approaches that would consider the uniqueness of each specific people group.[66] This idea of a unique strategy specifically tailored to a specific people group was one of the important elements of the NRM paradigm. Through extensive research on the targeted population segment leading to the development of a people group profile, the NRM then sought to develop a comprehensive strategy aimed at the evangelization of the specific people group or population segment.[67] In summarizing the role of the NRM to the Board in 1988, Myers emphasized, "Based on knowing the culture and language of the people, extensive research on the population segment, interaction with others who have information and activities relating to the population group, and the power of the prayers of the global Christian community, ministries with maximum evangelization potential will be undertaken."[68]

Ted Ward

In September 1980, Ted Ward, then professor of education at Michigan State University, presented a challenging report to the FMB Trustees. The thrust of Ward's presentation was that the world was radically changing, thus the Board must change in response to what was happening in the world.[69] The Board was already aware of the reality of vast numbers of unreached and "hidden" peoples in the world. Ward, in his presentation, emphasized this reality again by graphically showing the board that eighty-four percent of the world's non-Christian peoples were out of the reach of most Christians and that North American mission agencies deployed only a marginal number of missionaries for work among this eighty-four percent of the non-Christian world.[70]

The FMB integrated a number of Ward's suggestions into their global strategy. Further, a number of the suggestions and issues emerged within the

---

[65] Crawley, *Report to the Board,* February 10, 1981.

[66] Smith, "Thoughts for Bruce, "November 28, 2004; Winter, "Penetrating the New Frontiers," 61-62.

[67] See V. David Garrison, *The Non-residential Missionary: A New Strategy and the People It Serves*, Innovations in Mission, ed. Bryant L. Myers (Monrovia: MARC, 1990), 51-62; 147-55. Garrison presents an outline of the NRM training process as well as extensive information on researching a population segment. In addition, he includes several people group profiles as examples.

[68] Myers, *The World of Gaps.*

[69] Winston Crawley, *Report to the Board: Vice-President for Planning* (Richmond: Southern Baptist International Mission Board, Accession Number 751, October 13, 1980).

[70] Crawley, *Report to the Board,* October 13, 1980.

NRM paradigm that resulted from this global strategy. Crawley, in summarizing Ward's presentation to the Board the following month, mentioned the following ten emphases that warranted the Board's consideration:

1. The importance of understanding changing world conditions.
2. Openness to new ways that have not been a part of traditional missions.
3. More effective personalizing of missions for people in the churches.
4. Intensified missionary education for youth, in a time dominated by local concerns.
5. New appreciation for the frontier challenge in missions, including the vast areas of the unreached and changed plans for missionary development.
6. The urgency of finding ways to cross inhospitable borders for Christian witness in so-called "closed nations."
7. The growing importance of a legitimate "cover" reason for missionary presence, with the greatly increased role of bi-vocationalism in missions.
8. Capitalizing on the presence of potential "lay missionaries" in large numbers overseas, with plans for providing training and support systems.
9. Adjustment to the helping role in relationship to the "planted church."
10. Culturally appropriate institutions that will minimize dependency.[71]

Looking back, Ward's presentation to the Board was prophetic. Such issues as non-traditional approaches, the personalization of missions, innovative access to unreached peoples and closed countries, legitimate "cover" reason for missionary presence and capitalizing on large numbers of lay missionaries were important elements of the NRM paradigm that emerged within the FMB. Further, as the NRM paradigm evolved with the growing emphasis on church-planting movements (CPM)[72], the final two emphases presented by Ward received increasing attention by the Board and its missionaries.

David B. Barrett

Although the FMB constructed the term "non-residential missionary", mission researchers at the Board affirm that the creator of the concept is David Barrett.[73] The NRM concept arose out of the massive and remarkable research on the status of global Christianity conducted by Barrett, which culminated with the publication of the *World Christian Encyclopaedia* in 1982.[74] Barrett, who became a missionary in Africa with the Church Missionary Society in 1957,

---

[71] Crawley, *Report to the Board,* October 13, 1980.

[72] Chapter 5 will discuss and analyze the church-planting movement phenomenon and its impact on this missiological paradigm.

[73] Garrison, *Non-residential Missionary,* 23; Garrison, "Response to Bruce."

[74] Garrison, *Non-residential Missionary,* 23.

had a background in scientific research.[75] In 1965, Barrett began a unit of missionary research under the auspices of the Anglican Consultative Council and the Lambeth Conference where he was able to apply his scientific research skills to the global mission endeavour.[76]

Through his extensive research, Barrett discovered that in 1980, there were forty-nine countries, with a combined population of 1.3 billion, closed or partially closed to missionary presence.[77] Barrett's research further revealed 2,100 various ethno linguistic people groups whose populations were less than 60% evangelized, including around one thousand people groups that were considered unreached or less than 20% evangelized.[78] What is remarkable about Barrett's research is his systematic approach in seeking to quantify the global status of evangelization, as Barrett himself notes:

> No systematic attempt at measuring or quantifying the impact of Christianity on the world's populations as a whole has yet been attempted. We have therefore attempted here a first step in this direction by elaborating on the idea and concept of evangelization. The term is often used incorrectly as if it were synonymous with conversion, or Christianization. In fact it has, throughout Christian history, always been used in a broader sense to mean the spreading of the Good News of Jesus Christ and the proclamation of the gospel of the Cross; in other words, to include the impact and influence of Christianity on the non-Christian world as well as on the church and on Christians themselves. We have therefore evolved here a scale which depicts the status of evangelization in any particular country, or region, or ethno linguistic population.[79]

---

[75] David B. Barrett, *Towards a Global Strategy for World Evangelization* (Richmond: Southern Baptist Foreign Mission Board, Accession Number 625, May 24, 1983). Barrett's first major work arising out of his research in Africa was *Schism and Renewal in Africa: An analysis of six thousand contemporary religious movements* (Nairobi: Oxford University Press, 1968). Many today still consider Barrett's work as authoritative in the area of missiological research, particularly his findings on the African Indigenous Churches (AIC).

[76] Barrett, *Towards a Global Strategy.*

[77] David B. Barrett, *World Christian Encyclopaedia: A Comparative Study of Churches and Religions in the Modern World AD 1900-2000* (New York: Oxford University Press, 1982), 17. Barrett also concluded from his research that another 18 countries restricted missionary presence in varying degrees, which brought the total number of people in the world beyond the reach of traditional cross-cultural missionary witness to 3.1 billion.

[78] Barrett, *World Christian Encyclopaedia,* 19.

[79] Barrett, *World Christian Encyclopaedia*, 119. On pages 120 and 121 in his volume, Barrett reveals the scale that he developed to quantify the status of evangelization. While many within evangelical circles affirmed Barrett's research, including Southern Baptists, at the same time, there were some vocal critics of this quantitative approach,

The quantification of evangelization regarding the world's peoples and countries provided a visual picture of the status of global Christianity as never before. It confronted missiologists with the realities of the disparity of Christian witness around the world. It challenged mission agencies, like the FMB, to confront their own strategic deficiencies regarding the task of global evangelization.

Not only did Barrett's research highlight the fact of 1.3 billion unevangelized persons and 2,100 unevangelized ethno linguistic people groups, his research also revealed the enormity of the Christian resources in the world. His topical directory *World Christian Encyclopaedia* provides exhaustive information on Christian resources throughout the world.[80] Therefore, while Barrett's research revealed the gaps in global evangelization, it also served as an encouragement as the church began to awaken to the wealth of resources available for the task.

Barrett's analysis of the world's population as well as documentation on the extent of Christian resources throughout the world gave shape to the NRM paradigm as it emerged within the FMB. These two areas of research were essential to the NRM role. As the NRM researched his or her assigned people group and researched the world of GCC resources, he or she would then begin to develop a strategy to bring these two worlds together, leading to the evangelization of that particular people group.[81]

Barrett brought to the attention of mission agencies the critical need of research in the global missionary enterprise. Barrett was convinced that the missionary enterprise needed "a Christian parallel to contemporary scientific research, medical research, market research, academic research, which, day by day, year in and year out, discovers completely new facts, findings,

---

especially from missiologists outside of the West. See Samuel Escobar, "Evangelical Missiology: Peering Into The Future," in *Global Missiology for the 21st Century The Iguassu Dialogue,* ed. William D. Taylor, 101-22 (Grand Rapids: Baker Academic, 2000). Escobar, a leading Latin American missiologist, refers to this quantitative approach as "managerial missiology." By this, Escobar asserts that by describing the world through a quantitative, statistical approach, missiologists believe they can manage the mission task. He criticizes those who espoused this methodology as defining the mission task solely in terms of the numerical growth of the church, then coupling this with a challenge to evangelize those who had not yet had opportunity to hear and respond to the gospel message. Therefore, all that one needs to do is produce a picture of reality with statistics and then develop missionary activity in response to that reality. Thus, for Escobar, managerial missiologists are overly pragmatic, de-emphasizing theological problems and overlooking any part of the mission task that they cannot reduce to statistics.

[80] Barrett, *World Christian Encyclopaedia*, 893-978. In this directory, Barrett lists Christian resources according to seventy-six different topics.

[81] Garrison, "Response to Bruce."

information, trends, concepts, theories, methods, interpretations, remedies, and which on our application would lead to new theology and missiology."[82] Barrett convinced Board leadership of the value of such research, and, in 1985, the FMB extended a three-year contract to Barrett leading to the establishment of a global research department at the Board.[83] Within a few years after signing the contract with Barrett, the FMB had developed the most extensive mission database in the world.[84] Further, the signing of the contract with Barrett was the stimulus for bringing the NRM concept to fruition.

Innovations in Missions: Their Influence

Not only did the twentieth century see the emergence of movements aimed toward closure in global evangelization, but it also saw the rise of some innovative approaches in missions. As the church grappled with the realities of a changing world and the closing of doors to traditional missionary presence, some began to spawn creative ideas on how to penetrate these peoples and regions with the gospel. Several of these innovative approaches exerted influence on the NRM paradigm as it developed within the FMB. Smith identifies three innovative approaches as Brother Andrew and Open Doors International's (ODI) strategy, tent making, and radio broadcasting.[85]

Brother Andrew[86]

In 1955, Brother Andrew, who at that time was attending the World Evangelization Crusade (WEC) training college, made his first trip behind the Iron Curtain.[87] Brother Andrew had read in a communist propaganda magazine about a youth festival scheduled for Warsaw, Poland in July of that year.[88] This incident led Brother Andrew into new frontiers, both in physical and missiological terms.

In physical terms, it led Brother Andrew to develop a plan to take the gospel to those behind the Iron Curtain and into other countries such as China that did not allow missionary presence. He knew that his own organization,

---

82 Barrett, *Towards a Global Strategy.*

83 "Board of Trustees Minutes," (Nashville: Southern Baptist Foreign Mission Board, Accession Number 589, April 15, 1985).

84 Estep, *Whole Gospel Whole Word,* 353.

85 Smith, "Thoughts for Bruce."

86 See Brother Andrew with John and Elizabeth Sherrill, *God's Smuggler* (Old Tappan: Fleming H. Revell Company, 1967). Due to the sensitivity of his ministry, neither this book nor subsequent writings reveal Brother Andrew's real name. Most Christians would not be aware of his real name and would know him only as "Brother Andrew."

87 Brother Andrew, *God's Smuggler,* 75.

88 Brother Andrew, *God's Smuggler*, 72.

WEC, had never once deployed anyone behind the Iron Curtain.[89] In reflecting upon the circumstances of that year, Brother Andrew remarked, "If the Communists had attracted me to their country with literature, I was going to carry in literature of my own."[90] Brother Andrew demonstrated that it was physically possible for Christians to go into areas or countries considered closed to the gospel.

In missiological terms, Brother Andrew, and subsequently the organization ODI that he birthed, "dealt head-on with the ethical issue of whether Christians were duty bound to obey legal systems which prohibited mission activity and evangelism."[91] Brother Andrew's ministry demonstrated that government restrictions forbidding missionary presence were not barriers to evangelization, and mission agencies.

The following story demonstrates one way that Brother Andrew dealt with this ethical dilemma. On one occasion, Brother Andrew applied to travel into Yugoslavia, and on the application, he listed his occupation as missionary. The government denied his visa. This denial caused Brother Andrew to reflect on the Great Commission command to go and teach, so he reapplied listing his occupation as a teacher. The government approved the visa.[92]

Although the FMB would not advocate for working illegally in a country, it did confront the reality that there were many places in the world closed or closing to missionary presence. In August 1983, a major dialogue between Board staff and trustees took place in which this issue came to the forefront. Parks had proposed to the trustees that they consider establishing a separate legal entity that would facilitate the deployment of personnel into these closed countries.[93] Parks stated, "If we are serious about reaching all of the world, we are presently restricted by our organization, and part of my reason for giving consideration to this is to try to find ways of getting into places where we now cannot enter legally."[94] There was some opposition from within the trustees. However, the Board eventually would develop a separate entity called Cooperative Services International (CSI). Further, as the NRM paradigm developed, missionaries creatively found ways to access previously inaccessible countries and peoples, albeit not openly as missionaries and, at times, working contrary to government laws and regulations.

---

[89] Brother Andrew, *God's Smuggler*, 82.

[90] Brother Andrew, *God's Smuggler*, 75.

[91] Smith, "Thoughts for Bruce."

[92] Brother Andrew, *God's Smuggler*, 95-7.

[93] "Board of Trustees Minutes," (Glorieta: Southern Baptist Foreign Mission Board, Accession Number 618, August 08, 1983).

[94] "Board of Trustees Minutes," August 08, 1983.

Tentmakers[95]

On the one hand, Brother Andrew and ODI challenged conventional thinking in terms of government restrictions over against Christian responsibility, and, at the same time, demonstrated the ability of Christians to penetrate areas considered closed to missionary presence. On the other hand, the modern-day tentmaker movement was also demonstrating that there were additional avenues for Christian access besides traditional missionary presence. Tentmakers, however, did not so much seek to circumvent government restrictions on missionary presence and activity as much as they sought to find legal channels for lay Christians to gain access to restricted countries. Two men who championed and popularized the tentmaker movement among evangelicals in the twentieth century were J. Christy Wilson and Ted Yammarori.[96] Ruth Siemens, who served as a tentmaker in Latin America for over twenty years, formed the first tentmaker organization, Global Opportunities, designed to facilitate the placement of Christians in secular occupations overseas.[97]

Further, the tentmaker movement challenged the conventional thinking regarding the missionary profession, advocating that those "who are deeply involved in the economic, social and political structures and who represent every profession and field of knowledge, must be challenged to work out the meaning of the gospel in today's world."[98] Therefore, the tentmaker movement not only provided an avenue for Christian access into restricted areas or countries, but it began to open up missions to highly-qualified and capable professional men and women who might not otherwise consider missions as a vocation.

As the FMB developed its global strategy in the 1980s, the Board considered tentmakers as one of several viable options for accessing restricted areas or countries. Because the Board was a denominational sending agency with an emphasis on an incarnational approach focusing on career missionaries,[99] it

---

[95] The concept "tentmaker" derives from Acts 18:1-5. This term implies someone who is fully committed to the missionary task, but is self-supporting as opposed to drawing support from a mission agency or denomination.

[96] See J. Christy Wilson, Jr.. *Today's Tentmakers: Self-support – An Alternative Model for Worldwide Witness* (Wheaton: Tyndale House Publishers, 1979) and Ted Yammarori, *God's New Envoys: A Bold Strategy for Penetrating Closed Countries* (Sisters, OR: Multnomah Press, 1987).

[97] Mike Barnett, "Innovation in Mission Operations: Creative-Access Platforms," in *The Changing Face of World Missions: Engaging Contemporary Issues and Trends,* ed. Michael Pocock, Gailyn Van Rheenen, and Douglas McConnell (Grand Rapids: Baker Academic, 2005), Encountering Mission Series, ed. A. Scott Moreau, 216.

[98] Wilson, *Today's Tentmakers,* 65-6.

[99] See R. Keith Parks, *Will the Recommendations from the Transition Committee Change Our Foreign Mission Effort?* (Richmond: Southern Baptist Foreign Mission Board, Accession Number 447, February 09, 1987). As Parks was relating to the Board

found it difficult to incorporate an effective tentmaker component into its strategy. However, at the April 1989 Board meeting in Little Rock, home office staff recommended to the trustees that a tentmaker category of personnel "be established for Southern Baptists who are fully funded from non-Foreign Mission Board employment and who have also been selected by personal qualifications and commitment to join in a covenant relationship with the Foreign Mission Board in response to requests from area directors or the CSI director."[100] The tentmaker program never did develop as anticipated, and it is now no longer a formal category of personnel service for the Board.

What did develop was a variation of the tentmaker role within the NRM paradigm. Wilson describes one variation of the tentmaker role as Christians appointed by a mission agency, but who obtain a secular vocational position overseas.[101] As the NRM paradigm developed and efforts made to place personnel inside of restricted or closed countries, the Board progressively utilized this avenue of access for a number of its missionary personnel, enabling the deployment of increasing numbers of personnel to serve among unreached people groups or in restricted-access countries.[102] The Board continues to exploit this variation of the tentmaker role as a viable alternative for Board personnel where missionary visas are difficult or impossible to secure. The term "platform" refers to this concept within the NRM paradigm. One definition of a "platform" is a secular entity that provides missionaries

---

the transition to a more global strategy for evangelization, he reaffirmed the seven foundational concepts of the Board, which, he said, had been foundational for the Board since its inception.

[100] "Board of Trustees Minutes," (Little Rock: Southern Baptist Foreign Mission Board, Accession Number 436, April 09, 1989).

[101] Wilson, *Today's Tentmakers,* 142.

[102] This increase in appointments of personnel with secular, professional backgrounds over against the traditional method of appointing career missionaries with seminary degrees has not been without controversy within the IMB. No longer do career missionaries appointed by the Board need a seminary degree, although some seminary study is required, the number of hours determined by the type of assignment. Keith Eitel raised this issue in a dialogue with Jerry Rankin in 2003-4. Eitel raised the issue again in February 2004 with the Board of Trustees. Eitel believed there was an increasing de-emphasis on theological education for career missionary appointment. This dialogue is captured in Keith E. Eitel, "Vision Assessment: The International Mission Board of the Southern Baptist Convention," Electronic Letter to Jerry Rankin, October 2003; Keith E. Eitel, "Reply to Rankin," Electronic Letter to Jerry Rankin, November 6, 2003; and Keith E. Eitel and Robin Hadaway, "Points of Discussion," Paper submitted to the Board of Trustees of the International Mission Board, February 2004, Electronic document. All are available from the author.

with a "legitimate access to an unreached people group or area otherwise hostile to Christian missionaries, allowing them to carry out their ministries."[103]

Radio-Broadcasting

A third innovative approach in missions identified by Smith as influencing the NRM paradigm is that of gospel radio broadcasting. Smith asserts that gospel radio broadcasters "consistently reported the impact of long range Christian media on populations that were closed to traditional missions."[104] Radio broadcasters such as Trans World Radio (TWR) and Far East Broadcasting Corporation (FEBC) confirmed that the gospel message via radio broadcasts could go where people could not go. Evangelicals began to realize that radio broadcasting was one approach to overcoming barriers set by governments and regimes intolerant of missionary presence.

Within the NRM paradigm, media ministry, particularly radio broadcasting, was one of the four pillars of the comprehensive evangelization strategy developed by every NRM.[105] The underlying belief was that radio was indeed an invaluable tool for introducing the gospel message into those areas where incarnational missions was not yet possible or not allowed.[106] Garrison states, "Few societies today are without radio receivers, and virtually all non-residential missionaries depend on radio broadcasts to transmit the gospel into unevangelized hinterlands."[107]

As the NRM paradigm developed, radio broadcasting was one of the innovative approaches employed, and, in some situations, it proved to be a hugely successful methodology of penetrating areas and peoples closed to traditional missionary presence.[108] Besides proving, in and of itself, to be an effective evangelization tool for unreached people groups and restricted areas, radio broadcasting stimulated the search for creative and innovative

---

[103] R. Bruce Carlton, *Project Thessalonica: Acts 29 Training for Churches,* (Singapore: by the author, 2004), 10.

[104] Smith, "Thoughts for Bruce."

[105] Garrison, *Non-residential Missionary,* 16-9.

[106] Garrison, *Non-residential Missionary*, 18.

[107] Garrison, *Non-residential Missionary*, 18.

[108] See Garrison, *Church Planting Movements: How God is Redeeming a Lost World* (Midlothian: WIGTake Resources, 2004), 103. Garrison reports that over 16,000 Berber Muslims came to Christ with radio broadcasts being one of the key media employed. All of this occurred without the presence of foreign missionaries. On pages 39-43, Garrison also reports Christians effectively employed radio among a people group in India to facilitate rapid church growth. See also R. Bruce Carlton, *Amazing Grace: Lessons on Church-Planting Movements from Cambodia* (Singapore: by the author, 2004), 100-4. I describe the effectiveness of FEBC radio in the rapid church growth that occurred among the Khmer people during our six and a half years of ministry among them.

methodologies within the NRM paradigm. Even more, radio broadcasting effectively confirmed technology as a valuable ally of the global evangelization effort.

Radio was one of the first technologies used to usher in the information age of the twentieth century, an age that has spawned even more innovative and effective technologies for communication. The NRM paradigm embraced technology as an integral part of a strategy to reach into restricted areas and peoples, believing the information age and world missions were partners, not competitors. Parks expressed this belief as follows:

> The information age that has dawned is an age in which the explosion of the gospel ought to supersede that of the first century. Everything is now in place which should enable Christians to gossip the good news of the gospel to all of the peoples of the world. The technologies, the transportation, the communication, the resources of today are the equivalent of the Roman government and its system of roads, along with the Greek language of Paul's day. The world has come into the information arena where we as Christians have lived all of our history. This is who we are. If we would but recognize and be wise enough, sacrificial enough, and creative enough, we will move into the greatest day Christian missions has ever seen.[109]

Conclusion

From Edinburgh to Lausanne, the challenge of global evangelization was gaining momentum. The proliferation of conferences and consultations focusing on global evangelization created an atmosphere that increasingly encouraged innovative approaches to missions. Such an environment stimulated Southern Baptist missiologists, leading to the birth of the NRM paradigm.

The NRM paradigm was a unique response to a major challenge before the church, the challenge of completing the evangelization of every nation and every people group in the world. Although the FMB initiated and developed the NRM concept, the reality is that many individuals contributed to the creation of this pioneering missions concept. The NRM paradigm truly was a product of the creative minds of various Christians passionate about completing global evangelization.

As Southern Baptist missiologists within its FMB confronted the discrepancy between the desire to complete global evangelization and the tangible efforts of mission agencies toward fulfilling those desires, they stepped out in faith with some risk to create this new missions paradigm. The leaders at the Board were walking into unknown territory, but the need to take the gospel

---

[109] R. Keith Parks, *The Information Age and World Missions Are Made For Each Other* (Richmond: Southern Baptist Foreign Mission Board, Accession Number 571, December 10, 1990).

message to over one billion people virtually untouched by the church compelled them to walk down this path. Thus, a new era of missions began for Southern Baptists and their FMB.

CHAPTER 2

A New Paradigm Emerges

Introduction

The convergence of various factors within the evangelical Christian community created a ripe environment for the development of the non-residential missionary (NRM) paradigm. Aware of and influenced by all these events taking place, leaders at the Foreign Mission Board (FMB) of the Southern Baptist Convention (SBC), earnestly desiring to have a truly global strategy deployed the first NRM in 1987. The NRM concept was the brainchild of David Barrett, who in 1985, contracted with the Board to base his World Evangelization Research Center at its headquarters in Richmond, Virginia. Although Barrett conceived the idea of a non-residential missionary approach to the world's unreached peoples, he did not have the resources needed to implement this novel missionary concept. However, the partnership between Barrett and the FMB created the fertile environment that allowed this innovative paradigm to emerge. Baldridge explains this reciprocal relationship:

> Parks had in Barrett the new practical concept and the database, and in the FMB the financial and human resources necessary for a massive shift toward the most neglected peoples on earth. Most important of all, Parks championed the strategy that would open the doors through which many Great Commission people could walk.[1]

In Parks, Barrett found the benefactor he needed to execute this paradigm. Yet, at the same time, Parks and Barrett needed to call upon the services and expertise of other key leaders to successfully implement this paradigm and shepherd it from a fledgling concept towards maturity. Winston Crawley, Lewis Myers, David Garrison and Bill Smith were some of those key individuals. This chapter will explore further the development of the Board's global strategy under Parks' leadership: a strategy that ultimately led to the birth of the NRM paradigm. The unique contributions of these key leaders at the Board also warrant exploration. Finally, this chapter will focus on the initial progress of this paradigm as it was developing as well as the impact of the paradigm on the mission efforts of the Board.

---

[1] Gary Baldridge, *Keith Parks,* 4.

Cultivating New Approaches

Tilling the Soil for Change

From the beginning of his leadership at the Board, Parks challenged Southern Baptists to have a futuristic look regarding the global task facing them in the final quarter of the twentieth century and beyond. As already pointed out, the Southern Baptist Convention's (SBC) Bold New Thrusts provided the stimulus for Parks' challenge to develop a genuine global strategy. Parks' visionary leadership and his consuming passion for reaching the entire world with the gospel message provided a dynamic environment out of which new missiological paradigms could emerge.

During his initial year at the helm of the FMB, Parks provided a thought-provoking picture of the future of missions; a picture that implied the direction his leadership would guide the Board. Although the exact outcome arising from Parks' leadership was yet unclear, he was explicit in challenging Southern Baptists to embrace change in their mission efforts. In October 1980, Parks wrote:

> I expect there will be:
>
> | MORE | LESS |
> |---|---|
> | Change | Rigidity |
> | Mobility | Structure |
> | Partnerships | Unilateralism |
> | Financial Needs | Buying Power |
> | Missionary personnel | Dependence on missionaries |
> | Accountability | Defensiveness |
> | Strategy planning | Confusion and ambiguity |
> | Administrative guidance | Frustration and waste |
> | Local leadership | Missionary control |
> | Poverty | Equality |
> | Hunger | Food |
> | Danger | Stability |
> | Urgency | Complacency |
> | Witnessing | Tolerance |
> | Responsiveness | Neutrality |
>
> Each pair of words or phrases represents two sides of one concept. Each expression bulges with meaning and implication. The inevitability of these changes is certain. Our options are simple:
>
> 1) We can ignore the onrushing tide and be engulfed.
> 2) We can resist it and be shattered.

3) We can initiate some change and adapt to others and be blessed and a blessing.

May we have courage and clarity of vision as we keep the world in view.[2]

At the June 1980 Board meeting, the trustees elected Crawley as the Vice-President for Planning,[3] a role that would thrust Crawley into a key strategic position regarding the formulation and communication of the Board's global strategy. During the next few years, Parks and Crawley would continually articulate the components of this comprehensive global strategy through their regular articles in *The Commission* and in their various reports to the Board.[4] Crawley's *magnum opus* would be his 1985 book *Global Mission A Story to Tell* in which he extensively elucidated the global strategy vision of the FMB under Parks' leadership. Parks' *tour de force* would be his 1987 publication *World in View* in which he consolidated much of what he had written through his articles in *The Commission* and articulated his vision of leading Southern Baptists to fulfil their commitment to reach every person on earth to hear the gospel by the end of the century.

Change in the board's mission strategy was a major emphasis of Parks during the early years of his leadership. By creating a climate calling for change, Parks was laying the groundwork for the emergence of the NRM paradigm. For Parks, the historical setting of the latter twentieth century made change inevitable:

> Many good things are happening in Bold Mission Thrust; however, in foreign missions it seems that the time has come for igniting new spiritual rockets to thrust us out into a different orbit. Circumstances demand this....What a time in history! We should be trembling with excitement over the potential of the era we have entered. We must not pause to enshrine the accomplishments of our past, or we will never claim our future. Nor can we allow ourselves to be intimidated by the present. We must risk, in faith, to achieve what God has laid before us. The time has come for us to move into the future of world missions with daring and boldness lest by failing to adapt we become a spiritual dinosaur in the religious museums of tomorrow.[5]

Throughout this process of developing a global strategy, one primary theme that continually surfaced from FMB leadership was the need to include a

---

[2] R. Keith Parks, "The Future of Missions: Change," *The Commission* (October 1980):

[3] "Board of Trustees Minutes," (Ridgecrest: Southern Baptist Foreign Mission Board, Accession Number 733, June 24, 1990).

[4] In *The Commission,* Crawley's articles appeared under the banner "Horizons" from 1980 until 1989. Parks' articles appeared under the banner "World in View" from 1980 until 1992.

[5] Parks, *Foreign Missions-The Next Thrust.*

strategy component that would focus on the people groups untouched by the gospel message. As noted in chapter 1, the influences of the Lausanne Movement and Ralph Winter contributed to the FMB leadership's recognition of the need to include such an emphasis if it was serious about fulfilling the Convention's Bold New Thrusts in Foreign Missions.

As early as 1981, Crawley introduced the concept of "hidden peoples" to Southern Baptists in *The Commission* when he wrote, "The term 'hidden' identifies any people still without any churches of their own, and unable to evangelize their own group."[6] A year later, during a panel presentation with the Board of Trustees, Crawley raised once again the need to include in the Board's strategy an emphasis on "major blocks of mankind that are relatively untouched by the gospel."[7] Several months later, Crawley presented as one of the strategy concerns needing the attention of the FMB "a focus of effort on unreached people groups and perhaps especially on those with the least contact with the gospel."[8] The next month, Charles W. Bryan, Senior Vice-President for Overseas Operations, reported to the Board that a key concept in the development of the Board's strategy would necessitate prioritizing the need to expand outreach to new people groups and penetrating countries closed to traditional missionary presence.[9] Several months later, Bryan would once again present a challenge to the Board to "expand witness to unreached peoples of ethnic or cultural groups."[10]

Throughout this process of infusing the FMB with an awareness of unreached people groups and the need to include a people group approach within its broader global strategy, leaders at the Board were not seeking to shift entirely away from a geopolitical approach regarding missionary deployment.[11] Because of the Board's historical relationship with Baptist entities in countries where its missionaries served, FMB leadership believed it could not forego a country approach; however, within this geopolitical framework for planning the Board would now add a new emphasis on people groups.[12] Board leaders wanted to be sensitive to its various Baptist partners around the world. Crawley succinctly expressed this sensitivity, stating, "Thus in planning, both

---

[6] Winston Crawley, "Horizons: 'Hidden Peoples,'" *The Commission* (February-March 1981), 78.

[7] "Board of Trustees Minutes," (Richmond: Southern Baptist Foreign Mission Board, Accession Number 1511, February 08, 1982).

[8] "Board of Trustees Minutes," September 14, 1982.

[9] Charles W. Bryan, *Report to the Board: Office of Overseas Operations* (Richmond: Southern Baptist Foreign Mission Board, Accession Number 989, October 13, 1982).

[10] Bryan, *Report to the Board,* February 08, 1983.

[11] Crawley, *Global Mission,* 250.

[12] Crawley, *Global Mission,* 250.

in the Foreign Mission Board offices and on the fields, concern for people groups is expressed within the context of concern for partnership."[13]

A second theme that continually emerged was the need to focus on countries closed to traditional missionary presence. In a presentation to the Board of Trustees in 1982, Crawley explicitly stated that one of the major strategic concerns was reaching into countries sealed off from traditional missionary presence.[14] In his regular articles in *The Commission*, Crawley also addressed this concern.[15] According to Bryan, prioritizing within the Board's strategy would require looking at how the Board could access these closed countries.[16]

All this talk of concerns, priorities and challenges confronting the Board as it faced a changing world in the latter part of the twentieth century culminated with the "Strategic Priorities for the Foreign Mission Board 1985-1988," presented by Parks to the trustees in February 1985.[17] This report explicitly stated that Parks and FMB leadership were now ready to launch new missiological paradigms in response to this rapidly changing world. One of the strategic priorities presented was to "develop coordination and evaluation of current involvement in lands where missionary residence and/or activities are restricted and identify ways of strengthening these approaches and experimenting with new approaches."[18] At that time, it was not clear what new approaches the FMB leadership had in mind.

It was obvious in the strategic priorities that the FMB had not yet moved beyond a geopolitical framework regarding its strategic planning. However, although the new strategy did not explicitly mention unreached people groups or the NRM concept, Parks and FMB leadership had perspicaciously tilled the strategic soil out of which the NRM paradigm would spring forth.

Planting the First Seed of Change

Parks and FMB leadership took the first step in the development of a new missiological paradigm by recommending in April 1985 the formation of Cooperative Services International (CSI).[19] The Board established CSI primarily to respond to needs in China where traditional missionary presence

---

[13] Crawley, *Global Mission,* 250-1.

[14] "Board of Trustees Minutes," September 14, 1982.

[15] For example, see "Horizons: Gates to Closed Places Could Swing Open," *The Commission* (September 1983), 65 and "Horizons: Which Ones Are 'Closed?'" *The Commission* (August 1984), 7.

[16] Bryan, *Report to the Board,* February 08, 1983.

[17] "Board of Trustees Minutes," (Richmond: Southern Baptist Foreign Mission Board, Accession Number 598, February 11, 1985).

[18] "Board of Trustees Minutes," February 11, 1985.

[19] "Board of Trustees Minutes," April 15, 1985.

was no longer an option.[20] At the same time, the Board expanded the new office's mandate to include other closed or restricted countries where traditional missionary presence was not feasible.[21]

The formation of CSI as the arm of the FMB responsible for mission efforts in so-called closed countries was the culmination of a strategic process initiated as early as 1980. Chapter 1 revealed how Ted Ward challenged the Board to seek ways for penetrating countries closed or antagonistic to Christian missionaries.[22] In May 1983, the Office of Overseas Operations unveiled a ministry plan for countries where, at that time, the Board could not deploy missionary personnel.[23] A few months later, Parks and FMB staff convened a dialogue with trustees regarding the need for the creation of a separate legal entity that would allow personnel to penetrate countries resistant to missionaries and mission organizations.[24]

For Parks, it was critical to shape "change rather than allowing change to shape the Foreign Mission Board."[25] Thus, Parks viewed the formation of CSI as a vital step in the Board's plans to shape change or reshape foreign missions for Southern Baptists.[26] It would be more than a year later before the emergence of the NRM role within the FMB; nonetheless, the course had been set and the groundwork laid. As Parks noted:

> Changes are coming more rapidly than ever before. Pressures are stronger from more directions than they have ever been. In order to function appropriately, all of us must take the time and expend the effort to have a thorough understanding of foreign missions as it now is and as it ought to be....The awesomeness of our task is seen in the fact that the decisions recommended by staff and determined by this board will affect the eternal destiny of souls around the world. It is a sobering responsibility.[27]

For Parks, the global emphasis of the FMB necessitated planting three seeds of change into its strategy. The first seed of change was the formation of CSI, thrusting the Board into a new arena of mission activity – countries closed to traditional missionary presence. The other seeds of change were on the horizon.

---

[20] "Board of Trustees Minutes," April 15, 1985.
[21] "Board of Trustees Minutes," April 15, 1985.
[22] Crawley, *Report to the Board,* October 13, 1980.
[23] "Board of Trustees Minutes," (Richmond: Southern Baptist Foreign Mission Board, Accession Number 625, May 24, 1983).
[24] "Board of Trustees Minutes," August 08, 1983.
[25] R. Keith Parks, *Shaping Change in Foreign Missions* (Richmond: Southern Baptist Foreign Mission Board, Accession Number 636, October 07, 1985).
[26] Parks, *Shaping Change in Foreign Missions.*
[27] Parks, *Shaping Change in Foreign Missions.*

Planting the Second Seed of Change

With the signing of a three-year contract with David Barrett in 1985, the FMB began planting another seed that would produce significant shifts in Southern Baptist mission strategy. Before the signing of this contract, Barrett had been cooperating with the FMB in the area of researching the world's cities.[28] Barrett also had already published his *World Christian Encyclopaedia* and was a prominent, yet at times controversial, researcher within the Christian world.[29] Bringing Barrett into the inner sanctum of the FMB confirmed that he had convincingly demonstrated to Parks how comprehensive demographic research could serve as part of the solid foundation needed to build an effective global evangelization strategy.[30]

Barrett had decried the dearth of research among Christian mission agencies and denominations. According to Barrett, research was indispensable to the task of global evangelization, and mission efforts had often struggled because

---

[28] "Board of Trustees Minutes," April 15, 1985.

[29] Barrett's *World Christian Encyclopaedia*, although a significant contribution to the task of global evangelization, raised various questions that prompted dialogue among various missiologists within both Southern Baptist circles and the wider Christian community. Two years after its publication, *Missiology*, vol. 12, no. 1 (January 1984) dedicated several articles to a discussion about the significance of Barrett's research. The parameter of church membership was one issue that surfaced because of Barrett's research. For example, see Stephen Neill, "A World Christian Encyclopaedia," *Missiology*, 12, no. 1 (January 1984): 5-19. Neill states that this is one of the key issues raised by the *World Christian Encyclopaedia.* Barrett's parameters of church membership were broad and inclusive of many groups, whom a number of evangelicals would have opted to exclude. Some, like David N. Stowe, "A New Perspective on the World Christian Mission," *Missiology*, 12, no. 1 (January 1984): 49-54, considered Barrett's inclusiveness correct and one that should be allotted serious missiological consideration. This issue was later raised within Southern Baptist circles by Dr. Keith E. Eitel, "Vision Assessment: The International Mission Board of the Southern Baptist Convention," Electronic Letter to Jerry Rankin, October 2003. Eitel criticized Barrett's inclusiveness and the IMB's subsequent use of his data in its strategy planning, claiming that Barrett "imposes theological categories whereby he counts any grouping that calls itself Christian as being so." Eitel criticized the Board for accepting Barrett's inclusion of Roman Catholics, Orthodox and Mormons as Christian. This perspective of Barrett, according to Eitel, distorted the picture of the need for evangelical presence and witness in various places around the world.

[30] In Barrett's 1983 report to the Board entitled *Toward A Global Strategy for World Evangelization*, he presented a compelling argument on how substantial Christian research could serve the cause of global evangelization. In his presentation, Barrett also made recommendations to the Board that he hoped would bring research more into the forefront in its efforts to build a global strategy.

they lacked the vital information that research could provide.[31] Further, Barrett pointed out to FMB leadership that, although the Board's expenditure on research outpaced all other mission boards and agencies, its percentage of income spent on research was a paltry 0.2 percent.[32] Barrett spoke and Parks listened, leading to the establishment of a global research department at the FMB in 1985.

Bringing Barrett to the FMB, according to Garrison, was "the trigger that changed everything."[33] The research generated by Barrett's office brought to the attention of FMB leadership a significant gap in its global mission effort, a gap of over one billion people in the world neglected by the mission effort primarily because these people resided in countries where traditional missionary presence was not a viable option.[34] According to Hiebert, Barrett's research would benefit mission agencies by providing "a better basis for planning a diversity of mission strategies that are responsive to the complex realities of the modern world."[35] Undoubtedly, leadership at the Board believed Barrett's research was beneficial and broadly depended upon it while formulating the Board's global strategy.

Not only did Barrett's research highlight the gaps in the board's mission strategy, he also awakened FMB leadership to a world of Christian resources

---

[31] David B. Barrett, "Silver and Gold Have I None: Church of the Poor or Church of the Rich?" *International Bulletin* 7, no. 4 (October 1983): 149. Just as in his presentation to the FMB earlier in 1983, so Barrett, in this article, issues an urgent cry for more research by mission agencies. He demonstrates how research has revealed a wealth of Christian resources available to reinforce his plea. See also David B. Barrett, "Five Statistical Eras of Global Mission," *Missiology* 12, no. 1 (January 1984): 21-39. This issue of *Missiology* focused on various evaluations of Barrett's *World Christian Encyclopaedia.* Barrett's article focused on five eras in Christian mission. In the fifth era, which he called "The Global Discipling Era," he asserted that this fifth era would see the emergence and dissemination of Christian information on a global scale, thus making the message of the gospel available to all the peoples of the world.

[32] Barrett, *Toward a Global Strategy.*

[33] Garrison, "Response to Bruce."

[34] Garrison, "Response to Bruce." See Paul G. Hiebert, "Barrett and Beyond," *Missiology,* 12, no. 1 (January 1984): 64-73. Hiebert also points out that Barrett's categories of "evangelized," "unreached" and "hidden" peoples derive out of his own theoretical framework and that his figure of 1.3 billion "unevangelized" people differs significantly from figures quoted by other researchers. While acknowledging Barrett's extensive scale for measuring a people group's status of evangelization, Hiebert criticizes Barrett for not clarifying how he computed his measurements. Despite differences of opinions concerning Barrett's research, the Board accepted Barrett's figure of 1.3 billion "unevangelized" and utilized this number as it formed its strategy during the late 1980s and early 1990s.

[35] Hiebert, "Barrett and Beyond," 65.

outside of Southern Baptist circles.[36] Barrett's *World Christian Encyclopaedia*, according to Moffett, confirmed a global swell in the number of evangelicals throughout the world.[37] Barrett's figures stated that nearly 157 million out of 262 million Protestants in the world were evangelical.[38] Further, Barrett's *World Christian Encyclopaedia* provided a directory of global Christian resources according to seventy-six different topics.[39] One of the most significant contributions of this research to the global mission enterprise was its portrayal of an ever-increasing missionary effort, not just from the Western churches, but also from the church around the world.[40] Neill points out that Barrett's research had revealed that by 1983 "the Christian church does exist in every country of the world with the possible exception of Tibet."[41]

Barrett's research did awaken Parks to the need for closer consultation and partnership with others. Initially, Parks called for Southern Baptists and the FMB to pursue partnership with like-minded Baptist entities around the world.[42] However, as the Board developed and began to implement its global strategy, there was an increasing movement toward extending partnership to other Great Commission Christian (GCC) groups. The idea of networking with other GCC groups inevitably raised some concerns with some of the Board's Southern Baptist constituency. Parks sought to quiet some of these concerns by stating that Southern Baptists would not be relinquishing any of their distinctive doctrinal beliefs, would not necessarily be endorsing fully the theological beliefs of other groups and would not be funding other mission agencies.[43] At

---

[36] Hiebert, "Barrett and Beyond," 65.

[37] Samuel Hugh Moffett, "The Filaments of a World Mission," *Missiology,* 12, no. 1 (January 1984): 71.

[38] Barrett, *World Christian Encyclopaedia,* 6.

[39] Barrett, *World Christian Encyclopaedia*, 893-978.

[40] Wade T. Coggins, "God at Work Around the World," *Missiology,* 12, no. 1 (January 1984): 76.

[41] Neill, "A World Christian Encyclopaedia," 9.

[42] See Parks, *Foreign Missions-The Next Thrust* and Parks *World in View*, 37.

[43] R. Keith Parks, "World in View: Networking What It Is and Isn't," *The Commission,* January 1988, 6. As the Board progressed in partnerships with other evangelical groups, concern rose within some Southern Baptist circles about the possible dangers this might create to the theological moorings of Southern Baptist missionaries. See Keith E. Eitel, "Vision Assessment," October 2003. In his correspondence to Jerry Rankin, he addresses this issue, and Eitel's primary concern is that charismatic groups would influence the Board's missionary personnel because of no evaluative tool in which to guide these personnel in forming partnerships with other evangelical groups. During the 1980s, there was a shift within the Southern Baptist Convention toward a more conservative theological position, one in which those leading the resurgence claimed was a movement to lead Southern Baptists back to their historical roots. Eitel and others interpreted this trend within the Board toward increasing partnerships with other

the same time, Parks stated that the parameters of networking with other GCC groups would involve the sharing of research data, sharing of information regarding opportunities, sharing of plans, sharing of best mission practices and sharing for the purpose of prayer mobilization.[44] Functionally, this networking and partnership with other GCC groups and individuals served as an avenue for the FMB and its personnel to "avoid the problems of more formal ecumenical ties while advancing the cause of Christ around the world."[45]

One product that flowed out from Barrett's research and influence upon the FMB was the AD2000 Series of publications. This series of publications was one of the products of 1985 FMB-sponsored global evangelization meeting held in Ridgecrest, North Carolina.[46] The first book in this series was Barrett's *World-Class Cities and World Evangelization*, published in 1986.[47] The AD2000 Series provided Barrett a much-needed platform for disseminating his ongoing research. Through the various publications, Barrett also was able to enunciate simple concepts by which Christians could begin to define the world around them. Barrett divided the world into three segments – World A, World B and World C.[48] Barrett had already developed a methodology for quantifying evangelization; however, there needed to be a simpler way of communicating the results of this research, a way that would capture the hearts and minds of Southern Baptists and other Great Commission Christians. Williard would later summarize the impact of these new classifications:

evangelical groups as having potential for eroding Southern Baptists' historical emphasis on "personal evangelism, church planting, and discipleship of the nations."

[44] Parks, "World in View: Networking What It Is and Isn't."

[45] Estep, *Whole Gospel Whole World,* 353-4.

[46] David B. Barrett, *Evangelize! A Historical Survey of the Concept,* AD2000 Series (Birmingham: New Hope, 1987), 8. Parks and Barrett had attended this meeting convened by FMB leadership for the purpose of dialogue regarding partnership in the task of global evangelization. It brought together seventy participants representing twenty-one international Baptist groups with whom the FMB had a historical relationship.

[47] The Foreign Mission Board launched the AD Series, published by New Hope, the publishing arm of the Southern Baptist Women's Missionary Union. Early titles in the series include Parks' *World in View* (1987) and *Unreached Peoples: Clarifying the Task* (1987). The Board did not publish the full series planned, most likely because of Parks' retirement in 1992 and Barrett's subsequent departure from the Board shortly thereafter. However, significant publications did emerge, which provided Southern Baptists and others with a wealth of demographic knowledge about the world, and which provided a forum for propagating information regarding the unevangelized and unreached people groups. This series helped propel the FMB into the forefront of efforts to evangelize the 1.3 billion people Barrett identified as World A.

[48] Smith, "Thoughts for Bruce."

> Although missiologists for years recognized the concept of an "unreached" or "unevangelized" world, it remained relatively undefined. Hard data was missing. A model was missing. But perhaps most of all, a vision was missing that could bring the necessary resources together to identify it, enunciate it and act upon it.[49]

World C or the Christian world included the people groups and population segments where over 95 percent had heard the gospel in ways they could understand and respond and identified as having more than 60 percent church members.[50] World B peoples had less than 60 percent church members, but more than half of them had heard the gospel in ways they could understand.[51] World A comprised those people groups and population segments where less than 50 percent had never had opportunity to hear of Jesus Christ.[52]

The majority of unevangelized and unreached peoples resided in World A. World A, as defined by Barrett and his staff, included 3,030 unevangelized population segments – 2,000 people groups, 1000 metropolises, and 30 countries.[53] The total population of these 3,030 unevangelized population segments was a staggering 1.3 billion or nearly 26 percent of the entire world population.[54] O'Brien later pointed out that 85 percent of all the unreached

---

[49] David Williard, "Shaping New Strategies: Adjusting FMB vision in light of World A," *The Commission*, October-November 1991, 39.

[50] David B. Barrett and Todd M. Johnson, *Our Globe And How To Reach It: Seeing the World Evangelized by AD2000 and Beyond*, AD2000 Series (Birmingham: New Hope, 1990), 25. Some leaders at the Board, most notably those in places such as Latin America, were reluctant to accept Barrett's description of World C as the Christian world. They believed it incorporated many people in so-called World C countries who were genuinely lost. Therefore, they argued, one cannot call such people as evangelized. Barrett acknowledged that his model was a generalization, but that such generalization was necessary for the purpose of assessing the status of people groups around the world and guiding the Board's strategic processes. See Williard, "Shaping Strategies: FMB Vision," 38-45.

[51] Barrett and Johnson, *Our Globe And How To Reach It*, 25.

[52] Barrett and Johnson, *Our Globe And How To Reach It*, 25.

[53] Barrett and Reapsome, *Seven Hundred Plans*, 24. The fact that Barrett's data and classifications of evangelization appeared in a publication of the FMB indicated the Board's endorsement of his research. See William R. O'Brien, "'World A': Unbegun task?," *The Commission*, October-November 1990, 70. O'Brien uses the terminology of World A, B, and C developed by Barrett as well as his figures, again indicating the Board's acceptance of Barrett's research for its strategic planning. See also David Williard, "Evangelized?," *The Commission*, October-November 1991, 58. In this article, Williard publicly affirms that Board researchers were utilizing the evangelization factors developed by Barrett in his *World Christian Encyclopaedia*.

[54] Barrett and Reapsome, *Seven Hundred Plans*, 24.

peoples of World A lived in closed countries.[55] Barrett joined Parks in calling for change in mission strategies, concluding, "Unless changes are made now in how we think and carry out world evangelization, we could see this decade slip by as well and be no closer to taking the gospel to the whole world."[56]

Barrett's research also vividly revealed the inequity of the distribution of Christian resources deployed by mission agencies and denominations. In 1988, Barrett and Reapsome, reporting the results of this research, indicated there were over 241,300 foreign missionaries deployed to World C, 20,000 deployed to World B, but only 1000 targeting the peoples in World A.[57] Further, they reported that of all the money spent on Christian work each year, $130 billion was spent at home (World C) while only $1 billion was spent for work in World B and about $0.1 billion spent for work in World A.[58] Their research also reported that less than 0.1 percent of all Christian literature and less than 0.01 percent of Christian radio and television was utilized for efforts in World A while an overwhelming 99 percent of all Christian literature and 99.9 percent of Christian mass media was in World C.[59]

Barrett's research also confirmed the wisdom of the Board's decision to form CSI in 1985 as his research revealed an alarming trend regarding the openness of countries to foreign missionary presence. According to Barrett:

> Back in 1900, virtually every country was open to foreign missionaries of one tradition or another....Today, some 65 countries are closed to foreign missionaries of any kind, with three more closing their doors every year. If the trend continues, by the year 2000 we may well be faced with 120 closed countries.[60]

The startling realities about the world and the challenges presented by this collection of unevangelized and unreached people groups called World A captured the attention of Parks and Board leaders. For Parks, the information continually flowing to him from Barrett's office and other places was challenging him to alter his view of reality. Parks, in turn, challenged the Board to revise its reality maps:

> We're daily bombarded with new information as to the nature of reality. If we are to incorporate this information we must continually revise our maps and sometimes when enough information is accumulated we must make very major revisions. Sometimes excruciatingly painful....What we do more often than not

---

55 "Board of Trustees Minutes," (Glorieta: Southern Baptist Foreign Mission Board, Accession Number 543, July 21, 1990).

56 Barrett and Johnson, *Our Globe And How To Reach It,* 3.

57 Barrett and Johnson, *Our Globe And How To Reach It,* 27.

58 Barrett and Johnson, *Our Globe And How To Reach It,* 27.

59 Barrett and Johnson, *Our Globe And How To Reach It,* 27.

60 Barrett and Johnson, *Our Globe And How To Reach It*, 28.

> and usually unconsciously is to ignore the new information....Sadly such a person may expend more energy ultimately in defending an outmoded view of the world than would have been required to revise and correct it in the first place.... Therefore, I have to ask myself, our staff and this board if that's where we are in transforming the vision of Bold Mission Thrust into reality. Have we tended to keep our maps of reality as they were in 1976...deluded ourselves as to believing that, in fact, we were on the road to accomplishing the overarching objective...to have our part in preaching the gospel to all of the people in the world by the year 2000.[61]

As he began to revise his map of reality, Parks believed the Board needed to consider altering the administrative structure of the Board and field entities, the deployment of missionary personnel, the use of its financial resources, and the relationship of the Board with other Baptist and Great Commission Christian groups.[62] Two significant issues emerged from his thinking. First, Parks recognized the need for a "group charged with the development of global strategy on the staff level and the need for a 'strategy room.'"[63] Second, Parks realized a need to define unreached people groups and make decisions regarding the Board's responsibility and role in evangelizing these unreached peoples.[64]

In December 1986, Parks raised the issue of creating a Global Strategy Group (GSG) comprised of key administrators at the Board.[65] Parks presented a formal recommendation for a complete reorganization of the Board to the trustees a few months later at the February 1987 meeting.[66] In presenting the recommendations, Parks declared, "Today, for the sake of our Lord Jesus Christ, let us also call on this board, this staff, missionaries, our Baptist co-workers around the world, Southern Baptists and other Christians to pay the price of making the difference between life and death for the multitudes of the earth."[67]

This reorganization led to the approval of four new regional vice-presidents who would represent the major continents where Board personnel served, each

---

[61] R. Keith Parks *Transforming a Vision into Reality* (Richmond: Southern Baptist Foreign Mission Board, Accession Number 584, February 10, 1986).
[62] Parks *Transforming a Vision into Reality.*
[63] "Board of Trustees Minutes," (Ridgecrest: Southern Baptist Foreign Mission Board, Accession Number 575, June 24, 1986).
[64] "Board of Trustees Minutes," June 24, 1986.
[65] R. Keith Parks, *Charting a Course – By Candlelight* (Richmond: Southern Baptist Foreign Mission Board, Accession Number 587, December 08, 1986).
[66] "Board of Trustees Minutes," (Richmond: Southern Baptist Foreign Mission Board, Accession Number 447, February 09, 1987).
[67] Parks, *Will Recommendations Change Our Effort.*

of which would serve on the GSG.[68] At the same meeting, the board elected Lewis Myers, the director for CSI since its inception in 1985, as vice-president for CSI, thus placing him as another one of the key members of the GSG.[69] Besides Parks and the five area vice-presidents, other members of the GSG would be the executive vice-president, vice-president for administration and human resources, the director of research (David Barrett), and the vice-president for finance.[70] By naming Myers as vice-president for CSI and placing him as a member of the GSG, Parks was indicating that he firmly was committed to leading Southern Baptists in reaching the 1.3 billion people of World A identified through Barrett's research.

The formation of the GSG radically changed the manner in which the Board would form and implement its strategy. Historically, the Board developed its strategy geographically, focusing on countries that allowed for the deployment of missionary personnel.[71] The GSG would now focus on "how to reach people who have not had opportunity to respond to the Christian gospel, no matter in what country or under what political system they live…finding how best to expend funds and personnel to give every person on earth a chance to hear and respond to the message of Christ."[72] Within a few years, Williard, writing for *The Commission*, incisively revealed that Parks successfully had steered the Board in a direction from which it was unlikely to retreat:

> One thing is certain: World A has become part of the FMB mix; every strategic decision at the board will henceforth factor in, directly or indirectly, the urgency of reaching out to the unreached world. Out of that process of repeatedly weighing diverse needs of the entire world – at the administrative level, but equally at the local mission level – the balance ultimately will emerge.[73]

With the establishment of an office of global research and the reorganization of administrative structure in response to the realities of the world defined by Barrett's massive research efforts, Parks had firmly planted the second seed of change. Barrett and the Global Strategy Group soon would plant yet another seed of change – the non-residential missionary. This third seed, like the first

[68] Bob Stanley, "Parks Proposes Major Changes to Carry out Global Strategy," (Richmond: Southern Baptist Foreign Mission Board, December 10, 1986); available from https://solomon. imb.org; Stories database.

[69] Stanley, "Parks Proposes Major Changes."

[70] Stanley, "Parks Proposes Major Changes."

[71] Leland Webb, "Re-targeting the Planet," (Richmond: Southern Baptist Foreign Mission Board, September 01, 1990); available from https://solomon.imb.org; Stories database.

[72] Webb, "Re-targeting the Planet."

[73] Williard, "Shaping Strategies: FMB Vision," 45.

two, would lead the Board and Southern Baptists to rewrite their maps of reality regarding their mission efforts.

The Third Seed Planted

Toward the end of his tenure as President of the FMB, when asked from where the NRM concept came, Parks replied, "It actually emerged out of our research unit…researching the unreached people groups."[74] Parks, as he led Southern Baptists to have a global strategy to match their global vision as expressed in its Bold Mission Thrusts, knew the journey involved re-writing the Board's maps of reality. The research originating from Barrett and the World Evangelization Research Center at the Board provided the essential information, and in due course, the journey led to the development of the non-residential missionary concept. Parks describes the journey:

> Traditionally – and I'm not being critical, just descriptive – the way we have advanced has been to appoint a missionary or a missionary couple and send them to a country, and then we've added up the places we've done that, and that's been our world program….In the fall of '86 I began grappling with this. I asked a simple question of myself: Suppose we fulfil all of the goals of Bold Mission Thrust – 5,000 missionaries, 125 countries and all those good things. Will we as Southern Baptists have fulfilled our appropriate share of taking the gospel to the whole world?
>
> They keep telling me we're the largest evangelical mission board; 125 nations is roughly half of the nations of the world. It overwhelmed me that our goal was simply to place people in half of the nations of the world. But as we began looking at the other nations at that time…many of the nations we couldn't send missionaries. So we began grappling with how can we fulfil our biblical mandate. How can we really share the gospel with the rest of the world if we can't do it the way we've done it? It was out of that we began to talk about and ultimately adopt what [has been] called the "non-residential program."[75]

As noted earlier, the NRM concept was the brainchild of David Barrett. It was one of many creative ideas that emerged from the World Evangelization Research Center.[76] Garrison recalls hearing the term "non-residential missionary" for the first time in early 1986 when he met Barrett while attending

---

[74] Martha Skelton, "Reflecting on a Missions Career," (Richmond: Southern Baptist Foreign Mission Board, October 01, 1992); available from https://solomon.imb.org; Stories database.

[75] Skelton, "Reflecting on a Missions Career,"

[76] Garrison, "Response to Bruce."

a mission conference in Chicago.[77] Garrison summarizes his meeting with Barrett:

> We had lunch together, and then he came to our apartment for tea and dessert that evening. Even then, he was asking, "Have you ever heard of the Zhuang people?" After explaining to me who they were, he began describing the kind of missionary who might reside outside of a restricted country and then work through others to project the gospel back into that country. Before the evening was over, David had asked me if I would like to join him as a research associate at the Foreign Mission Board.[78]

Garrison accepted Barrett's offer and joined the World Evangelization Research Center team in March 1987.[79]

An even more significant meeting would take place in December 1986 in Richmond. The director of the Global Desk at the FMB James Maroney introduced Bill Smith, a furloughing missionary from Thailand seeking some guidance for his Doctor of Ministry project, to Barrett.[80] During their meeting that December day, Barrett asked the same question to and shared the same information with Smith as he had done with Garrison earlier that year.[81] Smith's wife Susan recalls, "By the end of the conversation Dr. Barrett agreed to be Bill's field supervisor on a D. Min. project to find ways, as a Non-Resident Missionary (NRM), to get the gospel to [an] unreached people group in a restricted access country."[82]

Smith began his research and at a meeting of the GSG in June 1987 shared with this group of Board strategists the manual he was developing for initiating a non-residential ministry among an unevangelized people group in Asia.[83] At the same meeting, Parks instructed Myers and Smith to draft a NRM plan for this unevangelized people group with the intent that the Board might begin

---

[77] Garrison, "Response to Bruce."

[78] Garrison, "Response to Bruce." The Zhuang people were a populous minority people group in Asia, one of the many categorized by Barrett as unevangelized.

[79] Garrison, "Response to Bruce."

[80] Smith, "Additional Document."

[81] Smith, "Additional Document."

[82] Smith, "Additional Document."

[83] "Global Strategy Group Minutes," (Richmond: Southern Baptist Foreign Mission Board, Accession Number 393, June 29, 1987). The Board has a stated policy of not disclosing publicly specific NRM assignments because of the concern of opposition or reprisal from non-Christian peoples in countries targeted by these NRM personnel. See "Board Appoints its first NRMs," *The Commission*, August 1989, 71. This paper will use the real name of unevangelized people groups and NRM personnel. However, this paper will seek to avoid coupling the name of the specific people group to the name of the NRM personnel assigned by the Board in order to respect this policy.

experimenting with such an approach.[84] At the September 1987 GSG meeting, Smith and Myers reported to the GSG, and the GSG administratively placed the Smiths under the CSI-China office while approving them to return to Asia to begin implementation of the NRM plan they had developed.[85] By that time, Smith had already taken the brief amount of information on this unevangelized people group provided to him by Barrett and converted it into over three thousand pages of research information, including the beginning of a list of possible options on how to present the gospel to this people group.[86] There was no formal action taken by the Board of Trustees transferring the Smiths to this new assignment.[87]

The GSG had planted the third seed of change. Parks took little time in seizing the initiative and capitalizing on this experimental NRM approach. In presenting the Board's Strategic Objectives to the trustees in December 1987, Parks stated that two of its goals would be to deploy twenty-five NRM personnel and establish a network whereby the Board could help link other GCC organizations with World A people groups by December 31,1988.[88] Although the Board did not reach this ambitious goal, by December 1988, it had deployed five NRM couples to unevangelized people groups totalling approximately 60 million in population.[89]

With the emergence of the NRM role, the Board was paving a new road that presented a vast array of possibilities for achieving its vision of global evangelization. No one truly knew what were those possibilities, yet it was a road that Parks and others at the Board were convinced they must pave. In reflecting on those early days of this new paradigm, Garrison expresses the attitude of the Board leadership, "We had no idea what was possible, but we

---

[84] "Global Strategy Group Minutes," June 29, 1987.

[85] "Global Strategy Group Minutes," (Richmond: Southern Baptist Foreign Mission Board, Accession Number 356, September 08, 1987); Smith, "Additional Document;" *Cooperative Services International Non-residential Missionary Program Review*, Preview Committee Edition (Richmond: Southern Baptist International Mission Board, January 1992), 65. There is some discrepancy on dates. At the August 1987 Board Meeting, Parks introduced Smith as someone developing plans for reaching an unevangelized people group, and Smith states that he was approved by the GSG to do this in August 1987. However, there is no formal record of GSG minutes for August 1987. The earliest written Board record of GSG minutes indicating approval for the Smiths to begin this assignment is September 08, 1987.

[86] Smith, "Additional Document;" Garrison, "Response to Bruce;" *Cooperative Services International Review*, 4.

[87] Smith, "Additional Document."

[88] "Board of Trustees Minutes," (Richmond: Southern Baptist Foreign Mission Board, Accession Number 444, December 07, 1987).

[89] R. Keith Parks, *The State of Southern Baptist World Mission Efforts* (Richmond: Southern Baptist Foreign Mission Board, Accession Number 622, December 12, 1988).

had a strong sense that God demanded us to obey the Great Commission and thus, He would enable us to do so."[90] Years later, reflecting upon the birth of the NRM paradigm and its subsequent impact, Baldridge would add, "Few people recognized it then, and few were aware of it more than a decade later, but this administrative move of freeing up personnel and budget to experiment with the new World A strategy unleashed forces that would revolutionize frontier missions well into the twenty-first century."[91]

The New Seed Grows

As any new seed planted, the NRM concept needed nurturing and protection in order to grow and blossom. Parks along with a small number of leaders at the Board created the environment that allowed the concept to develop. With the nurturing and protection of these key leaders, often in the face of strong opposition from within the Board's ranks, the NRM paradigm matured as it developed its own unique ethos, and slowly over the first few years, witnessed an increasing numerical growth in terms of personnel.

Structuring for Growth

While there is little doubt that Parks' unflinching support for this innovative paradigm was the primary ingredient allowing it to successfully manoeuvre its way from infancy to maturity;[92] at the same time, it was the pulling together of key people, each playing a unique role in the development of the paradigm that truly revealed Parks' ingenuity. Parks was committed to the success of this new paradigm because he was committed to providing every person in the world with an opportunity to hear and respond to the gospel message.

The GSG initially placed Smith under the administrative responsibility of the CSI-China office, but quickly discovered that major philosophical differences created an atmosphere of conflict and distrust.[93] The CSI-China office was committed to deploying workers solely through the Amity Foundation, which was the government-approved channel for non-Chinese seeking to be involved as Christian workers within China.[94] The CSI-China

---

[90] Garrison, "Response to Bruce."

[91] Baldridge, *Keith Park*, 42.

[92] Baldridge, *Keith Park*, 42., 48; Smith, "Additional Document," and Garrison, "Response to Bruce."

[93] Smith, "Additional Document."

[94] Smith, "Additional Document:" Garrison, "Response to Bruce;" *Cooperative Services International Review*, 6. The Amity Foundation was the Three Self Patriotic Movement's interface with the Christian world outside of China. The Three Self Patriotic Movement and the Chinese Christian Council are government sanctioned and controlled organizations for the purpose of monitoring and regulating Christian activity

office was convinced that personnel should only engage in activities, programs or projects that had official approval of the Amity Foundation.[95]

However, the Smiths believed that the unevangelized people group they were targeting would likely not have access to the gospel if they had to carry out their work strictly through government-approved channels; therefore, they bypassed the Amity Foundation and sought other channels for ministry among this unevangelized people group.[96] For the CSI-China office, working outside official channels was unethical, yet, for the Smiths, working outside the official channels was the best opportunity to get the gospel to this unevangelized people group.[97] It did not take long for these two parties, espousing divergent philosophical approaches, to reach an impasse.

Aware of the conflict, the GSG grappled with how to administer the NRM approach. The Director of Research and Planning, Clark Scanlon, proposed three possibilities: 1) place NRM personnel under a regional vice-president working with an area director; 2) develop a special unit within CSI; or 3) create a unique unit specifically dedicated to the NRM approach.[98] In less than one year's time, two of Scanlon's three recommendations became reality.

On October 10, 1988, the Board of Trustees approved Garrison to serve as the Associate to Coordinate Non-residential Missions under the auspices of CSI.[99] Garrison's role was "to nurture and develop the concept and program…a bridge between David Barrett's unparalleled Global Research Database and the implementation vehicle of CSI,…in a unique position to identify, prioritize, and pursue the least unevangelized unreached people groups in the world."[100]

CSI would administer both the NRM program and the CSI-China office;

---

within the country. The government mandates through the Three Self Patriotic Movement and the Chinese Christian Council that Christian activities occur in government-designated facilities, at government-specified times, and under government-approved leadership.

[95] Smith, "Additional Document:" Garrison, "Response to Bruce;" *Cooperative Services International Review*, 6.

[96] Smith, "Additional Document:" Garrison, "Response to Bruce;" *Cooperative Services International Review*, 6.

[97] Smith, "Additional Document;" Garrison, "Response to Bruce." At one point, a Board-appointed missionary with the CSI-China office wrote a letter to Parks and sent a copy of that letter to Bishop Ting, head of the Chinese Christian Council. In the letter, this man accused the NRM personnel as being clandestine missionaries. This was a frequently heard criticism of the NRM approach, creating a stigma that was difficult to shed. As people, such as Garrison and Barrett enunciated the NRM paradigm, they dismissed as erroneous the idea that a NRM was a clandestine or illegal missionary.

[98] "Global Strategy Group Minutes," November 24, 1987.

[99] "Board of Trustees Minutes," (Richmond: Southern Baptist Foreign Mission Board, Accession Number 528, October 10, 1988).

[100] Garrison, "Response to Bruce."

however, in May 1990 the Board separated the two programs.[101] Despite the friction between the CSI-China office and the NRM program, the decision to create a separate NRM program under the supervision of a regional vice-president was liberating. According to Garrison, Myers, an experienced missionary to Southeast Asia and now the vice-president for CSI, provided "a departmental umbrella under which the fledging NRM program could find protection from its many potent critics."[102] Within the GSG, Myers provided another strong voice of support for this new approach, and to the NRM program's new director and personnel he provided veteran counsel.[103] With the needed structure in place, the stage was set for this emerging paradigm to begin to flourish.

Defining the New Paradigm

One of the first tasks undertaken by Board strategists was to define the term "non-residential missionary." In November 1987, the research department under Barrett's direction submitted to the GSG a rather lengthy definition:

> A non-residential missionary is a full-time, appointed, salaried, professional career foreign missionary who is assigned by his or her board or agency, through a matching-up process designed to concentrate on priorities of first evangelization and to avoid gaps or inadvertent duplications with other agencies, to a ministry to one unevangelized population segment of the unevangelized world (one metropolis, or one people, or one country), who resides outside that segment or its country (because legal residence is prohibited or otherwise impossible) and who then networks with all other concerned Great Commission Christians both local and non-local, denominations and agencies, in order to do the following: (1) research and survey the whole situation of that single segment, becoming expert in the subject within six months, (2) learn and become fluent in that segment's main language, (3) draw up and help to see implemented a wide range of ministry options directed towards that segment, (4) report briefly on a monthly standard form to his board outlining progress with that segment, in order to enable adequate monitoring and assistance to proceed, (5) relate throughout to the World Evangelization Database and the associated network, and (6) relate as part of a global team to his board's other non-residential missionaries each of whom has been assigned to a different segment; with the overarching objective of seeing to it that through the whole vast network of Christian influences all persons in his population segment become evangelized by AD2000 (have the opportunity by that date to hear and respond to the gospel) with at least a dozen converts made and a

---

[101] *Cooperative Services International Review,* 7.
[102] *Cooperative Services International Review,* 7.
[103] *Cooperative Services International Review,* 7.

> beachhead church (one or more local groups, or churches, or organized church fellowships) planted in that segment by that time.[104]

The definition, although lengthy and cumbersome, did provide a thorough description of this emerging missionary paradigm. It reflects some avant-garde mission concepts for Southern Baptists. First, the NRM concept, by design, sought to include networking and partnership with other GCC individuals and groups.[105] Second, by its very definition, the NRM approach would focus exclusively on population segments that, according to Barrett's research, had yet to have access to the gospel message.[106] Third, the NRM approach would deliberately focus on the over one half of the global population who resided in countries where acquiring missionary visas was extremely difficult or impossible.[107] Bridges describes the innovative approach of the NRM concept in this way:

> The genius of this approach…is the way it can multiply evangelization. The non-residential missionary is not a solitary witness, but an "agent of evangelization." Working as a non-resident, he coordinates the efforts of hundreds, perhaps thousands of others who have a cumulative impact by their sheer number. He becomes a funnel for the wealth of evangelistic resources that have been going into the same places again and again and channels them into areas that previously had no evangelistic witness at all.[108]

In the early days of this emerging paradigm, there was some misunderstanding of this new concept, a misunderstanding inherent in the name

[104] *Cooperative Services International Review,* 4. In 1988, the same definition appeared publicly for the first time in Barrett and Reapsome, *Seven Hundred Plans,* 35. See Appendix C for Barrett and Reapsome's exhaustive list of the twelve dimensions and eighty-four characteristics of a non-residential missionary, which elaborate further on the key components of the definition. At its March 02, 1998, meeting the GSG would approve a much shorter definition for its use – "personnel with a full-time assignment to evangelize an unevangelized population segment and who resides and works from a location outside that segment." A few years later, Garrison's book *The Non-residential Missionary* (Monrovia, MARC, 1990) would elaborate extensively on the NRM paradigm, making it understandable for the wider evangelical community. In introducing a related article, which was an excerpt from Garrison's book, entitled "An Unexpected New Strategy," *International Journal of Frontier Missions,* 7 no. 4 (October 1990): 107-15, the editor raised the question of whether or not this new strategy might alter the course of mission history.

[105] *Cooperative Services International Review,* 4.

[106] *Cooperative Services International Review,* 6.

[107] *Cooperative Services International Review,* 6.

[108] Erich Bridges, "New Kid on the Block: the 'Non-residential Missionary'," *The Commission,* August 1988, 45.

"non-residential missionary." Some understood the term to indicate an "approach…exclusive of residential, incarnational ministries."[109] Others mistook the term to mean tentmaker itinerant missionary, or even a missionary on furlough.[110] Therefore, there was a need, at times, to explain what was not a NRM. For example, Garrison points out that a NRM was neither a missionary unable to obtain a residence visa, a tentmaker nor a covert missionary.[111] To the contrary, Garrison asserts, "A non-residential missionary is a frontier evangelist committed to the use of every God-given means possible to present the gospel to the unevangelized world."[112]

The Board consistently emphasized that the overall thrust of the NRM was the same as any of its missionary personnel, evangelizing the targeted population segment resulting in the planting of indigenous churches.[113] In a report to the Board of Trustees, Myers explained that although advocacy, networking and collaborating with GCC groups were instrumental aspects of the NRM role, the goal of evangelization remained central.[114] Myers pointed out the catalytic nature of the NRM role led to the emergence of residential, incarnational presence, which, in turn, generated evangelistic ministries.[115]

One of the key concepts unique to the NRM paradigm in comparison to the traditional, incarnational paradigm, which had been the foundation of the Board's missiological model since its inception, was the attitude toward the task. According to Smith, the NRM had the attitude that "it is more important to get the gospel there than it is to get me there."[116] In other words, the NRM approach asked the question, "What will it take to evangelize the people group?" Whereas, the incarnational approach primarily began with the question, "What can I do to evangelize the people?" This was a subtle, yet significant shift in missiological thinking, a shift more towards a catalytic approach to the mission task.

Smith further asserts the NRM model had a different standard of success, which further set it apart from the traditional, incarnational approach.[117] This standard, according to Smith was that success was measured by progress made

---

[109] *Cooperative Services International Review,* 6.

[110] *Cooperative Services International Review,* 108.

[111] Garrison, *Non-residential Missionary,* 20.

[112] Garrison, *Non-residential Missionary,* 21.

[113] Garrison, *Non-residential Missionary,* 14; *Cooperative Services International Review,* 6; Mark Harvey, "Missionaries Needed: Non-residential Missionaries," *The Commission,* August 1990, 71.

[114] Lewis I. Myers, Jr., *Two Roads, One Destination* (Richmond: Southern Baptist Foreign Mission Board, Accession Number 570, February 11, 1991).

[115] Myers, *Two Roads.*

[116] William Smith, interview by author, January 07, 2005, Singapore, written transcript, available from the author, 1.

[117] William Smith, interview by author, January 07, 2005, 1.

toward the overall evangelization of the people group with church planting as a means to that end; whereas, for most incarnational missionaries the end was viewed as the planting of churches coupled with the forming of a denominational structure.[118] Thus, the NRM paradigm challenged conventional thinking. Parks explained it this way:

> Part of our emphasis, not just in World A, but wherever our missionaries are, is to really encourage them to move out beyond existing churches and stay on the cutting edge of the gospel....
>
> ...In my estimation, the initiation of leadership training and the institutionalizing of church activity is a temporary detour for missionaries, and once local churches have come to the place where they ought to be doing that, we need to keep aware that our thrust is a 'missioning' thrust. We do not go overseas to build up the institutions of a denomination....
>
> ...You need that, but that's not our calling. Our calling is to be out on the cutting edge of spreading the kingdom of God.[119]

Finally, there were some overly optimistic expectations presented in the initial definition of the NRM. For example, it was idealistic thinking to presume that a NRM could become an expert on his or her population segment in the short time span of six months.[120] Some considered it somewhat unrealistic to expect every person within an unevangelized population segment, most numbering in the millions, to have opportunity to hear and respond to the gospel message by the year 2000.[121] While some considered these expectations as romantic thinking, others believed that this idealism infused a "sense of urgency and focus which has generally proven beneficial."[122]

The NRM training manual and process developed by Garrison with input and assistance from Bill Smith, Jim Maroney, Dale Hooper and Mike Stroope provided the scaffolding upon which to construct this new missionary paradigm.[123] The training manual and process fleshed out the concepts

---

118 William Smith, interview by author, January 07, 2005, 1.

119 David Williard, "Q's and A's on World A," (Richmond: Southern Baptist Foreign Mission Board, October 01, 1991); available from https://solomon.imb.org; Stories database.

120 *Cooperative Services International Review,* 6.

121 *Cooperative Services International Review,* 6.

122 *Cooperative Services International Review,* 6.

123 Garrison, "Response to Bruce." Maroney served as the director of the Board's Global Desk. Hooper worked in the Board's Research and Planning Office. Stroope initially served as a Board missionary in Sri Lanka and later served as the associate director of the Missionary Learning Center. The Board approved Stroope to serve as a non-

delineated in the definition. Garrison's initial step involved taking Smith's research and developing a process to assist missionaries in understanding how to research a population segment.[124] Then, in conjunction with Smith, Maroney and Hooper, Garrison developed a section on one hundred ministry options for reaching an unevangelized population segment.[125] Based on the research of the people group, the NRM would engage in a brainstorming exercise, listing at least one hundred different ways to begin evangelizing the population segment. This component of the training helped the NRM respond to the question, "What will it take to evangelize this people group?" One purpose of this training component was to lead the NRM to visualize the vastness of the task, a task much bigger than what one could accomplish alone.

In conjunction with Stroope and others, Garrison made several revisions to the NRM training manual, completing a final revision in late 1992.[126] The training centred around five key elements: (1) researching the unevangelized population segment; (2) researching the world of GCC resources; (3) developing a strategy to bring the GCC resources to the unevangelized population segment; (4) training in computer skills; and (5) training in administrative and logistical issues.[127]

Built into the NRM training and, consequently, the NRM paradigm was a firm commitment to strategic planning. Initially, the strategic planning focused on four key areas: (1) prayer; (2) scripture and literature; (3) media; and (4) incarnational presence ministries.[128] The NRM strategy focused on the mobilization of a wide array of evangelization resources with the overall objective of the evangelization of the target population segment or people group.

Strategic planning was not new to the FMB and its missionaries, but conventional planning focused on specific goals and objectives that a mission entity in a country sought to accomplish each year in cooperation with local Baptist entities.[129] Often these plans were the sum total of the plans of the individual missionaries assigned to that particular mission entity. Further, these plans often led to a mono-denominational approach to the task. The NRM

---

residential missionary. From 1992-7, Stroope served as the director for Cooperative Services International.

124 Garrison, "Response to Bruce."

125 Garrison, "Response to Bruce."

126 Garrison, "Response to Bruce."

127 Garrison, *Non-residential Missionary*, 51. In Chapter 7 of his book, Garrison outlines the four-and-a-half week NRM training developed by the Board. *Cooperative Services International Review*, 126.

128 Garrison, *Non-residential Missionary*, 17-19.

129 Crawley, *Global Mission*, 136. A "mission" entity comprised the missionaries assigned to a specific country or a particular region within a country. Upon deployment, the board assigned its missionaries to a specific mission entity.

strategic process intentionally shifted the thinking of the missionary toward the wider GCC community, recognizing that a mono-denominational approach was inadequate for the task. As Garrison points out, "By using every possible Christian contact…the non-residential missionary is able to catalyze hundreds – and even thousands – of agents in a concerted effort to serve a specific population segment."[130]

Initial Growth

Not only did the Board need to define this new missiological paradigm, but it also had to answer the unavoidable question, "From where will we find appropriate personnel to step into these new NRM roles?" Recognizing this as a potential problem for this new, emerging role within the Board's ranks, Parks, as early as 1987, began proposing that a plan be put into place for recruiting existing missionary personnel who felt led to shift toward an unevangelized people group focus in their ministry.[131] Initially what Parks sought was a redeployment of personnel from World C assignments to World A assignments. This proved to be a formidable task.

By projecting the deployment of three hundred NRM personnel within ten years, the Board had set a challenging, seemingly impossible, goal. Within the first year, the Board had deployed only five NRM couples, all who had transferred from other missionary assignments.[132] By October 1989, the NRM program reported sixteen NRM couples focusing on sixteen World A population segments.[133] By June 1990, the number of NRM couples rose to nineteen.[134] By January 1992, the NRM program reported forty-eight career units working among World A population segments, of which only twenty-five had transferred from other areas of the world.[135] The GSG, recognizing the slow growth of the NRM program via redeployment "attempted to rectify the problem with the creation of a 'Global Priority Deployment Policy.'"[136] Further, recognizing the need for speedier deployment of NRM personnel, the Board began to open up NRM assignments to new personnel appointed from

[130] Garrison, *Non-residential Missionary,* 15.

[131] "Global Strategy Group Minutes," June 29, 1987.

[132] R. Keith Parks, *State of Southern Baptist Efforts.*

[133] "Global Strategy Group Minutes," (Richmond: Southern Baptist Foreign Mission Board, Accession Number 381, October 03, 1989).

[134] Lewis I. Myers, Jr., *And Yet There is More* (Richmond: Southern Baptist Foreign Mission Board, Accession Number 542, June 08, 1990).

[135] *Cooperative Services International Review,* 55. One couple or one single person constitutes a career unit.

[136] *Cooperative Services International Review,* 57. See Appendix D, "Policy: Deployment of Missionary Personnel in Response to Global Priorities."

the US.[137] However, the Board initially intended to recruit missionaries with cross-cultural experience before opening up the selection process to new appointees.[138]

Despite the formation of a Global Priority Deployment Policy, the number of missionary personnel redeploying into World A assignments was painstakingly slow.[139] The Board cited various reasons contributing to the difficulty in recruiting experienced missionaries for redeployment to the strategically identified NRM positions. For some missionaries, the thought of deployment created anxiety as it would involve uprooting from one culture to a new culture as well as shift in ministry roles.[140] The Board challenged its missionary personnel to revisit their missionary call. There was a challenge to be more Pauline in thinking about the missionary role. In other words, missionaries perhaps should see their role as being itinerant, initiating the evangelization process in one place and then shifting to a new place to repeat the process.[141]

Even though the rate of deployment initially was slow, the Board's challenge indicated the beginning of a significant reinterpretation of the missionary role. Since its inception, the Board had espoused a strong incarnational approach in its mission efforts. This strong incarnational approach often led missionaries to interpret their calling as living and working in one location for an extended period or even the entirety of one's missionary career. With the emergence of the NRM paradigm came the beginning of a shift in interpreting and understanding the missionary role. It was not a shift away from the incarnational approach, but more a reinterpretation of the incarnational approach. However, in order to fulfil its vision of taking the gospel message to the unevangelized peoples of World A, the Board had to challenge itself and its missionary personnel to reconsider the nature of the missionary call and role.[142]

---

137 "Board Appoints its first NRMs," *The Commission,* August 1989, 71. Al and Cathy James were the first personnel directly from the United States appointed for a NRM assignment.

138 David Williard, "Erecting Foundations in World A," (Richmond: Southern Baptist Foreign Mission Board, October 01, 1991); available from https://solomon.imb.org; Stories database.

139 *Cooperative Services International Review,* 57. One year after the deployment policy was put into effect, only one missionary unit had redeployed into the NRM program indicating that the Board's efforts to redeploy experienced personnel into World A was not bearing fruit.

140 Webb, "Re-targeting the Planet."

141 Webb, "Re-targeting the Planet."

142 Two anecdotes from my own missionary career illustrate the issue raised here. My wife and I served in Cambodia from 1990 to 1996. In 1996, we felt led to initiate work among another unevangelized people group in India as we had done among the Khmer people in Cambodia. When discussing our redeployment with leaders of the Board, one

Opposition from other area directors[143] within the Board further contributed to the slow success of redeployment of personnel into World A assignments. The NRM program review presented to the GSG in 1992 indicated that only seven out of the twenty-five transfers from other areas into the NRM program had transferred receiving the support of their area directors.[144] Some of the early transferees into the NRM program "were give the impression that they had betrayed their colleagues and area administrators by their desire to transfer out of the area and into the NRM program."[145] In addition, misinformation regarding the NRM program circulated throughout the FMB leading to a hesitancy on the part of some to transfer.[146]

One issue surrounding the redeployment of missionaries into the NRM program, in particular, and the NRM approach, in general, was one of 'turf.' Some area directors simply were not pleased with a new paradigm that challenged some of their traditional beliefs regarding mission work.[147] According to Smith, some area directors were jealous that they had not developed this innovative approach, thus were reluctant to give their approval.[148] On the other hand, the issue could have been simply that Parks and

---

leader indicated that he was concerned because, in his opinion, we needed to "take root and bear fruit." While we had understood our missionary call as being itinerant – shifting from place to place to begin the work of evangelization – our beliefs put us at odds with the thinking of a large number of our colleagues. Further, there seemed to be an assumption in comments made to us that we were neglecting the incarnational aspects of our role. However, we had functioned fluently in the language of the Khmer people and we had painstaking learned and adapted to their culture during our time there. Nonetheless, there was a misperception that an itinerant missionary role lacked the incarnational emphasis. The issue surfaced again a few years later at a mission conference in a local US church. During that conference, there was a session in which I was to be interviewed by someone regarding our work in Cambodia and, subsequently, in India. While discussing the interview process with the interviewer, a leader from the IMB interjected and asked the interviewer, "Why don't you ask him why he cannot stay in one place a long time?"

143 The board divided its work overseas into specific geographical areas. An area director oversaw the mission work within the defined geographical parameters for his area.

144 *Cooperative Services International Review,* 55-6.

145 *Cooperative Services International Review*, 56.

146 *Cooperative Services International Review,* 56. For example, rumour circulated that NRM personnel were non-evangelistic, individuals who could not function in face-to-face ministry or missionaries who operated outside the scope of the law. Another rumour circulating said that personnel would lose some of their missionary benefits if they transferred into the NRM program. The misinformation slowed the flow of potential NRM redeployments.

147 Smith, interview by author, 1; Baldridge, *Keith Parks,* 47.

148 Smith, interview by author, 1.

other leaders were naïve in believing that area directors would gladly accept the idea of some of their best and most experienced personnel leaving their area to work with an experimental mission paradigm.[149] All of these factors, coupled with the fact that area directors were the first line of screening for potential transferees out of their region into the NRM program, greatly reduced the numbers of potential redeployments.[150]

What is true is that there existed an atmosphere of intense opposition to the NRM program emanating primarily from the area directors of traditional fields, an opposition that had a debilitating effect on the redeployment of experienced personnel into this new program. Nevertheless, the fledging program did grow and by 1992, the number of personnel within the NRM program outnumbered at least one of the traditional administrative areas of the Board – Middle East and North Africa.[151]

Although the growth of NRM personnel was slower than perhaps some expected, millions of people previously without access to the gospel were now within the scope of Southern Baptist mission efforts. In 1988, Parks commented, "The assignment of five non-residential missionary couples to groups totalling 60 million people is an important step in trying to penetrate areas where there is virtually no gospel witness."[152] By the end of 1989, the number of World A population segments engaged by the Board increased to sixteen representing a population of 120 million people.[153] Within a few short months, Board personnel were focusing on twenty unevangelized groups with a population totalling nearly 172 million.[154] Toward the end of 1990, Board personnel were working among population segments that totalled approximately 238 million.[155] By January 1992, the NRM program was targeting forty major unevangelized population segments with a cumulative population approaching 350 million.[156] Furthermore, by January 1992, the GSG had approved 113 different population segments for NRM assignments.[157] Thus, within a few short years the Board had made significant progress toward fulfilling its vision of targeting ten percent of World A population segments.[158]

---

149 *Cooperative Services International Review,* 57.

150 *Cooperative Services International Review,* 57.

151 *Cooperative Services International Review*, 8; Smith, "Additional Document."

152 Parks, *State of Southern Baptist Efforts.*

153 "Global Strategy Group Minutes," October 03, 1989.

154 "Global Strategy Group Minutes," (Richmond: Southern Baptist Foreign Mission Board, Accession Number 832, April 24, 1990).

155 "Global Strategy Group Minutes," (Richmond: Southern Baptist Foreign Mission Board, Accession Number 655, November 16, 1990)

156 *Cooperative Services International Review,* 18-9.

157 *Cooperative Services International Review*, 11-5.

158 "Global Strategy Group Minutes," (Richmond: Southern Baptist Foreign Mission Board, Accession Number 350, May 12, 1987). Parks had suggested to the GSG that

The New Paradigm's Impact

From the inception of the NRM role, this emerging missionary paradigm began to have an impact within the wider FMB. Not only did the World A strategy and the resulting NRM paradigm break down a number of barriers that hindered ministry among previously unevangelized people groups, it also had an immediate impact on the other, more traditional, areas of the FMB. At times, this impact was evident in the conflicts that arose between the NRM program and these other areas of the Board. At other times, the NRM concept spawned new creative approaches in other areas. Regardless, the NRM paradigm did begin to awaken many of the other areas of the Board to the unevangelized population segments and people groups within their geographical areas.

The NRM paradigm widened Southern Baptists involvement with the larger GCC community. Another contribution of the NRM paradigm was the use of intercessory prayer as a primary tool for ministry among the unevangelized people groups. Finally, through the NRM role, FMB missionaries increasingly utilized and applied information technology to the mission task.

Tension and Conflict

From the inception of the NRM role, conflicts arose between this new paradigm and the traditional missionary paradigm of the Board. The development and implementation of the NRM paradigm created tension at various levels. At one level, the emphasis on World A and the resulting NRM paradigm created tension with the conventional mission philosophy of many within the FMB. By its definition, the NRM role focused specifically on the unevangelized people groups or population segments identified by Barrett's research. However, for a number of years a major influence on Board strategy was the Church Growth movement that had grown out of Donald McGavran's work.[159]

Southern Baptists, who made up approximately five percent of the evangelical Christian community, should target ten percent of the World A population segments.

[159] One can trace the origins of the Church Growth movement back to McGavran's classic work *The Bridges of God* (London: World Dominion, 1955) in which he expressed most of the underlying principles and foundations of this movement. A later work *Understanding Church Growth* (Grand Rapids: Eerdmans, 1970) also expounds on the foundations of this movement. McGavran spent thirty-six years as a missionary in India, and this experience shaped his views on church growth. One of his classic works on his analysis of the church in India is *Ethnic Realities and the Church: Lessons from India* (Pasadena: William Carey, 1979). One of the most ardent supporters of the Church Growth movement was C. Peter Wagner. For example, see Wagner's *Your Church Can Grow* (Glendale: Regal Books, 1976). The Church Growth movement has created a large amount of dialogue among missiologists. For example, McQuilken, in his book *Measuring the Church Growth Movement: How Biblical Is It?* (Chicago: Moody Press, 1974), seeks to defend the movement against its critics within the mission community,

One of the key missiological concepts expounded by the Church Growth movement was the idea that mission agencies and missionaries should focus the majority of their resources on those people groups identified as the most responsive to the gospel.[160] At the same time, mission agencies should not neglect the unresponsive or resistant peoples, but the Church Growth movement advocated for less emphasis of resources among such peoples.[161] Although the strategy of the FMB was eclectic in nature; nonetheless, Crawley asserted that the Board's strategy specifically incorporated this concept of the Church Growth movement.[162]

As a result of this influence from the Church Growth movement, some within the FMB saw the unevangelized people groups of World A as being resistant and unresponsive, thus not truly harvest fields. At the same time, there was concern that the global strategy adopted by the Board would lead to an imbalance in the deployment of mission personnel in favour of World A, an imbalance that would pull missionary personnel away from the harvest fields. Such concern eventually precipitated a dialogue between the Board of Trustees and the FMB leadership in 1991 where the issue of deployment into World A and continued deployment into traditional fields was discussed.[163]

---

asserting that the Biblical and missiological principles of the Church Growth movement are sound. On the other hand, Orlando E. Costas in *The Church and Its Mission: A Shattering Critique from the Third World* (Wheaton: Tyndale, 1974), Chris De Wet in "The Church Growth Movement – Does it Foster Churches that Challenge the World," *Missionalia* 14, No. 2 (August, 1986): 85-99 and David J. Bosch in "Church Growth Missiology," *Missionalia* 16, No. 1 (April 1988): 13-24 seek to expose a number of weaknesses that they see in this movement. In his book *Global Mission: A Story to Tell* (Nashville: Broadman, 1985), 269-79, Winston Crawley devotes an entire chapter explaining how the Church Growth movement has influenced FMB strategy.

160 De Wet, "Church Growth Movement," 86. Crawley, *Global Mission,* 273.

161 De Wet, "Church Growth Movement," 86. This dual emphasis of focusing on the responsive people or harvest fields while not neglecting the unreached (often considered unresponsive) was a major emphasis of "New Directions," an effort of the IMB launched in 1997 under Jerry Rankin. Chapter 4 will explore the impact of the NRM/SC paradigm on "New Directions." See R. Bruce Carlton, "Towards a New Understanding of Missions: A Challenge to the Conventional Missions Thinking of Our Day," in *Strategic Coordination in Mission: Training Manual for the Nehemiah Institute for Strategic Coordination,* eds. S.D. Ponraj and R. Bruce Carlton (Chennai: Mission Education Books, 2001), 8-12. In this article, I challenged this thinking on Biblical grounds. I argued that the issue was that the church had neglected taking the gospel to many people groups and the issue was not one of responsive or unresponsive. In the article, I coined the term "neglected harvest fields," which has gained wider acceptance within the IMB.

162 Crawley, *Global Mission,* 275.

163 "Board of Trustees Minutes," (Richmond: Southern Baptist Foreign Mission Board, Accession Number 654, August 12, 1991).

Board leaders continually addressed this issue of finding balance in the deployment of missionary personnel between World A peoples and traditional fields.[164] Myers, in an article for *The Commission*, wrote:

> The field is the world. There is no indication that our field is anything less than the whole world. Though the New Testament often speaks of the urgency of "white fields," there also is the inescapable mandate that our responsibility is "panta ethne" – all the nations or peoples.
>
> There is no ambivalence or polarization in the mandate between "seed time" and "harvest." Our field is the world, responsive and unresponsive. Open or restricted. Old fields and new fields; seeding, harvesting – the whole world....
>
> ...The needs of our world and the basic thrust of the New Testament speak to variety and balance, not to polarization....
>
> ...how much resource should be allocated to the resistant or restricted areas of our world? Whether resources of money and personnel should be allocated is not the question. But missions and administrators wrestle continually with the proportion that good stewardship dictates.[165]

Myers further asserted that no people group or population segment should be neglected, and it is premature to label a people group as responsive or unresponsive without first having gone among them to sow the gospel seed.[166]

In addressing the Board of Trustees, Don Kammerdiener, Executive Vice-President, sought to address this issue of balance in the deployment of personnel between World A and traditional areas.[167] In doing so, he addressed the Church Growth movement's harvest theology. In words that have a prophetic tone, Kammerdiener states:

> A more recent emphasis that is attracting the attention of the missionary world is that of pushing back the frontiers and planting the gospel seed in those parts of the world and among those peoples who have never yet had an opportunity to respond to the gospel. *Increasingly, this role is seen as the true function of missionary agencies*. [emphasis mine] The Foreign Mission Board will, of necessity, wrestle with the question of balance between these two emphases. Can we as a missionary

---

[164] The majority of FMB missionaries in traditional areas served by the Board were focusing on people groups that Barrett categorized as World B or World C. See Note 50 above.

[165] Lewis I. Myers, Jr., "New Horizons: Seed Time and Harvest," (Richmond: Southern Baptist Foreign Mission Board, January 01, 1991); available from https://solomon .imb.org; Stories database.

[166] Myers, "New Horizons: Seed Time and Harvest."

[167] Don R. Kammerdiener, *Report to the Board: Executive Vice-President* (Richmond: Southern Baptist Foreign Mission Board, Accession Number 570, February 11, 1991).

family maintain a sense of balance and proportion or will we be stampeded into accepting one emphasis or the other?[168]

While the NRM paradigm challenged some of the conventional missiological thinking; nonetheless, the NRM paradigm did have a positive impact. The NRM paradigm with its World A people group emphasis created a World A people group awareness among leadership within some of these traditional areas. This increasing awareness of the World A population segments within the geographical boundaries of the traditional areas created tension and conflict with the NRM program, and turf battles ensued.

In November 1990, the GSG approved the Fulani people group of West Africa for a NRM assignment.[169] However, the area director for West Africa argued that with the ability to place missionary personnel almost anywhere in West Africa where the Fulani people lived, the GSG should reconsider assigning the Fulani to the NRM program.[170] Further, the area director claimed there had been evangelistic efforts among the Fulani for nearly forty years, and there already was a large multi-group, cross-denominational collaboration for those focusing on this major people group.[171] The NRM program leadership, advocating for the NRM approach, raised the issue that the Fulani lived in fourteen different nations of West Africa, some of which FMB residential personnel could not access.[172] The GSG decided there was a need for a study group to resolve the conflict, and three months later, the study group recommended that the Board form a Fulani task force of three missionaries – a coordinator, a NRM and a residential missionary from the West Africa area.[173]

Turf issues came to the surface time after time. According to Garrison the majority of the nine area directors and four regional leaders continually questioned the validity of the NRM approach and "were virtually united in their effort to either keep CSI (i.e., the NRM Program) out of their area or lobbied to have it broken up and assimilated into their respective areas."[174] Sometimes, the NRM program and the areas were able to collaborate. For example, when Jerry Rankin, area director for the Southeast Asia area, expressed hesitancy regarding the deployment of NRM personnel to people groups in Indonesia, both the area leadership and the NRM program achieved a compromise and affirmed the

---

[168] Kammerdiener, *Report to the Board,* February 11, 1991.

[169] "Global Strategy Group Minutes," (Richmond: Southern Baptist Foreign Mission Board, Accession Number 574, March 04, 1991).

[170] "Global Strategy Group Minutes," March 04, 1991.

[171] "Global Strategy Group Minutes," March 04, 1991.

[172] "Global Strategy Group Minutes," March 04, 1991.

[173] "Global Strategy Group Minutes," March 04, 1991; "Global Strategy Group Minutes," (Richmond: Southern Baptist Foreign Mission Boar, Accession Number 824, July 24, 1991).

[174] Garrison, "Response to Bruce."

value of multiple approaches.[175] Sometimes, area directors sought to pre-empt any decision by the GSG to assign a country or people group to the NRM program. They were convinced that a residential approach and a non-residential approach could not coexist within the same area. Such was the situation as the GSG in 1989 grappled with how to best engage the nation of Turkey.[176] At other times, the NRM program complained that when the GSG assigned to the NRM program specific World A people groups that resided within the geographical boundaries of another area, at times that area's leadership would seek to place personnel to work among that people group as well.[177] The picture presented resembles somewhat the situation the Apostle Paul painted in his letter to the Philippian church, saying, "Some indeed preach Christ even from envy and strife, and some also from goodwill" (Phil. 1:15 NKJV). Whatever the motive of the other area leaders may have been, it was clear that the NRM paradigm stimulated a World A awareness.

Spawning Creative Approaches

Not only did the NRM paradigm stimulate an awareness among the traditional, geographically defined areas to World A people groups within those areas that had previously been neglected, but as this awareness developed the area directors sought to develop new, creative approaches for reaching into restricted-access countries and unevangelized population segments. The issue is not the motive behind some of these creative ideas. To the contrary, whether the motive was sincere or not, the result was that creative ideas began to be generated because of the NRM paradigm.

First, in 1987 the Board of Trustees was asked to consider a proposal whereby missionaries could enter into restricted-access or limited-access countries through a process of becoming citizens of such countries.[178] This

---

175 "Global Strategy Group Minutes," (Richmond: Southern Baptist Foreign Mission Board, Accession Number 379, April 04, 1989).

176 "Global Strategy Group Minutes," (Richmond: Southern Baptist Foreign Mission Board, Accession Number 378, March 06, 1989). The vice-president for Europe, Middle East and Africa recommended to the GSG that a traditional, residential missionary approach be used to engage a specific World A people in a restricted-access country. The area had plans to mobilize personnel for English-language work. On the other hand, the office of Research and Planning advocated for a NRM approach. Parks tended to favour the NRM approach, indicating that a nation of over fifty million people needed more than just several couples. This was the first discussion held by the GSG regarding entry into a new country, and it revealed the gaps in mission philosophy that existed between the NRM program and the geographically defined area leaders.

177 "Global Strategy Group Minutes," (Richmond: Southern Baptist Foreign Mission Board, Accession Number 826, October 03, 1991).

178 "Board of Trustees Minutes," (Richmond: Southern Baptist Foreign Mission Board, Accession Number 444, December 07, 1987).

proposal was the direct result of a problem that arose in one Asian country. The government of Indonesia began revoking the visas of missionaries, thus the proposal to allow missionaries to consider taking a second citizenship.[179] It took almost ten years before any FMB missionary received citizenship![180] Obviously, this approach was not widely adopted among FMB missionaries; however, it does illustrate how the NRM paradigm with its emphasis on doing what it takes to get the gospel message to unevangelized peoples was stimulating creative thinking.

A second idea generated because of the influence of this new paradigm was the concept of an itinerant missionary force. This idea was the brainchild of leadership within the Southeast Asia and the Pacific area and developed as one possible avenue for gaining access into restricted or closed countries.[181] The itinerant missionary force did not focus on unevangelized people groups, rather the effort focused on training and equipping Baptist leaders within those countries throughout South and Southeast Asia where missionaries were not able to secure long-term residency visas.[182] Although not a specific World A strategy as the NRM paradigm, the itinerant missionary force was one creative response to a world that was growing less and less tolerant of long-term residential missionaries. Launched initially to focus on one country in Asia, this concept expanded into numerous other countries throughout Asia.[183]

Wider Involvement with Other Christians

As noted above, a major component of the global strategy pursued by Parks and the Board involved widening Southern Baptist involvement with other like-minded Christian individuals, agencies and denominations. Inherent within the NRM role as conceived by Barrett was the concept of "joint efforts of a range of mission-minded agencies and individuals."[184] The NRM training that

---

[179] "Board of Trustees Minutes," October 06, 1996.

[180] "Board of Trustees Minutes," October 06, 1996.

[181] "Global Strategy Group Minutes," (Richmond: Southern Baptist Foreign Mission Board, Accession Number 369, October 16, 1990). Jerry Rankin, who would become the President of the FMB after Parks, was the area director for Southeast Asia and the Pacific. As already noted, Rankin was hesitant regarding the deployment of NRM personnel to his area even though he did reach a compromise with the NRM program over the deployment of NRM personnel into his area. Rankin had a reputation among the NRM personnel -and later among the SC personnel within CSI – as being one of the most vociferous opponents of the new paradigm. At that time, the Southeast Asia and the Pacific area included most of the Asian and Pacific Rim countries outside of China, Mongolia, Japan, Taiwan and the Koreas.

[182] "Global Strategy Group Minutes," October 16, 1990.

[183] "Global Strategy Group Minutes," October 16, 1990.

[184] Garrison, *Non-residential Missionary,* 41.

developed as the paradigm began to take shape involved identifying the vast amount of GCC resources in the world and matching those resources with specific needs identified within the targeted unevangelized population segment. Parks had continually emphasized the need for networking with other GCC groups, believing that such collaboration was essential in taking the gospel message to the entire world. The empowerment of NRM personnel in mobilizing and catalyzing GCC resources in an effort to take the gospel message to a specific unevangelized population segment was the tangible expression of Parks' vision.

NRM personnel sought to mobilize hundreds of GCC individuals, agencies and denominations to become involved in the evangelization of the targeted population segment or people group. As Myers points out, the goal was to create an "interlocked web of Great Commission Christendom which plays to each other's strengths to produce a 'varicolored' tapestry, against which backdrop effective witness can take place."[185] This interlocked web of GCC resources included both Baptist entities as well as non-Baptist entities.[186]

The Smith's NRM ministry among their targeted unevangelized people group vividly illustrates how they created such an interlocked web. When the Smiths began their assignment in December 1986, their targeted people group had "no missionaries, no Bible, no Christian institutions such as hospitals, clinics or schools, no Gospel radio broadcasts, and no known organized efforts to pray for their salvation."[187] Within three years, the Smiths had mobilized a wide array of GCC resources for ministry among this people group. This included Southern Baptist churches committed to prayer for the people group, Wycliffe Bible Translators for scripture translation, International Bible Society for printing and distribution of literature, Campus Crusade for Christ for translation of the *Jesus Film*, other agencies for radio broadcasting and several residential personnel who were able to live among the people group.[188]

The NRM paradigm and the creative missionaries who implemented it thrust the FMB into a new era of mission activity. Not only did NRM personnel build partnerships with other GCC groups for ministry among specific unevangelized people groups, but the FMB was also involved in training personnel from other

---

[185] Lewis I. Myers, Jr., *Netweaving As A Shaping Concept* (Richmond: Southern Baptist Foreign Mission Board, Accession Number 444, December 07, 1987).

[186] Myers, *Netweaving As A Shaping Concept.*

[187] Lewis I. Myers, Jr., *Report to the Board: Cooperative Services International* (Richmond: Southern Baptist Foreign Mission Board Accession Number 539, December 11, 1989).

[188] Myers, *Report to the Board,* December 11, 1989. See also Garrison, *Non-residential Missionary,* 63-9. Garrison presents two case studies that highlight the success of the NRM role in mobilizing GCC resources for work among an unevangelized people group.

GCC organizations to become NRM trainers.[189] For the FMB, this was a major innovation. Yet, as Smith points out, while NRM personnel found this empowerment to collaborate with GCC groups as liberating, this innovative approach created tension and controversy within the FMB and some wider Southern Baptist circles.[190]

Prayer as a Strategy

One of the first initiatives that Parks undertook upon becoming president of the FMB was to appoint Catherine Walker as a special assistant to his office responsible for intercessory prayer.[191] In 1987, this office became the International Prayer Strategy Office.[192] Several years later, Parks, in reflecting back on this significant decision remarked, "All I wanted was to get specific prayer requests from missionaries, share them with Southern Baptists and then share back with the missionaries and Southern Baptists how God answered those prayers."[193] Although Parks' vision at the time was limited, his decision to put a high priority on prayer would prove to be momentous.

The NRM paradigm took the concept of prayer in ministry and expanded it beyond just praying for missionaries and their work. NRM personnel began enlisting GCC partners to intercede on behalf of the targeted unevangelized people group as well as for mobilizing workers for the task. Prayer was one of the foundational pillars on which a NRM would build his or her strategy. Garrison, in pointing out the value of prayer within a NRM strategy, states:

> The least evangelized countries, cities and peoples on earth have long been under the spiritual domination of Satan; only fervent and concerted prayer can break this oppressive control. As people begin to pray for these great unevangelized areas, not only are new doors opened for witness, but God also works a miracle of grace in the hearts of the praying people. Once their hearts are changed by prayer, Christian who never before considered participating in missions begin to discover ways they themselves can participate in reaching out to the ends of the earth.[194]

As noted earlier, within three years of beginning their NRM assignment, the Smiths had mobilized five hundred Southern Baptist churches to pray for their targeted unevangelized people group. Garrison reports how another NRM,

---

[189] Williard, "Q's and A's on World A."

[190] Smith, "Thoughts for Bruce." See Note 43 above.

[191] "Board of Trustees Minutes," (Richmond: Southern Baptist Foreign Mission Board, Accession Number 1314, March 10, 1981).

[192] David Williard, "Shaping New Strategies: Praying Forth the Harvest," *The Commission,* January 1992, 59.

[193] Skelton, "Reflecting on a Missions Career."

[194] Garrison, *Non-residential Missionary,* 17.

within a six-month period, had mobilized three hundred churches to pray for his targeted people group.[195] Other NRM personnel were successful in launching worldwide days of prayer and fasting for the evangelization of their focus people groups.[196] Parks recalled the effectiveness of these prayer strategies utilized by NRM personnel:

> We can trace so many places where churches were enlisted, the focus was given. We began praying. At the time we began praying, we knew very little that was happening. The Lord might have done that without a bunch of Baptists praying, but the beautiful evidence is that again and again we find that where our prayers are focused, He does begin doing some things that He wasn't doing before.[197]

Parks' conviction of the priority of prayer in mission and the NRM paradigm's practical application of prayer as an evangelization tool created an environment within the FMB as whole whereby prayer became a primary component of mission strategy.

Several years later as they trained personnel around the world in many of the key concepts and methodologies of the new paradigm, Myers and Slack cited the prayer strategies of NRM personnel as one of the paradigm's most significant contributions to the global evangelization effort.[198] Because NRM personnel could not publicize their work due to tight security, the prayer supporters in these networks became a close-knit family of supporters for the work; consequently, as a result these prayer networks became the primary pipeline for both human and material resources needed to evangelize the specific people group.[199]

Information, Technology and Mission

Parks understood the value of information and the technologies developed to store and transmit information. Without the information database developed by Barrett, the FMB may never have been able to develop the global strategy that spawned the NRM paradigm. The availability of information on the countries and peoples of the world altered the way the FMB and Southern Baptists viewed the world around them. A major component of the NRM paradigm as it emerged within the FMB was the utilization of information technology as a strategic tool in the mission endeavour.

---

[195] Garrison, *Non-residential Missionary*, 64.

[196] Garrison, *Non-residential Missionary*, 66.

[197] Skelton, "Reflecting on a Missions Career."

[198] Lewis I. Myers, Jr. and Jim Slack, *To The Edge: A Planning Process for People Group Specific Strategy Development* (Richmond: Southern Baptist International Mission Board, 1999), 3.6-7.

[199] Myers and Slack, *To The Edge,* 3.6-7.

A tactical component of the NRM training focused on developing computer skills, and every NRM was provided a computer by the Board for his or her ministry.[200] The role computers played in facilitating the ministry of NRM personnel during the initial years was significant. First, NRM personnel used their computers to do e-mail, which allowed them to communicate with other NRM personnel around the world as well as with key GCC contacts.[201] Second, the computers were used to store valuable people group and GCC research data, data that could easily be transferred back into the Board's global database in Richmond or shared with others.[202] Third, the computers allowed the NRM personnel to utilize word processing programs that enabled them to take their research data and publish them into formats, creating valuable tools for advocacy and mobilization.[203]

Computers were not the only technology utilized by NRM personnel. NRM personnel consistently sought to mobilize radio broadcasts in the language of their targeted population segment.[204] Partnerships developed with Campus Crusade for Christ to translate the *Jesus Film* into many different languages. Although many FMB missionaries utilized information technologies in their specific ministries, NRM personnel not only utilized such technologies, but excitedly embraced them as strategic tools for penetrating into places and peoples who had previously lacked access to the gospel message.

Conclusion

The first decade of Parks' leadership at the helm of the FMB brought significant changes to the Board, changes that led Southern Baptists to new frontiers in its mission efforts. The research of David Barrett, resulting in the establishment of the World Evangelization Research Center at the Board, stimulated the Board's efforts to develop a genuinely global strategy. The process of developing this global strategy led to the development of CSI and the NRM program. CSI, with its mandate to focus on restricted-access countries, and the NRM program, with its mandate to focus on the unreached and unevangelized people groups (World A), pushed the FMB beyond the 125 or so countries that permitted traditional missionary presence into a world, for the most part, neglected by the church and mission agencies.

As CSI and the NRM program developed, Board strategists discovered that these paradigms were "opening even larger gaps in the walls that have separated us from the unreached and previously inaccessible peoples of the

200 *Cooperative Services International Review*, 136-8.
201 *Cooperative Services International Review*, 127.
202 *Cooperative Services International Review*, 127.
203 *Cooperative Services International Review*, 127.
204 See above, where I discuss the influence of radio broadcasting and other information technology on the development of the NRM paradigm.

world."[205] NRM personnel discovered that, in many situations, it was possible to place personnel living and working among these previously inaccessible people groups. The Board discovered that unreached did not necessarily translate into unreachable, neither should unreached be understood as unresponsive.[206] Parks expressed it in these words:

> The other surprise has been much more response, more quickly than I had anticipated in many places. I somehow had envisioned that [in] all these places you'd work for years with no visible response. But to our amazement, we found many of these people were not that resistant as much as they just never had a chance to respond.[207]

Like most things that usher in change, the NRM paradigm faced difficult challenges. Many within the Board's ranks did not welcome the NRM concept. Yet, Parks and other key leaders supported the paradigm and protected it during its years of infancy. The Board had planted the seed. It took root and began to grow. Nothing would uproot it.

---

[205] Don Kammerdiener, *Linking Strategy and Administration* (Glorieta: Southern Baptist Foreign Mission Board, Accession Number 543, July 21, 1990).
[206] Smith, "Additional Document."
[207] Skelton, "Reflections on a Missionary Career,"

CHAPTER 3

The Paradigm Matures

Introduction

During its initial five years of existence, the success of non-residential missionaries (NRM) demonstrated the validity of the new paradigm. The new paradigm took root in the soil of the Foreign Mission Board (FMB) and began to grow despite the fact that some considered the NRM program to be a tare among the wheat of the established, incarnational missiological paradigm of the Board Some desired to pull up the so-called tare, but Parks and other key leaders of the Board believed in the NRM paradigm and, therefore, provided the shelter and nurturing needed for the paradigm to take root firmly within the FMB structure.

By 1992, the Board had NRM personnel targeting forty major unevangelized people groups, and the NRM program was gaining momentum. The next five years saw accelerated growth of the NRM program and maturation in the development of the NRM paradigm. The visionary leadership of Mike Stroope provided the impetus for this growth and maturation. Baldridge, a former NRM and later an associate to Stroope, notes that the Board's World A ministry under Stroope's leadership "mushroomed in an unprecedented explosion of manpower and financial investment."[1] Garrison describes the development of the NRM paradigm in this way:

> I nurtured the program from its healthy birth, through early struggles for survival, until it emerged from the nursery and onto the playground. Once this early childhood was completed (1987-1992), Mike Stroope took over the program shepherding it into maturity.[2]

This chapter will examine the years of the NRM program and Cooperative Services International (CSI) under the leadership of Stroope. This chapter will explore the events leading to the merger of the NRM program with the CSI-China office, resulting in the establishment of CSI as the tenth administrative area of the Board and equal with the other nine geographically designated

---

[1] Baldridge, *Keith Parks,* 45.

[2] Garrison, "Response to Bruce."

administrative areas. This chapter will further explore the statistical growth of CSI. Not only did CSI experience significant growth in the number of personnel, but it also demonstrated through increasing numbers of new churches planted in World A that the unevangelized peoples were not necessarily unresponsive. During Stroope's tenure as the leader of CSI, tensions between CSI and the other administrative areas remained, and some of these tensions warrant examination. Further, this chapter will explore and analyze the NRM paradigm's most noteworthy contribution to the Board's missiology, that is, the ethos created by CSI. The ethos developed and nurtured under Stroope's leadership was a source of tension between CSI and other areas of the Board. Yet, at the same time, the ethos left an indelible imprint on the Board's missiology, an imprint that remains to this day. This chapter will also compare the emerging paradigm with Bosch's postmodern paradigm, noting both points of convergence and divergence. Finally, this chapter will explore some of the elements within the new paradigm that correspond to the emerging postmodern, ecumenical missiological paradigm described by Bosch.

From Provisional to Permanent

During its initial years of existence, the NRM program had a seemingly provisional status within the structure of the FMB. Parks and other leaders affirmed the NRM program, but the program functioned outside the main administrative structures of the Board. Perhaps the main reason for this centred on the fact that the Board defined its administrative areas overseas along geographical lines, while the NRM program was not geographically defined. The NRM program was a functional program, that is, it existed for the function of engaging World A peoples regardless of their geographical location. However, there was a growing awareness by those associated with the NRM program that changes were needed if the NRM program was going to survive.

Assessment and Recommendations

Recognizing the increasing growth of the NRM program and the tense environment within the Board because of this new paradigm, in 1991, Garrison proposed to Parks that the NRM program become an official administrative area of the Board.[3] In response to this proposal, Parks asked for a review of the NRM program, and the Global Strategy Group (GSG) formed a subcommittee to oversee this review process.[4] The subcommittee consisted of Don Kammerdiener (Executive Vice-President), Harlan Spurgeon (Vice-President of the Office of Mission Personnel), Betty Law (Vice-President for the

[3] Garrison, "Response to Bruce."

[4] Garrison, "Response to Bruce"; Michael W. Stroope, interview by author, July 07, 2005, Lexington, KY, written transcript, 1.

Americas), and Clark Scanlon (Director of Research and Planning).[5] Garrison was responsible for designing the review and presenting the findings of the subcommittee to the GSG.[6]

Garrison presented the findings of the subcommittee at the April 14, 1992, meeting of the GSG.[7] There was discussion with some suggested changes, and the GSG asked Garrison to rewrite the document to reflect the suggested changes.[8] One area of concern expressed by some members of the GSG was that they believed the NRM program was receiving a disproportionate share of budget funds, and they wanted to establish parity in the budget process.[9] Garrison reworked the study document and presented it again to the GSG at its May 1992 meeting, at which time the GSG approved the recommendations of the subcommittee.[10]

The GSG subcommittee assessed the NRM program along several lines. The review process assessed the NRM program's personnel selection process, the NRM training program, the financial/economic situation of the program, its relationship with the other administrative areas of the Board, the measurable results of the NRM program and the administration of the program.[11] Along with the findings from the assessment process, the subcommittee presented its conclusions and recommendations.

A valuable part of the subcommittee's report involved a re-evaluation of some of the initial assumptions pertaining to the NRM program. By challenging these assumptions, the subcommittee was establishing the basis for the NRM program moving off the sidelines and into the mainstream of the FMB.

First, the report asserted that the assumption that an unevangelized people group was an unresponsive people group needed to be challenged. Based on their assessment of the work of various NRM personnel, the report stated, "Since the inception of the NRM program, literally thousands of these so-called 'unresponsive peoples' have responded positively to the invitation of Christ," thus the NRM program has "helped to dispel the myth of World A as an unresponsive wasteland beyond the bounds of prudent strategy."[12]

The NRM paradigm was beginning to dispel the myth that unevangelized and unreached people groups were resistant to the gospel message. In an effort

---

[5] Stroope, interview by author, 1.

[6] Garrison, "Response to Bruce."

[7] "Global Strategy Group Minutes," (Richmond: Southern Baptist Foreign Mission Board, Accession Number 955, April 14, 1992).

[8] "Global Strategy Group Minutes," April 14, 1992.

[9] "Global Strategy Group Minutes," April 14, 1992.

[10] "Global Strategy Group Minutes," (Richmond: Southern Baptist Foreign Mission Board, Accession Number 1034, May 05, 1992).

[11] *Cooperative Services International Review,* i-ii.

[12] *Cooperative Services International Review,* 107.

to chip away at this myth, the subcommittee's report presented several case studies and church planting results from work among various unevangelized people groups targeted by NRM personnel.[13] The report cited thirty new groups of Christians formed within one people group.[14] Since the beginning of NRM ministry among two other people groups, the number of Christians had doubled in size within both groups.[15] Residential personnel in the NRM program reported that among another World A people group, the number of Christians had grown from three believers at the end of 1990 to over one hundred in just over one year.[16]

The NRM paradigm clearly was beginning to demonstrate that as unevangelized people encountered the gospel message, they indeed were responsive. Although the numbers of new Christians among these World A people groups were not massive, unreached could not be translated to mean resistant or even unresponsive. The NRM paradigm was confronting another false assumption, which was the tendency to refer to an entire people group as unresponsive or resistant. Individuals might be resistant to the gospel, but it was unfair to place such a label on an entire people group.

Another assumption that the report asserted needed re-evaluation was that NRM personnel would not be able to establish incarnational presence among most, if not the overwhelming majority of World A people groups.[17] Coupled with this was another false assumption that the NRM paradigm, by definition, excluded the possibility of any residential personnel.[18] However, since 1987, NRM personnel had facilitated placing residential personnel among World A peoples for incarnational witness. Indeed, the NRM paradigm included "residential as well as non-residential ministries into its purview."[19] At the time of the subcommittee's report, 49 percent of NRM program personnel were residential.[20] Conventional thinking contributed to the belief that these assumptions were a picture of reality. At the same time, although the NRM paradigm anticipated the placement of residential personnel among World A peoples, no one at the Board could have predicted such success within a few short years.

---

[13] *Cooperative Services International Review,* 64-86.
[14] *Cooperative Services International Review,* 69.
[15] *Cooperative Services International Review,* 75, 79.
[16] *Cooperative Services International Review*, 85.
[17] *Cooperative Services International Review,* 85.
[18] *Cooperative Services International Review,* 85.
[19] *Cooperative Services International Review*, 108.
[20] *Cooperative Services International Non-residential Missionary Program Executive Overview,* Preview Committee Edition (Richmond: Southern Baptist Foreign Mission Board, January 08, 1992), 1.

A fourth assumption, which likely contributed to the confusion regarding residential personnel within the NRM program, focused on the name itself. As the subcommittee's report stated, "Ample responsibility for the confusion is inherent to the name 'non-residential' missionary."[21] The continued use of the name non-residential missionary would need re-examination in light of the present realities within the NRM program. As the NRM role moved from an abstract concept to a concrete missiological paradigm, there was a need for a name that more adequately defined the scope of this role.

The final two assumptions that the report sought to challenge dealt specifically with the administration of the NRM program itself. The Board had assumed a matrix approach as the most effective way to administer the NRM program, that is, asking CSI to provide strategic direction to the program while relying upon other administrative areas to step in with logistical assistance and support.[22] Not only did the matrix approach prove itself unwieldy and ineffective, it added to the tension between CSI and other administrative areas of the Board.[23]

Besides the NRM program administrative structure, the subcommittee also raised some questions regarding the Board's overall administrative structure at that time. However, in order to pave the way for the NRM program to gain equal status with the other administrative areas of the Board, it was crucial to challenge the Board's standard practice of defining its formal administrative areas exclusively along geographical lines.[24] The NRM program was functional in nature, not geographical, in that its focus was on the unevangelized ethno linguistic peoples of the world. The NRM paradigm viewed the world neither geographically nor geo-politically. The subcommittee was asserting that since the Board was assigning personnel to ethno linguistic groups it should recognize the need to designate formally the NRM program as a peer of the other administrative areas. As the report cited, "It may now be time for the Foreign Mission Board's administrative designations to catch-up with its personnel designations."[25]

The subcommittee brought several recommendations to the GSG based on its findings in the assessment process. The main recommendation was that the FMB "formally designate CSI's Non-residential Missionary Program its tenth administrative area with all the implications inherent to this designation."[26] At the same time, they also recommended that upon approval of the primary recommendation by the Board, Garrison, the present NRM program director,

---

[21] *Cooperative Services International Review,* 108.
[22] *Cooperative Services International Review,* 108.
[23] *Cooperative Services International Review,* 108.
[24] *Cooperative Services International Review,* 108.
[25] *Cooperative Services International Review,* 108.
[26] *Cooperative Services International Review Executive Summary,* 1.

should be elected as the new area director.[27] These recommendations sought to move the NRM program from a provisional status to a permanent position within the Board's administrative structure.

Affirmation

After much discussion and debate within the GSG regarding the recommendations brought by the subcommittee, the GSG presented the following recommendation to the full Board of Trustees at its June 1992 meeting:

> That Cooperative Services International be formally designated the Foreign Mission Board's fifth strategic region functioning with one administrative area; and that the trustees proceed with the process to elect an area director.[28]

The Board approved the recommendation.[29] The approval of this recommendation was an affirmation by the Board of the NRM paradigm's valuable contributions to its global evangelization efforts. The approval of this recommendation also was an acknowledgement of the increasing emphasis by the Board to view the world in terms of ethno linguistic classifications as opposed solely to geo-political or geographical entities.

This decision by the board effectively merged the NRM program and the CSI-China program into one administrative region called Cooperative Services International. According to Garrison, the Board did not merge the two programs, but rather the NRM program grew more rapidly than the CSI-China program and demonstrated itself to be more effective than the CSI-China program; therefore, the CSI-China program simply was assimilated into the NRM program.[30] As Garrison states:

> In retrospect, it is easy to see that on virtually every front, the NRM outperformed the CSI-China Program. It was far more effective evangelistically, it was very

---

[27] *Cooperative Services International Review Executive Summary,* 1.

[28] "Board of Trustees Minutes," (El Paso: Southern Baptist Foreign Mission Board, Accession Number 1033, June 22, 1992). At this time, the FMB had four administrative regions: Asia, Africa, Americas, and Europe/Middle East. Each administrative region had a vice-president, and each region included one or more administrative areas with an area director. For example, the Board divided the Asia region into the East Asia area and the South Asia and Pacific area, each area having its own area director under the leadership of the Asia region's vice-president. Before this decision, Myers served as the vice-president for CSI, but CSI lacked official regional status. Myers remained the CSI region's vice-president.

[29] "Board of Trustees Minutes," June 22, 1992.

[30] Garrison, "Response to Bruce."

> attractive to new candidates and to transferees, and it proved itself highly adaptable, capable of addressing any type of country or people group, from Muslims, to Hindus, to Communists in the USSR or China.[31]

When the Board approved the recommendation to designate CSI as its tenth administrative area, the Board changed the name from 'non-residential missionary' to 'strategy coordinator (SC).'[32] As noted above, the GSG subcommittee had assessed it was no longer appropriate to define this missionary role by what it was not. The NRM name was, in and of itself, a source of some confusion. Some NRM personnel had discovered ways to establish residential ministries among their targeted people group; therefore, there was a need to change the name to more accurately reflect the primary emphasis of the role. Furthermore, according to Smith, given that most of the World A people groups lived in restricted-access countries often hostile to missionary presence, there was a need to drop the word 'missionary' from the name.[33] The taxonomy change from NRM to SC was more elucidatory, one that was a coordinator of a comprehensive evangelization strategy for a World A people group, population segment or unevangelized city.

Although the Board approved the recommendation to designate CSI as an administrative region with one administrative area, the Board did not automatically accept Garrison, the NRM program director since its inception, as the new area director. The recommendation approved in June 1992 explicitly stated that the Board would initiate a process to elect an area director for this new administrative area. The search for a new area director to lead this new administrative area did not take long. Within a few months, the Board of Trustees elected Mike Stroope as CSI's new area director.[34] Stroope and his wife Kay initially served as Board missionaries in Asia.[35] Stroope then served in the missionary enlistment department of the Board and as the associate director of missionary orientation.[36] In 1988, the Stroopes were the first NRM personnel officially approved by a vote of the Board of Trustees, approved to focus on a major unevangelized people group in the Middle East.[37] The election of Stroope to become the area director for CSI injected the NRM/SC paradigm with the vision and leadership needed to move it out of its fledgling status toward maturity. Under Stroope's leadership, CSI developed a unique ethos, an ethos that permeated almost every area of the Board.

---

[31] Garrison, "Response to Bruce."

[32] Smith, "Additional Document."

[33] Smith, "Additional Document."

[34] "Board of Trustees Minutes," August 17, 1992.

[35] "Board of Trustees Minutes," (Richmond: Southern Baptist Foreign Mission Board, Accession Number 1362, February 08, 1988).

[36] Stroope, interview by author, 1.

[37] "Board of Trustees Minutes," February 08, 1988.

A Change at the Helm

While the GSG was reviewing the NRM program leading to the recommendation that CSI become the tenth administrative area of the Board, Parks resigned as president of the FMB, citing an atmosphere of distrust with the Board of Trustees.[38] Parks began his presidency of the FMB in January 1980, the same time a conservative resurgence began within the Southern Baptist Convention (SBC). Therefore, his entire presidency took place in the atmosphere of controversy swirling within the convention. Finally, after various conflicts with Trustees and others in the convention associated with this conservative resurgence, Parks tendered his resignation. Eight years later, reflecting back on his decision, Parks stated:

> I came to believe that the emphasis that was being made by the Trustees was focused more on a political effort to take over the denomination and the convention than it was focused on what was best for missions....I became aware in (19)'82 of some developments that caused me to believe that those who were trying to take control of the convention were approaching things from a way that had not been the traditional Baptist heritage as I understood it. There were several elements in that as I said a while ago from a constitutional standpoint, there's no question that the SBC came into existence in order to do missions. The constitution says that the purpose is to elicit, combine and direct the energies of the people called Baptists for the propagation of the gospel at home and abroad. That was the purpose....My assessment is that they're coming more from an independent Baptist viewpoint where conventions are built around doctrine than from the heritage that we as Southern Baptists have had that the convention is built around missions.[39]

---

[38] "Board of Trustees Minutes," (Clemson: Southern Baptist Foreign Mission Board, Accession Number 1029, April 06, 1992).

[39] R. Keith Parks, Interviewed by Philip O. Hopkins, April 04, 2000, transcript Southeastern SBC Historical Missiology Oral History Collection, Southeastern Baptist Theological Seminary, Wake Forest, NC: 10. Hopkins' interview of Parks provides a detailed account of Park's understanding of the issues surrounding his resignation from the FMB and his subsequent election as the leader of the Cooperative Baptist Fellowship's (CBF) mission efforts. The Cooperative Baptist Fellowship was a group started by Southern Baptist leaders who were opposed to the conservative resurgence within the convention. The controversy regarding the Board's relationship to the Rűschlikon Baptist Seminary in Switzerland was the pivotal event leading to Park's realization that he needed to step aside as the leader of the FMB. See Estep *Whole Gospel Whole World,* 359-65, for a summary of events regarding this controversy. For a perspective on the conservative resurgence and its impact on the Southern Baptist Convention similar to that expressed by Parks, see Bill Leonard, *God's Last and Only Hope: The Fragmentation of the Southern Baptist Convention* (Grand Rapids: Eerdmans, 1990). For a perspective on the conservative resurgence as viewed by those

Parks believed that the controversy surrounding the conservative resurgence was a distraction to the Board's efforts to focus on unreached people groups, especially during the latter part of his presidency as conflicts with Trustees intensified.[40] Although the effort to focus on World A may not have grown as fast as Parks may have expected, the fact remained that the Board's World A efforts had grown and had become firmly embedded into the Board's global strategy.

Parks' resignation likely did raise some concern among some that the Board might draw back from its World A emphasis. However, the decision to designate CSI as an administrative area helped to overcome some of the anxiety Parks' resignation may have generated.[41] According to Stroope, Parks firmly supported this effort to make CSI an administrative area.[42] It seems that Parks did more than just facilitate efforts to solidify the NRM program's existence at the Board. Garrison claims that when there was strong reaction within the GSG to elevating the NRM program to the level of an administrative area, Parks simply outlasted the opponents.[43] Garrison's observation suggests that Parks was intent on solidifying the existence of CSI within the Board beyond his personal tenure as president.

Parks' resignation became effective on October 30, 1992, and a little over seven months later, the Board elected Jerry Rankin to serve as its next president.[44] In his letter to field personnel soon after his election, Rankin, a vocal critic of the NRM program, stressed that efforts to take the gospel to World A people groups would continue.[45] At the same time, Rankin affirmed that the World A efforts would not detract from the Board's efforts to "concentrate on reaping the harvest that God has ripened on fields that are open and responsive."[46]

---

involved in leading this effort, see Paul Pressler, *A Hill on Which to Die: One Southern Baptist's Journey* (Nashville: Broadman and Holman, 1999); Jerry Sutton, *The Baptist Reformation* (Nashville: Broadman and Holman, 2000); and Tom Nettles, *Ready for Reformation?: Bringing Authentic Reform to Southern Baptist Churches* (Nashville: Broadman and Holman, 2005).

40 Parks, Interviewed by Philip O. Hopkins, 28.

41 Stroope, interview by author, 2.

42 Stroope, interview by author, 2.

43 Garrison, "Response to Bruce."

44 "Board of Trustees Minutes," April 06, 1992; Erich Bridges, "Rankin Writes Missionaries, Calls Election 'a Miracle,'" (Richmond: Southern Baptist Foreign Mission Board, June 25, 1993); available from https://solomon.imb.org; Stories database.

45 Bridges, "Rankin Writes Missionaries."

46 Bridges, "Rankin Writes Missionaries." See also William Smith, "Response to Your Questions about the SC Paradigm vs. Church Growth," Electronic Letter to Bruce Carlton, September 14, 2005; and V. David Garrison, "Response to Your Questions about the SC Paradigm vs. Church Growth," Electronic Letter to Bruce Carlton,

Although Rankin sought to reassure those associated with World A ministry that the Board would not draw back from its World A efforts, clearly Rankin still held to the traditional Church Growth missiology prevalent throughout the Board. Rankin, by affirming the Church Growth paradigm of harvesting the responsive fields, revealed that he still viewed the unreached or unevangelized people groups of World A as unresponsive. In his report to the Board in April 1994, Rankin reveals:

> What is the primary task of missions? Some would define it as seed-sowing, proclaiming the gospel where it has never been heard, giving people an opportunity to respond whether they do or not. Others would give priority to following responsiveness and reaping the harvest since personal salvation is the goal of our witness. Should open, responsive fields where there are churches be neglected in order to reach World A? If priority is given to the fertile fields that are ripe unto harvest, will the seed ever be sown among the unreached nations and people groups who have yet to hear the gospel?[47]

Rankin's words vividly indicate the tension created by this missiological principle, and the tension in his own thinking. Although firmly committed to continuing the Board's efforts within traditional mission fields, Rankin was true to his word about not allowing the Board to draw back from its World A emphasis. To the contrary, under Rankin's presidency the Board's efforts to penetrate the unevangelized of World A expanded, both within CSI and within some of the other administrative areas of the Board.

Immediately upon assuming the presidency of the Board, Rankin also made it clear that he did not support the idea of the Global Strategy Group formed by Parks. In the same letter to field personnel, Rankin stated that he wanted to alter the strategy decision-making process of the Board in an effort "to find 'balance' between the heavily field-oriented approach under the 26-year presidency of Baker James Cauthen and the more centralized strategy during the 13-year presidency of…R. Keith Parks."[48] The Global Strategy Group under the leadership of Parks had provided a safety net for the fledgling NRM paradigm to develop. By the end of 1993, Rankin had dissolved the GSG and

---

September 14, 2005. Both Smith and Garrison report that Rankin, while an Area Director in Southeast Asia, opposed deploying a lot of resources to unreached people groups whom he considered unresponsive. This was a key area of friction between Rankin and CSI.

[47] Jerry A. Rankin, *Report to the Board* (Ft. Worth: Southern Baptist Foreign Mission Board, Accession Number 1513, April 25, 1994).

[48] Bridges, "Rankin Writes Missionaries."

reassigned the regional vice-presidents to various specialized positions within the Board.[49]

Rankin, while serving as an area director under Parks, had argued for the absorption of the NRM program into the various geographical areas. The October 1993 Board meeting provided a hint of what was to come under his presidency. Avery Willis, whom Rankin recommended become the Senior Vice-President for Overseas Operations, stated the following:

> With the streamlining of administration and the elimination of the Global Strategy Group, we are asking the remaining Regional Vice-Presidents to assume administration of specialized strategic assignments. These will include a World A advocacy that will keep the whole organization cognizant of the challenge of unreached people groups. This role will extend beyond CSI to mobilize other areas in applying strategies and resources to focus on this segment of our task.[50]

Myers, the regional vice-president for CSI, stepped into the role as Vice-President for World A Strategies.[51]

Another significant decision made by Rankin during his initial months as Board president was to end the contract that the Board had with Barrett.[52] Gone was yet another strong advocate for World A and the NRM paradigm. With Park's resignation, Rankin's immediate changes and the departure of Barrett from the Board, an atmosphere of anxiety swirled around CSI and the NRM paradigm. However, it was the Board's decision to elevate CSI to an administrative area that provided the necessary shelter that would allow it to expand and mature over the next several years.

From Movement to Institution

At this point, it is necessary to provide a brief analysis of the decision to solidify CSI as one of the Board's official administrative areas. The NRM role was an experimental paradigm developed to stimulate Southern Baptists' efforts in implementing a genuine global strategy that would include all the peoples of the world, focusing exclusively on those people groups considered inaccessible by missionaries. In essence, the NRM paradigm began as a movement, functioning outside the standard parameters of mission

---

[49] "Board of Trustees Minutes," (Richmond: Southern Baptist Foreign Mission Board, Accession Number 1358, October 10, 1993).

[50] "Board of Trustees Minutes," October 10, 1993.

[51] "Board of Trustees Minutes," (Richmond: Southern Baptist Foreign Mission Board, Accession Number 1395, December 03, 1993).

[52] "Board of Trustees Minutes," December 03, 1993; "Global Strategy Group Minutes," (Richmond: Southern Baptist Foreign Mission Board, Accession Number 1277, May 03, 1993). The GSG decided to terminate Barrett's contract, effective December 31, 1993.

administration and, as a result, creating tension with the conventional missiological wisdom prevalent at the Board.

Bosch, comparing the differences between institution and movement, states, "The one is conservative, the other progressive; the one is more or less passive, yielding to influences from the outside, the other is active, influencing rather than being influenced; the one looks to the past, the other to the future."[53] Bosch further adds, "The one is anxious, the other is prepared to take risks; the one guards boundaries, the other crosses them."[54] Clearly, the NRM paradigm during its formative years was progressive, active, future-oriented, risk-taking, and daring to cross boundaries. The conventional institutionalized paradigm of the Board at the time of the NRM paradigm's emergence, for the most part, was conservative, more averse to risk-taking, and prone to fiercely guarding its perceived boundaries.

On the one hand, the process leading up to the approval by the Board to accept CSI as its tenth administrative area was the beginning of the institutionalizing process of this movement. Guder asserts, "Movements do not remain movements; they either become institutions or they disappear."[55] For Guder, the shift from movement to institution is an inescapable reality.[56] According to Garrison, his proposal to Parks to elevate the NRM program to an official administrative area was the only way that the paradigm would survive.[57] If Guder and Garrison are correct, then the decision to create CSI as the tenth administrative area of the Board was inevitable for the paradigm's continued existence.

On the other hand, the events leading up to this decision seem to reflect a similar situation as that which faced the early church. In describing the early church's shift from movement to institution, Bosch states, "Their survival as a separate religious group, rather than their commitment to the reign of God, began to preoccupy them."[58] According to Guder and Bosch, the problem that often arises in the shift toward institution is the movement's loss of dynamism.[59] Guder goes on to assert that a movement's shift toward institution is not the issue, rather the issue "is what happens to the central and driving mission of the movement when this necessary transition takes place."[60] Bosch,

---

[53] Bosch, *Transforming Mission,* 50-1. See also H. Richard Niebuhr, *The Kingdom of God in America* (New York: Harper and Brothers, 1959).

[54] Bosch, *Transforming Mission,* 50-1.

[55] Darrell L. Guder, *The Continuing Conversion of the Church,* The Gospel and Our Culture Series, ed. Craig Van Gelder (Grand Rapids: William B. Eerdmans Publishing Company, 2000), 187.

[56] Guder, *Conversion of the Church,* 187.

[57] Garrison, "Response to Bruce."

[58] Bosch, *Transforming Mission,* 50.

[59] Bosch, *Transforming Mission,* 50., 53; Guder, *Conversion of the Church,* 187.

[60] Guder, *Conversion of the Church,* 187-8.

in evaluating the shift of the early church, states, "Our main point of censure should therefore not be that the movement became an institution but that, when this happened, it also lost much of its verve."[61]

After its initial years of development, there was a sense that those involved with the NRM paradigm were deeply concerned for its survival. Did this concern for survival overshadow the initial vision that gave birth to the paradigm? Did the paradigm lose its dynamism because of the shift toward institution? An examination of CSI under Stroope's leadership will show there is little evidence to suggest the quest for survival did supplant the initial vision. At the same time, CSI struggled with this issue over the next several years. Stroope's tenure as area director for CSI was a continual struggle to preserve the new paradigm within the Board while, at the same time, maintaining the vitality of the paradigm in order to prevent it from calcification.

The Stroope Years: Expansion

Stroope served as the area director for CSI from 1992 until 1997, five years of exceptional growth. The strategy coordinator (SC) paradigm during these tumultuous, yet exciting, years witnessed impressive numerical growth in terms of personnel, new people groups engaged and new churches planted among World A people groups.[62] These areas of growth helped to establish the validity of the new paradigm. Furthermore, not only did the SC paradigm stimulate growth within CSI, but the paradigm's influence and effectiveness stimulated other administrative areas to a wider involvement in World A. Although other administrative areas may not have adopted the SC paradigm in its entirety, these areas increasingly came to the realization that the World A emphasis by the Board was not just a passing fad.

CSI Expansion into World A

By January 1992, the Board was targeting 40 major World A people groups with an aggregate population near 350 million through its new paradigm. A little over a year later, SC personnel in CSI were targeting 52 major World A people groups totalling approximately 371 million in population.[63] By the end

---

[61] Bosch, *Transforming Mission,* 53.

[62] From this point forward, I primarily will use the term strategy coordinator (SC) instead of non-residential missionary (NRM) to denote the new paradigm.

[63] Michael W. Stroope, *Cooperative Services International 1992/93 Statistical Report: Area Director's Narrative Summary* (Richmond: Southern Baptist Foreign Mission Board, September 1993), 1; Erich Bridges, "Missionaries See Results in Unevangelized 'World A,'" (Richmond: Southern Baptist International Mission Board, May 10, 1993); available from https://solomon.imb.org; Stories database. Based on the statistical report

of 1993, CSI personnel were working in 32 countries among 63 unevangelized World A people groups, all of which the Board identified as unevangelized mega peoples - a people group of over one million in population.[64] In March 1995, Stroope reported on the success of the SC paradigm in terms of the engagement of people groups or population segments, stating:

> The focus of CSI from its inception was the unreached which the geo-political view of the world had overlooked. The names of groups…were not even in our vocabulary in 1998. Since targeting [the] first two groups, sixty-seven more unreached people groups and cities have become part of our commitment. In essence, this would be akin to opening sixty-seven new countries. The goal of CSI

---

submitted by Stroope for 1992-93, CSI initiated work among 12 new people groups, 22 cities over 100,000 population and 26 cities less than 100,000 population.

[64] David Williard, "World A: Out of the Shadows to Stay," (Richmond: Southern Baptist Foreign Mission Board, January 01, 1994); available from https://solomon .imb.org; Stories database. Through the World Evangelization database developed by Barrett and his research staff, the Board had identified 212 unevangelized mega peoples, which became a priority World A focus in the Board's strategy. These 32 countries mentioned by Stroope were primarily countries within the 10/40 Window. The 10/40 Window was a concept developed by the AD2000 Movement (see http://www. ad2000.org for an extensive description of this movement). Simply defined, the 10/40 Window was an imaginary window measuring 10 degrees north latitude to 40 degrees north latitude extending from North Africa to Asia. The AD2000 movement was a global movement of evangelical Christians who were intent on taking the gospel to every people group by the year 2000. The beginning of this movement stems from the Lausanne meeting in Manila in 1989. Luis Bush directed this global movement. His book *The Move of the Holy Spirit in the 10/40 Window,* eds. Luis Bush and Beverly Pegues (Seattle: YWAM Publishing, 1999) seek to explain this global evangelical movement. One of the groups formed because of the AD2000 Movement was the Joshua Project 2000 (see http://www.joshuaproject.net) that focused on the unreached peoples, which the FMB called World A. While many Southern Baptist strategy coordinators networked and cooperated with many other groups who were a part of this movement, there is evidence to suggest that Board leadership supported this wider evangelical effort. Willis attended the Global Consultation on World Evangelization in Seoul in May 1995. At that meeting, Willis admitted Southern Baptists had a 'lone ranger' attitude toward global evangelization for many years, and expressed a willingness on the part of the Board to openly share its massive research data and other resources with other evangelical groups who were part of the AD2000 movement. For the most part, however, the Board's World A efforts ran parallel to the AD2000 movement, intersecting primarily at those points where individual FMB strategy coordinators, strategists and leaders chose to interact with other evangelicals who were involved in ministry to unreached and unevangelized people groups. The FMB chose to use its own terminology rather than adopting the terminology used by the AD2000 movement. Rankin, however, would expand the Board's involvement and partnership with other Great Commission Christian groups and networks.

is to increase the number of targeted people groups and cities by 12 to 15 per year.[65]

In 1995/96, CSI entered 13 new World A people groups and cities.[66] CSI surpassed its goal of 12 to 15 new population segments the next year. In his October 1996 report to the board, Stroope stated that in the previous reporting year "CSI opened work among an additional 26 people groups."[67] This increase emboldened Stroope to lead CSI to set a goal to engage 65 new World A mega people groups and 20 non-mega people groups in 1997.[68] The phrase "All Peoples Nothing Less" became the rallying cry for CSI personnel, a rallying cry driven by the belief that all the peoples of the world had the right to hear and respond to the gospel. CSI considered no people group unreachable.

Accompanying this expansion in terms of the number of people groups targeted by SC personnel was comparable growth in the number of Board personnel assigned to work among these people groups. In January 1992, there were forty-eight career units (all couples) working in World A through CSI. Additionally, at that time, there were sixty International Service Corps (ISC) and Journeyman personnel working in CSI.[69] The number of personnel assigned to CSI doubled to three hundred personnel by the end of 1992.[70] The 1993 CSI statistical report indicated that by June 1993 there were 364 CSI personnel, almost evenly divided between career personnel and ISC/Journeyman personnel.[71] The overwhelming majority (83 percent) of these personnel were residential.[72] By November 1994, there were 383 personnel assigned through CSI.[73] The total of personnel assigned to World A through

---

[65] Michael W. Stroope, *Perspective and Prospects: A Proposal for Avery Willis* (Richmond: Southern Baptist Foreign Mission Board, March 02, 1995), 4.

[66] Michael W. Stroope, *One Day...Is Today!* The actual statistical reporting period ran from June 15 to June 15 each year.

[67] Michael W. Stroope, *Taking the Edge All Peoples Nothing Less* (Richmond: Southern Baptist Foreign Mission Board, Accession Number 2464, October 08, 1996).

[68] Stroope, *Taking the Edge.*

[69] Stroope, interview by author, 5. International Service Corps (ISC) personnel were short-term missionary assignments, ranging from three months to two-years. Within CSI, most of the ISC positions were two-year assignments. The Journeyman program, begun in 1964, was a two-year mission assignment for single young people. The Board eventually domiciled the Journeyman program within the International Service Corps.

[70] Bridges, "Missionaries See Results."

[71] Stroope, *1992/93 Statistical Report*, 1.

[72] Stroope, *1992/93 Statistical Report*, 1.

[73] Stroope, interview by author, 5.

CSI rose to 412 by mid-year 1995 with 47 percent of these as ICS/Journeyman personnel.[74]

Statistics confirm that CSI and its World A emphasis was attracting more and more personnel who were applying to serve overseas with the Board. In 1989, only 2 percent of the Board's personnel were focusing on World A people groups, yet at the beginning of 1994, this had grown to 8 percent - a 400 percent increase.[75] One of the reasons for the rapid growth of CSI during this time was the fact that CSI leadership empowered SC personnel to mobilize directly from the local church.[76] In his interview with Eitel in 1998, Stroope expressed the following:

> In many times we talked about drawing a straight line between the resources and the need and continually trying to cut the middle man out so that we could draw a straight line, not triangles which we felt were inefficient but we need a straight line between the field and those pockets of resources. So, continually, we were encouraging our people to go straight to the peer and straight to the resources and to mobilize them and in many cases they would come with someone ready to come to the field before there was ever a personnel request written and then would write the request, specifically for a particular person and then we'd work through the system as they had to in order to get the person to the field but they were working directly with those people in the churches.[77]

Another factor that stimulated the personnel growth within CSI was the recognition by SC personnel that ISC/Journeymen could play a significant role in opening doors among World A peoples. According to Smith, most of the other administrative areas of the Board treated these short-term, two-year personnel more as support personnel rather than potential front-line

---

[74] *Cooperative Services International Statistical Review 1992-1995* (Richmond: Southern Baptist Foreign Mission Board, February 02, 1996), 1.

[75] David Williard, "World A: Out of the Shadows."

[76] Michael W. Stroope, Interview by Keith E. Eitel, February 25, 1998, transcript, Southeastern SBC Historical Missiology Oral History Collection, Southeastern Baptist Theological Seminary, Wake Forest, NC: 8.

[77] Stroope, Interview by Keith E. Eitel: 8. Standard personnel deployment procedures at the Board involved field personnel generating generic personnel requests for specific assignments. Each administrative area then submitted its priority requests to the home office, and candidate consultants at the home office would then, via a lengthy application process, seek to link potential candidates to specific job requests listed at the Board. Field personnel who submitted the requests were not involved in the screening of potential candidates, which often led to mismatches of personnel to the requested position. SC personnel creatively learned how to circumvent the bureaucracy of the personnel selection process at the Board, which stimulated the growth of personnel within CSI.

missionaries.[78] SC personnel adopted a much different attitude toward these two-year personnel. Within CSI, the attitude was that everyone wears long pants; a saying that indicated CSI treated all of its personnel, career or short-term, as adults.[79] Smith illustrates how CSI demonstrated this attitude, stating, "Two year people were sent to…hazardous areas… difficult situations…and rose to the challenge, and in many cases greatly exceeded expectations."[80] Others at the Board increasingly became aware of the differing attitude between CSI and other areas toward these two-year personnel, reflected in the following:

> John Faulkner, FMB area director for Eastern and Southern Africa, said the feeling that some journeymen were falling short of expectations was shared by himself and other area administrators. In his area, roles at one time reserved for journeymen were redefined in past years to accommodate persons less-prepared to assume responsibility, he said.
>
> Cooperative Services International (CSI) had a different experience, however. In a sense, it may be seen as paradoxical. Prior to creation of CSI, journeymen serving through the area offices were seen primarily as apprentices, or helpers, to their career counterparts. As such, they generally worked within the framework of local Baptist missions. Under CSI…many journeymen served in "front-line" situations.
>
> James Hampton, assistant vice president for CSI, reported that journeymen and other ISC personnel "are meeting needs that we have had. There have not been many who haven't made contributions to CSI strategy. Some are making amazing contributions." Many serving under the journeyman option have shown "incredible maturity: in assuming responsibility in difficult situations," he said.[81]

A consequence of this attitude toward these short-term personnel was that the ISC/Journeyman program became a pipeline for CSI in its recruitment of career personnel. Stroope compared CSI's utilization of ISC/Journeymen personnel to a baseball farm system, "a way of stepping into the circle, getting your feet wet."[82] According to Smith, because CSI treated these short-term

---

[78] Smith, "Thoughts for Bruce."

[79] Smith, "Thoughts for Bruce;" Stroope, interview by author, 4.

[80] Smith, "Thoughts for Bruce."

[81] David Williard, "Shaping New Strategies: FMB Reinstates Journeyman Tradition," (Richmond: Southern Baptist Foreign Mission Board, April 01, 1993); available from https://solomon.imb.org; Stories database.

[82] Stroope, interview by author, 4. The professional baseball system in the United States has an extensive farm or minor-league system whereby teams provide opportunity to potential players for honing their baseball skills in preparation for a career at the major league level. Stroope claims that CSI utilized the ISC/Journeyman program as a time to

personnel as adults they "chose to come back to the part of the world where they had experienced fulfilling two year assignments."[83]

Not only did CSI skilfully develop a career force of missionary personnel through the ISC/Journeyman program, CSI also influenced the Board's appointment process for career personnel. A standard requirement for all career missionary personnel was two years of ministry experience before deployment. Up to this time, a two-year ISC or Journeyman assignment did not qualify as the necessary two-year full-time ministry experience. However, Stroope asserts, "CSI pushed to get the two-year ISC assignment credited as the two-year experience needed to be a career missionary, which shortened the turnaround time for these folks."[84] Today, the turnaround time for career appointment for ISC or Journeymen personnel averages about six months.

The steady growth in terms of new World A people groups targeted and the corresponding expansion in personnel deployed for ministry among these peoples solidified the role of CSI as an integral component of the Board's global strategy. At the same time that CSI was expanding its reach into World A, other administrative areas of the Board were responding to the success of CSI. As these other areas came to the realization that World A was an ever-growing emphasis of the Board, they quickly stepped into the World A arena to become players.

Beyond CSI: Expansion and Tension

As early as 1993, the Board reported, "Five of the 10 FMB area offices indicate they have personnel working with megapeoples…in World A."[85] By mid-1993, 150 personnel from these five other areas were deployed among World A people groups.[86] Adding these personnel to the number of CSI personnel raised the percentage of Board personnel working in World A to 11.1 percent.[87] By the end of 1993,other areas were reporting the deployment of 190 missionary personnel among 22 World A mega people groups.[88] In 1994, Myers, expounding on the progress of the Board since its initial thrust into World A, reported:

> You have seen the figures quoted often:
>
> - World A composes 23% of the world's population, 1.2 billion.

---

allow these short-term personnel to hone their skills and gifts in preparation for career missionary service.

[83] Smith, "Thoughts for Bruce."

[84] Stroope, interview by author, 5.

[85] "Busy in World A," *The Commission* (October-November 1993), 3.

[86] "Busy in World A," 3.

[87] "Busy in World A," 3.

[88] Williard, "World A: Out of the Shadows."

- .01% of the total mission force is focused on World A.
- .1% of all Christian literature is produced for World A.
- .01% of all Christian TV is produced for World A.
- Less than .01% of every mission dollar is spent on World A.

In the middle 80s, we at the Foreign Mission Board were faring only slightly better than the global average. In less than 10 years, we have made impressive strides.

- 14% of our mission force works in World A.
- 5% of our literature is produced for World A.
- 8% of our TV is focused on World A.
- 11% of our budget is spent in World A.[89]

World A was continuing to gain more of the attention of Board leadership. In fact, Rankin proposed a new vision statement for the Board that reflected World A as a priority. This statement read, "We will lead Southern Baptists to be on mission with God to penetrate the unevangelized world and accelerate making Christ known among all people."[90] This proposed vision statement expressed Rankin's belief that the Board must remain committed to "reach and eliminate World A."[91] Willis supported this growing emphasis on World A, stressing that the Board "must see this as a major, major direction that we go."[92] Although nearly 14 percent of the Board's missionary force now were targeting World A peoples, Willis challenged the Board to go even further.[93]

Reports to the Board given by various area directors are a clear indication that the new paradigm with its emphasis on people groups, especially World A peoples, was beginning to elicit a shift in their missiological thinking. Increasingly, the reports of these various area directors highlighted their area's efforts to target previously unengaged people groups.[94] At the same time, there

---

[89] Lewis I. Myers, Jr., *Roads Less Traveled* (Orlando: Southern Baptist Foreign Mission Board, Accession Number 1560, June 10, 1994).

[90] Jerry A. Rankin, *Report to the Board* (Alexandria: Southern Baptist Foreign Mission Board, Accession Number 1607, August 15, 1994).

[91] Rankin, *Report to the Board,* August 15, 1994. The Board approved a different vision statement in December 1994 that stated, "We will lead Southern Baptists to be on mission with God to bring all the peoples of the world to saving faith in Jesus Christ." See "Board of Trustees Minutes," (Richmond: Southern Baptist Foreign Mission Board, Accession Number 1677, December 12, 1994).

[92] Avery T. Willis, Jr., *Report to the Board* (Ridgecrest: Southern Baptist Foreign Mission Board, Accession Number 1922, August 14, 1995).

[93] Willis, *Report to the Board,* August 14, 1995.

[94] For example, see Clyde Meador, *Report to the Board: Southern Asia and the Pacific* (Ft. Worth: Southern Baptist Foreign Mission Board, Accession Number 1513, April 27, 1994); "Board of Trustees Minutes," (Richmond: Southern Baptist Foreign Mission Board, Accession Number 1639, October 10, 1994); Bill Phillips, *Report to the Board:*

was some tension as some believed the increasing emphasis on World A would lead to a decrease of emphasis in some of the traditional mission fields of the Board. Bruce's comments exemplify this concern:

> Certainly we need to place people and resources in the unreached regions, but in the process we must not cut back on doing everything within our power to bring in the harvest in our Samaria (Middle America and Canada) whose fields are white, and who still has millions of people that do not know Jesus and who are just as lost in their sins as those in the most remote parts of the world.[95]

This tension extended beyond area directors to the missionaries of the Board serving in traditional mission fields. Bridges summarizes the concern expressed by many of these missionaries as follows:

> The strategic shift toward seriously targeting World A - the 'A' means Priority No. 1 – has been anything but painless at the Foreign Mission Board and other evangelical agencies. Leaders have debated about whether to concentrate on more open or responsive areas. Thousands of missionaries work in so-called Worlds B and C – regions where people can hear the gospel relatively freely and traditionally 'Christian' countries or peoples. Many of them argue that their mission fields are just as needy and wonder if their ministries are being devalued by the emphasis on World A.[96]

It was evident that the Board's increasing attention toward World A, spurred by the success of CSI, created anxiety among missionaries in other areas as they sensed this push negated the many years of their faithful labour in these

---

West Africa (Richmond: Southern Baptist Foreign Mission Board, Accession Number 1677, December 12, 1994); William E. Goff, *Report to the Board: Spanish South America* (Richmond: Southern Baptist Foreign Mission Board, Accession Number 1677, December 13, 1994); Bill Phillips, *Report to the Board: West Africa* (Richmond: Southern Baptist Foreign Mission Board, Accession Number 1961, October 09, 1995); Joe W. Bruce, *Report to the Board: Middle America and Canada* (Ridgecrest: Southern Baptist Foreign Mission Board, Accession Number 1922, August 17, 1995); John H. Faulkner, *Report to the Board: Eastern and Southern Africa* (Knoxville: Southern Baptist Foreign Mission Board, Accession Number 2162, February 13, 1996); and Joe W. Bruce, *Report to the Board: Middle America and Canada* (Atlanta: Southern Baptist Foreign Mission Board, Accession Number 2438, August 13, 1996). Each of the area directors reporting to the Board emphasize their involvement with World A people groups who resided solely within the geographical boundaries of their respective area.

[95] Bruce, *Report to the Board,* August 13, 1996.

[96] Bridges, "Missionaries See Results."

traditional areas. However, the Board did not create this new paradigm to diminish the work of missionaries in these traditional areas.[97]

While it is evident that CSI was exerting an impact on the other administrative areas of the Board, this impact at times evoked a protectionist response on the part of some area directors. While becoming more aware of World A, they were still provincial in their outlook, seeing only the part of World A within their geographical boundaries. Area directors were advocates for their geographical areas, and expectedly they would advocate for more personnel and resources for their respective areas. Therefore, many area directors were willing to shift some of their focus on to the unreached or unevangelized peoples in their areas in order to preserve the number of personnel in their area and even attract more, but they lacked a truly global perspective.

According to Stroope, some other area directors simply began "picking up the terminology and talking about doing CSI-type of ministries in order to be participants in the World A strategy."[98] At the same time, these area directors were experiencing a decrease in personnel coming to their regions because of the rapid increase of personnel applying to CSI.[99] A major constraint that most of the other administrative areas faced was budget. Therefore, they could talk about engaging World A peoples, yet could do very little to finance such efforts. These areas were forced to utilize the lion's share of their budget funds to fulfil commitments "to help new Baptist churches and Baptist conventions develop sufficient resources to become self-sustaining."[100] CSI did not have the history of denomination building so prevalent throughout the geographical administrative areas; therefore, the majority of its budget was earmarked for starting new work in World A.[101] As a result, CSI soon became the fastest growing area of the Board, thus requiring more and more of the Board's resources and able to focus those resources on opening new work in World A. Understandably, an atmosphere of tension, and even competition, increased between CSI and other administrative areas.

---

[97] See *Cooperative Services International Review,* 58-61. This review of the new paradigm in 1992 highlights some of the tension created with other areas. The perception by some missionaries that this new paradigm was an indictment of their failure seems to have stemmed from the efforts of the Board in challenging missionaries in traditional fields to transfer to World A assignments. This redeployment effort seems to have communicated to some that World B or World C assignments were less important and/or that missionaries were failures in their traditional roles.

[98] Stroope, interview by author, 2.

[99] Stroope, interview by author, 2.

[100] Williard, "World A: Out of the Shadows." Many areas of the Board had drifted into denomination building activities overseas, which hindered any effort to initiate new work, especially new work among World A people groups.

[101] Stroope, interview by author, 2.

With the loss of the GSG and its global view, the Board's global strategy began to fragment. Rankin attempted to push strategy planning back closer to the field by dissolving the GSG; however, in this push the Board began to lose its ability to maintain a global perspective on its mission effort. In one sense, the Board's global strategy devolved into the sum total of each administrative area's strategy.[102] In another sense, this change in strategic planning increased competition for personnel between the various areas as each area sought to claim priority for the unreached people groups in their area. Willis words reveal the change brought about by Rankin's new approach to the strategic planning process:

> There is also a new direction as far as the overseas strategy and how we're trying to accomplish this work....From now on, we are defining the world in nine geographical regions, and those regions will continue to work as they are working. They will also be free to target people groups in their areas. So instead of saying 10% of what we're trying to do is going to be focused toward World A...[we] will target the people groups that are in our areas.[103]

In summary, the growth of CSI in the number of new World A people groups engaged as well as the growth in personnel did have a stimulating effect on the entire Board. CSI relentlessly advocated for World A among Southern Baptists, spurring a rapid growth in personnel desiring to serve in this new frontier of Baptist mission efforts. At the same time, the success of CSI in mobilizing more and more personnel created more tension with the other administrative areas. The SC paradigm was no longer an experimental missiological paradigm that some hoped might fade away into the horizon. As a functional area not limited to geographical boundaries as with the other areas, it was inevitable that territorial issues would emerge. Overlap naturally occurred as SC personnel often engaged World A peoples residing within the geographical boundaries of the other areas. Further, the growth of CSI led to a

---

[102] See Avery T. Willis, Jr., *Report to the Board* (Richmond: Southern Baptist Foreign Mission Board, Accession Number 1677, December 12, 1994); Avery T. Willis, Jr., *Report to the Board* (Memphis: Southern Baptist Foreign Mission Board, Accession Number 2093, December 11, 1995) and Avery T. Willis, Jr., *Report to the Board* (Atlanta: Southern Baptist Foreign Mission Board, Accession Number 2438, August 13, 1996). In these reports, Willis explains the planning process initiated under Rankin's leadership. Basically, every mission delineated its vision, critical issues, objectives and goals. These were then passed to the area leadership teams who then developed the major objectives for their specific area. Finally, all the area directors gathered together and examined all the plans from every mission (including CSI teams) and honed down this massive amount of information to eight basic objectives, which were then presented to the Board for approval.

[103] Avery T. Willis, Jr., *Report to the Board*, August 14, 1995.

diminishing share of Board resources for the other areas, thus adding to the tension.

Unreached but not Unreachable

From its inception, and to the surprise of many at the Board, this new missiological paradigm began to dispel the myth that unreached was synonymous with unreachable. As with the early NRM personnel, strategy coordinators were discovering that they could open doors in World A that allowed for residential, incarnational witness among these people groups. By the end of 1993, "83 percent of CSI's personnel, including strategy coordinators, creative access personnel, and others" lived and worked among their respective target population segment.[104] The success of SC personnel in placing residential personnel within World A "shattered what was, in effect, a missions myth: that some people were not being reached because it was impossible to penetrate perceived political and social barriers that existed."[105]

Because the SC paradigm had as its overall objective the evangelization of a World A population segment, an entry strategy was paramount to achieving this objective. The countries where the overwhelming majority of World A peoples resided were restricted or closed to traditional missionary presence. Therefore, SC personnel utilized creative means to place residential personnel in these countries in order to allow personnel to have daily, personal contact with the targeted population segment. Stroope stated, "Personnel were challenged to take the doors off the hinges if the door wouldn't open and to do whatever it takes to reach the people group."[106]

Within CSI, "platform" was the nomenclature used to describe the means of gaining access to the areas where these World A people lived. A platform typically provided a secular identity for personnel. SC personnel quickly discovered that by dropping the missionary identity and adopting secular identity, "it allowed all kinds of access into these places."[107] As SC personnel researched the needs and situation of their targeted people group, they would

---

[104] Williard, "World A: Out of the Shadows." CSI developed the term "Creative Access" personnel to denote non-SC, front-line personnel who resided among their target population segment.

[105] Williard, "World A: Out of the Shadows."

[106] Stroope, Interview by Keith E. Eitel: 8.

[107] Stroope, Interview by Keith E. Eitel: 16. For example, in 1990, my wife Gloria and I redeployed to Cambodia, a restricted-access country in terms of missionary presence. We could not enter that country to begin work among the Khmer people, a World A people group, with a traditional missionary identity. We were able to gain entry through providing humanitarian aid and community development services. In this way, we were able to establish residence and establish an incarnational witness among this people group.

then begin to strategize as to the most appropriate platform needed to secure access. Most of these platforms focused on such areas as education, health care or business.[108] Barnett, who served within CSI, describes the emergence of platforms within the NRM paradigm as follows:

> What had been considered restricted areas simply required some ingenuity on the part of the missionaries. It was not a question of restrictions but of creativity and determination. Mission workers simply needed to get out of their vocational ministry mind-set and enter the real world of marketplace witness – the modern-day version of the apostle Paul. The term *restricted-access* gave way to *creative-access*, and the strategy of developing creative-access platforms took root.[109]

These secular platforms not only created access, but they were highly conducive for creating effective incarnational witness. Stroope states that these platforms "created a different dynamic to where people were living out a secular identity rather than an ecclesiastical identity or religious identity, and that caused them just to have a different lifestyle and to relate differently."[110] Stroope further adds, "With these platforms, we were performing services that were needed and so much of the identity and much of the lifestyle of the people were involved in…providing significant services to people and so they related to them in that way rather than in someone coming and propagating this strange faith."[111] Barnett summarizes the value of these platforms as (1) providing access to the people group; (2) providing a valid rationale for living long-term among that people group; (3) providing the workers a credible identity within the host culture; (4) providing a practical means to establish relationships, which facilitate witnessing opportunities, with the local community; and (5) providing workers with the opportunity to model with integrity a Christ-like lifestyle through their daily lives.[112]

As noted in Chapter 1, the concept of establishing platforms was a variation of the tentmaker role. At times, some criticized the concept of utilizing platforms to gain access into restricted-areas as being illegal and unethical; however, the Board did not advocate for working illegally in a country. These platforms were legal entities. The development and maintenance of these platforms often required specialized skills such as business people, educators, agriculturalists and medical personnel. This further stimulated the personnel

---

[108] Lewis I. Myers, Jr., *Report to the Board* (Richmond: Southern Baptist Foreign Mission Board, Accession Number 1395, December 06, 1993). Myers points out that the access created by these platforms was not the end, but simply a means toward the end, which was the evangelization of the targeted people group or population segment.

[109] Barnett, "Innovation in Mission," 214.

[110] Stroope, Interview by Keith E. Eitel: 16.

[111] Stroope, Interview by Keith E. Eitel: 16.

[112] Barnett, "Innovation in Mission," 234-9.

growth within CSI. More and more people, who might not otherwise have considered missionary service, began to respond to the multiplicity of opportunities opening up that allowed them to use their education and life skills for cross-cultural witness and ministry.

Unreached but not Unresponsive

Not only did the SC paradigm persistently dispel the myth that unreached was synonymous with unreachable, it also continued to dispel the myth that these World A peoples were unresponsive. As noted above, when the GSG evaluated the NRM program, they cited several case studies that revealed World A peoples were responding to the gospel as they had opportunity to hear it. Based on its 1992 annual statistical report, the Board announced, "A blip appeared on the screen when Southern Baptist missionaries looked back on their efforts during 1992: Among 1,606 churches started by the Foreign Mission Board workers and their overseas partners, 20 were launched in a certain isolated part of the world….in World A."[113] In total, SC personnel reported 55 churches among World A peoples in 1992.[114]

The following year, CSI reported 75 new churches planted in World A, bringing the total of churches to 130, which was an increase of 136 percent.[115] By June 1994, Stroope reported, "The total number of churches to which CSI personnel relate increased from 130 to 299."[116] The next twelve months saw an additional 216 new church starts by CSI in World A.[117] By the end of 1995, the total number of new church starts in World A climbed to 367 or 15 percent of the total number of new church starts reported by Board personnel around the world.[118] The new church starts reported by CSI "ranked third-highest in new churches among the 10 world regions identified by the Foreign Mission Board."[119]

Year by year, the SC paradigm was demonstrating that World A people, upon having opportunity to hear the gospel, indeed were responsive. One of the last things that Barrett attempted to do before leaving the Board was to demonstrate quantifiably that World A peoples were more responsive harvest

---

[113] Bridges, "Missionaries See Results."

[114] Williard, "World A: Out of the Shadows."

[115] Williard, "World A: Out of the Shadows;" Stroope, *1992/93 Statistical Report,* 2.

[116] Michael W. Stroope, *Cooperative Services International 1993/94 Statistical Report: Area Director's Narrative Summary* (Richmond: Southern Baptist Foreign Mission Board, September 1994), 5.

[117] Stroope, *One Day...Is Today!*

[118] Erich Bridges, "367 New Churches Prove 'Last Frontier' Reachable," (Richmond: Southern Baptist Foreign Mission Board, March 14, 1996); available from https:// solomon. imb.org; stories database.

[119] Bridges, "367 New Churches."

fields than many of the Board's traditional mission fields. In an interview with a Board journalist, Barrett stated the following:

> Yes, the World A database…tells us the church-growth rates of every one of the 12,000 ethno linguistic peoples in the world….
>
> It also tells us the total of evangelism hours per year expended on every people in the world (the cumulative hours of Christian witness received by individuals within a people group). If you then count the number of new church members and divide by the number of evangelism hours, you can determine where the greatest per capita response occurs. That is the sensible place to invite new missionaries to tackle – where the harvest is ripest.
>
> Results vary. The lowest figure is something like 10; that is, 10 new church members for every 1 million evangelism hours. That's the situation in America. The average for the world is 90. But World A, in most cases, turns out to be far higher. We can definitely say that World A is a more responsive harvest field than World B or World C. Some World A peoples have current response rates over 500.[120]

Although Barrett's extensive use of quantifiable data to determine a people group's response to the gospel may not tell the whole story, his explanation was an attempt to challenge a wide-spread belief that certain people groups, as a whole, were resistant to the gospel. According to Barrett, missionaries and missiologists chose to label certain people groups as resistant as a way of justifying their neglect of these people groups.[121] In the same interview, Barrett added, "The experience of this board is that when you target even the toughest people in the world with a strategy-coordinator approach, within the first year you start to see things happen."[122]

Not only did SC personnel begin to see the initial church starts among previously unengaged World A peoples, they also began to witness the beginnings of church-planting movements among some of these people groups.[123] In some cases, SC personnel did not report the statistics on new

---

[120] David Williard, "World A: What it is; How to get there," (Richmond: Southern Baptist Foreign Mission Board, January 01, 1994); available from https://solomon .imb.org; stories database.

[121] Williard, "World A: What it is; How to get there."

[122] Williard, "World A: What it is; How to get there."

[123] See V. David Garrison, *Church Planting Movements* (Richmond: Southern Baptist International Mission Board, 2000), 7. Garrison formally stated what would become the Board's operating definition for church-planting movements – "a rapid and exponential increase of indigenous churches planting churches within a given people group or population segment." Up until this time, there was no standard definition of the term utilized by the Board, although some at the Board, as well as other evangelical missiologists, were employing the term.

church starts in their annual statistical reports or, in other cases, reports lagged behind realities on the field by a year or two. Nevertheless, within a few short years of implementing this new missiological paradigm, SC personnel began to see multiplication of new churches spontaneously occur among some World A people groups. In 2000, Garrison cited four specific case studies on church-planting movements, three of which originated in World A.[124] These case studies verified what SC personnel had asserted – World A was a harvest field as much as, if not more than, many of the traditional mission fields.

The Stroope Years: Ethos

The statistics show significant numerical growth in terms of personnel, new World A people groups targeted and new church starts within World A, but they only provide a partial picture of the development and impact of the SC paradigm. On one level, the statistics provide quantifiable data of the success of this new paradigm. In a less quantifiable manner, the ethos that emerged within CSI demonstrated the achievement of SC paradigm on a different level.

The decision to elevate CSI to the level of an official administrative area of the Board was a step of the paradigm toward institution. However, the ethos, so deftly developed and nurtured by Stroope, kept the paradigm from losing its vision and the creative tension fashioned at its birth. In fact, Stroope states that the new paradigm attracted him because he saw within it "a possibility of creating a new ethos and structure within mission life."[125] True, from the birth of this new paradigm, an unique ethos was emerging; however, it was under Stroope's visionary leadership that it truly matured. The Ten Guiding principles, initially written by Stroope at a meeting in Pakistan in 1995, grew out of the organizational ethos that CSI had already begun to develop.[126] Stroope stated that there was nothing new in what he wrote down, the ten principles were simply "verbalizing what already was….reflected who we already were."[127] The following paragraphs will describe the unique and challenging ethos that CSI developed as it matured, an ethos that eventually Stroope sought to encapsulate in those ten guiding principles.

---

[124] Garrison, *Church Planting Movements*, 11-32. Chapter 5 will explore this phenomenon in more detail as the identification of these movements created a major shift in the SC paradigm and throughout the entire Board.

[125] Stroope, Interview by Keith E. Eitel: 5.

[126] Stroope, interview by author, 4. See Appendix E for the complete list of these ten guiding principles, which seek to summarize the ethos of CSI. Stroope stated that he jotted these principles down while at a meeting of CSI personnel in Pakistan. Willis, Senior Vice-President for Overseas, attended this meeting. This was during a time of much tension within the Board regarding CSI. Stroope stated that he wanted to summarize for Willis the ethos of CSI.

[127] Stroope, interview by author, 4.

Vision

Almost every organization develops a vision statement. Vision statements serve to keep the big picture before the staff of the organization. They serve to help the organization understand its destination. CSI, under Stroope's leadership developed the following vision statement:

> To lead Southern Baptists and other Great Commission Christians to use all appropriate means to bring salvation through Jesus Christ to the unreached peoples and cities of the world; and to establish indigenous churches among every tribe, tongue and nation as we anticipate the imminent return of Christ.[128]

The vision statement above helped to focus the attention of CSI personnel on its unique role of evangelizing World A. However, the vision statement did not communicate the essence of the vision. Shorter phrases such as "All People Nothing Less" and "Taking the Edge" were much more effective in communicating the vision throughout CSI and the Board. When Stroope composed the ten principles in 1995, he expressed the vision with the simple phrase, "The Edge is where we belong."[129] For CSI, the cutting edge of missions was World A. To be on the "edge" meant to be active in witness among those untouched by the gospel. CSI personnel were convinced that God's plan was for His message to be preached to all peoples because God was not willing that any perish, inclusive of World A peoples (see 2 Peter 3:9; Matthew 24:14). It was this vision of all people groups having the opportunity to hear and respond to the gospel that created the enthusiasm within CSI and synergy among its personnel. As Stroope expressed it, "We said that the thing held us together, the glue that held us together…was the vision."[130] He added, "We lived and died for the vision, not for the board, not for policy, but for vision."[131]

Stroope understood his foremost responsibility as that of managing the vision not as an administrator of personnel and policy.[132] In his various reports to the Board during his tenure, Stroope consistently cast the vision, not just for CSI personnel, but also for the entire Board. Stroope was convinced that the Board "must continue to reach beyond the foundations which have been

---

[128] CSI vision statement adopted in October 1994.

[129] Michael W. Stroope, *CSI Guiding Principles* (London: Cooperative Services International, July 1995).

[130] Stroope, Interview by Keith E. Eitel: 7.

[131] Stroope, Interview by Keith E. Eitel: 6-7.

[132] Stroope, Interview by Keith E. Eitel: 7. In his interview with Eitel, Stroope talks about the esprit de corps between CSI personnel, and attributes it to vision. He was convinced that if he were vision-driven, those who he led would be the same.

established to those places where the gospel has yet to be preached."[133] In a later report, he would reiterate this consuming passion, stating, "CSI is to keep pushing until the church is established among the very last people group – at the Edge."[134] This emphasis on pushing to the "edge" rang out with a strong sense of urgency. As Stroope emphasized, "I believe our Lord would have us see clearly the Edge, call our generation to it, and take it while we live."[135]

Indeed, the key tool for sustaining the verve of the SC paradigm was this vision. Although from a human perspective the statistics demonstrating the growth of CSI were impressive, the vision was a constant reminder that God's "aim is not our small numbers, but His aim is all the peoples of the earth."[136] The consistent message focusing on moving toward the edge was intentional. Stroope believed that many of the Board's missionaries had drifted into institutional work and denomination building, and the vision of taking the edge was the fulcrum intended to move the Board away from these distractions back toward what he believed to be authentic mission.[137] In a report to the Board, Stroope expressed it as follows:

> To be missionary or apostolic means to be at the Edge. We must stop calling everything we do 'missionary.' Many of the things we call missions are in fact 'ministry.'...To be missionary is to be apostolic and to be at the Edge.[138]

From Vision to Empowerment

While vision expressed the destination for CSI, the empowerment of SC and other personnel created the drive needed to continually move toward reaching

---

[133] Stroope, *Report to the Board,* December 08, 1993.

[134]Stroope, *Taking the Edge.*

[135] Stroope, *Taking the Edge.*

[136] Michael W. Stroope, *Report to the Board* (Cape Girardeau: Southern Baptist Foreign Mission Board, Accession Number 2338, April 18, 1996).

[137] Stroope, interview by author, 3. Under Stroope's leadership, CSI continued emphasizing this message, a message that Parks strongly emphasized while at the helm of the Board. See Estep's *Whole Gospel Whole World,* 356-7. Parks realized that fewer and fewer Southern Baptist missionaries were directly involved in church planting efforts, so he proposed what became known as the 70/30 concept. The basic idea behind this concept was that 70 percent of Board missionaries would devote at least 50 percent of their time in direct evangelism and church planting while 30 percent of missionaries would provide support services. This created a great amount of tension among Board personnel as many missionaries felt that Board leadership was invalidating their ministry, ministry that Board leadership had appointed them to carry out. As CSI continued to underscore the need to move away from denomination building and support, it experienced a similar response from other missionaries. However, within CSI, this remained a core value of its ethos.

[138] Stroope, *Taking the Edge.*

that destination. The following guiding principle expressed it in these words, "Destination is the point and you are the key!"[139] The structure of CSI and the attitude of its leadership empowered SC personnel and their teams to plan and implement their ministries, recognizing that these personnel were the key if the new paradigm were to be effective and successful. Within this environment, SC personnel were "free to pursue their assignment without much constraint, ...[they] had the ability to make things happen."[140] CSI leadership intentionally sought to develop an atmosphere of mutual trust between field personnel and themselves. According to Stroope, CSI experienced success because leadership trusted personnel, stating, "We trusted people to make the right decisions for their work, we expected them to make the right decisions."[141] He concluded, "Really, it all gets back to the issue of how people were treated, the way we trusted people and the way we trusted that the Holy Spirit would work in people."[142] At the same time because of leadership's trust of field personnel, personnel "could receive decisions from leadership and believe that their heart was right...and that they were making the best decision possible."[143]

This atmosphere of trust allowed for the development of a structure within CSI that fostered the empowerment of SC personnel and their teams. A secondary factor that facilitated the emergence of a different structure was the reality that CSI personnel were scattered all over the world and did not live in close physical proximity of each other. The structure that emerged within CSI was noticeably different from the Board's traditional mission structure prevalent throughout the world and solidified over the course of 150 years. Implicit in the traditional mission structure was the fact that most missionaries lived in the same country or a smaller region within the country. Besides this characteristic, the traditional structure of the mission entity was based on "Southern Baptist congregational, democratic polity."[144] As the mission entity developed over the years, a bureaucracy of parliamentary procedure, committees, subcommittees, peer personnel review and corporate mission budgeting took root. Within the traditional mission structure there was pressure for missionaries to conform to the mission's operating procedures and policies, often designed to establish parity among the missionaries. Thus, in the mission entity an ethos developed where "everything was everybody's business and...everything had to be voted on."[145] For Stroope, who early in his missionary career had been a part of a traditional mission structure, "it seemed

---

[139] Stroope, *CSI Guiding Principles*.
[140] Stroope, interview by author, 3.
[141] Stroope, interview by author, 3.
[142] Stroope, interview by author, 3.
[143] Stroope, Interview by Keith E. Eitel: 8.
[144] Smith, "Thoughts for Bruce."
[145] Stroope, Interview by Eitel: 6.

like the mission structure beat people down, treated them like children, and rather than empowering people, it really crippled people."[146]

What emerged within CSI was a salient innovation. SC personnel had one supervisor who approved the strategic plan and to whom the SC was accountable for implementation of that plan. According to Smith, "Delegating creation of a Master Plan to a single unit, along with giving that unit the responsibility for implementing that plan, was entirely contradictory to previous FMB management principles."[147] However, this structure allowed SC personnel "to create structure for the team, to create spending policies,...to create strategy, to create relationships with Great Commission Christians, that they really had power at that point."[148] This simplified, yet efficient, structure allowed for rapid decision-making, a necessity for SC personnel and their teams working in the pioneer, and often hostile, areas of World A.

Not only did this structure allow for rapid decision-making, it also created an environment within CSI that encouraged and "rewarded innovation and risk taking."[149] Some of these innovations already mentioned previously included developing extensive networks with GCC groups outside Southern Baptist circles, generating advocacy materials on their target people group for wide distribution among Southern Baptists and GCC groups, developing creative platforms for access into World A, mobilizing personnel directly from churches and utilizing short-term, two-year ISC/Journeymen personnel in front-line mission efforts. Another innovation warrants mentioning. Not only did SC personnel go directly to the churches to mobilize personnel for their teams, they also "were authorized to work beyond the level of FMB regular budget constraints."[150] Because of the vast networks created by SC personnel both

---

[146] Stroope, Interview by Eitel: 6.

[147] Smith, "Thoughts for Bruce."

[148] Stroope, Interview by Eitel: 7.

[149] Stroope, Interview by Eitel: 8.

[150] Smith, "Thoughts for Bruce." The budgeting process within the Board was an intricate process whereby each administrative area would submit budget requests on an annual basis, after which time Board leadership and trustees would approve a specific percentage of the overall Board budget to each respective area. The Board then sent requests not approved through the regular budget process to the Board's development office and listed as "unfunded needs." The Board would then prioritize, publish and distribute these needs to the wider Southern Baptist constituency. SC personnel soon became skilled at drafting such requests. Once these requests were in the Board's development office, SC personnel would often, through their mobilization efforts, find donors to fill many of these needs. This innovative approach led to accusations of direct solicitation from Southern Baptists, which the Southern Baptist convention did not allow Board missionaries to do. SC personnel quickly found ways to circumvent the direct solicitation restriction. As they networked with Southern Baptist individuals and churches, they would not directly solicit funds. However, because these SC personnel

within and outside of Southern Baptist circles, they soon discovered a wealth of resources, financial and human, available for deployment among their targeted people group.

When Stroope set out to summarize the ethos of CSI during the eventful Pakistan meeting in 1995, he captured this concept of moving away from organizational conformity towards empowerment and innovation in several of the principles. The third principle stated, "Organizational conformity for the sake of conformity is death."[151] Elaborating on this principle, Stroope wrote:

> We are part of the FMB family, and yet we do not have to look or act exactly like our brothers and sisters. Our motivation must not be conformity to organizational standards, procedure and policies for the sake of conformity.[152]

While expounding on another key principle, "The greater our diversity, the greater our strength," Stroope added:

> Equity is not our way of operating. Each of you will be treated differently. Our aim must be the maximizing of everyone's unique gifts and personality so that the destination is reached.[153]

Because of the streamlined structure that emerged out of the CSI ethos, others often accused SC personnel as lacking accountability. However, inherent within the CSI structure were strong accountability relationships. The appearance of a lack of accountability arose because CSI operated without "the administrative constraints that were present in traditional mission settings."[154] Those within traditional mission settings, looking from the outside into CSI,

---

nurtured relationships directly with these groups, often these groups would ask the SC what needs he/she had for his/her ministry. Once asked by the group, the SC would then share the needs. Because the individual or church asked first, the SC was able to circumvent the direct solicitation restriction. The direct solicitation restriction only applied to Southern Baptist individuals, churches or agencies. It did not apply to other Great Commission Christians. Therefore, because the SC paradigm involved wide networking with GCC groups, SC personnel were able to mobilize both financial and human resources for ministry among their target people group. The only restriction that SC personnel faced was that they could only solicit resources from GCC groups based on funding requests that had been approved in the budgeting process, but which were not funded through the normal budgeting process. According to Smith, at one point, nearly 75 percent of all the "unfunded needs" requests in the Board's development office were generated by SC personnel and their teams.

[151] Stroope, *CSI Guiding Principles*.

[152] Stroope, *CSI Guiding Principles*.

[153] Stroope, *CSI Guiding Principles*.

[154] Stroope, interview by author, 3.

saw SC personnel who were trusted with decision-making responsibility and given a sense of ownership of their ministry. There was no voting, no committees and no policy manuals, thus for those on the outside it gave the appearance of a lack of accountability.

All SC personnel were accountable to a supervisor in a corporate-like structure. These supervisors approved the plan generated by the SC and had the responsibility to hold the SC accountable regarding the implementation of that plan. Monthly reports by all personnel to their respective supervisors became standard operating procedure.[155] The accountability structure with CSI was different from traditional mission settings, but different accountability did not mean there was no accountability. To the contrary, when Stroope composed the *CSI Guiding Principles* document, he clearly stated, "We all live under authority and are accountable."[156] While asserting that everyone within CSI was in an accountability relationship, Stroope was also clear that the purpose of this accountability structure was to empower people, not control them. Stroope highlighted the emphasis of the SC paradigm's accountability structure:

> The new mission paradigm calls into question policies written for missionaries and mission activity which operate under other directives. Some policies and procedures assume that people cannot be trusted to be good stewards or that they will not live as empowered individuals. New paradigm thinking assumes trust as the basis for administrative decisions and facilitation as the chief role of the administrator. New paradigm administration includes built-in accountability structures which in themselves automatically guarantee control while enhancing the potential for success.[157]

In a number of ways, CSI functioned as a counter-culture within the wider FMB culture. However, the culture that developed was not a denunciation of the status quo within the Board rather what emerged was the result of the

---

[155] Smith, "Thoughts for Bruce." Smith suggests that the concept of submitting monthly reports was a unique contribution of the SC paradigm to the Board. Although he states he cannot attest to the veracity of his statement, Smith concludes, "Never before in FMB history had missionaries been required to submit written monthly reports on their activity." I do not intend to assert that there was no reporting within the traditional mission setting. Area directors were required to submit reports back to the Board on a regular basis, and annual statistical reports were part of the Board's accountability structure. However, the practice of having individual missionary units submit monthly reports does not appear to have been widespread throughout the Board. On the other hand, monthly reporting by each missionary unit assigned to CSI was required. For the SC, progress toward implementing his/her overall plan was a major component of the monthly report.

[156] Stroope, *CSI Guiding Principles*.

[157] Stroope, *Perspective and Prospects,* 5.

common vision, the destination. In reading the ten principles set out by Stroope, it is evident that the destination of reaching the nations with the gospel compelled CSI to develop this unique ethos. In explaining the necessity of avoiding organizational conformity, Stroope said, "Our motives must be driven by what it will take to reach the nations."[158] The ninth principle states, "We will do whatever it takes to get to the destination."[159] This principle did not justify every method as being appropriate for reaching the nations with the gospel, but it sought to explicate the firm belief that in order to fulfil its vision, CSI must foster innovation and creativity.[160] What emerged in this counter-culture was an ethos of mutual trust, empowerment and innovation, ingredients perceived by CSI to be deficient in the traditional structures of the Board.

CSI leadership was convinced that if personnel were trusted and empowered, they would make the right decisions. Jennings and Haughton, writing about developing effective corporate culture in the business world, conclude, "If everyone within the organization knows and makes fast decisions within the parameters of the same set of guiding principles, the vast majority of the decisions made will be the right one."[161] This observation from the business world is a compelling description of the ethos of mutual trust and empowerment infused by Stroope into CSI.

Change as a Value

When Stroope stepped into the leadership role of CSI, he inherited a movement that was shifting toward institutionalization. A major part of nurturing the paradigm to maturity involved protecting this new paradigm from calcification as it moved toward institutionalization. Stroope recognized that the SC paradigm was shifting toward institution when he stepped into his role as area director.[162] If he had not recognized this reality, CSI well may have drifted into stagnation as often happens when movements transition to institution. Guder points out how important it is to recognize this transition:

> Movements that claim that they are not institutions are practicing self-delusion. In fact, the attempt to conceal the institutional reality, the attempt to maintain the

---

[158] Stroope, *CSI Guiding Principles.*

[159] Stroope, *CSI Guiding Principles.*

[160] Stroope, *CSI Guiding Principles.*

[161] Jason Jennings and Laurence Haughton, *It's not the Big that Eat the Small...It's the Fast that Eat the Slow: How to Use Speed as a Competitive Tool in Business* (New York: Harper Collins Publisher, 2000), 97.

[162] Stroope, interview by author, 4. In this interview, when asked whether he saw his role as nurturing the new paradigm to maturity, Stroope responded, "In a way, you might say we were moving toward the institutionalizing of CSI."

façade of a movement while actually functioning as an institution, is a very dangerous one.[163]

In order to prevent this new paradigm from losing its dynamism, Stroope established change as a value within the ethos of CSI. He captured this in the following guiding principle, "We must continually change."[164] Elaborating on this principle, Stroope added, "Unwillingness to challenge what has become status quo or conventional wisdom in CSI will mean stagnation."[165]

The task of trying to keep the SC paradigm dynamic was formidable. Even though Stroope kept the value of continual change in front of CSI personnel, by 1996 Stroope realized that the new paradigm was losing much of its vivaciousness.[166] It was this realization that led Stroope to convene a "Redreaming the Dream" conference in February of that year. Events that happened within CSI suggest there was a similar development to what Bosch perceived occurred in the early church:

> Its white-hot convictions, poured into the hearts of its first adherents, cooled down and became crystallized codes, solidified institutions, and petrified dogmas. The prophet became a priest of the establishment, charisma became office, and love became routine.[167]

The heart of the CSI ethos was a vision to continually push to the edge by entering new people groups. The success of the SC paradigm in recruiting new personnel, resulting in large teams throughout CSI, worked counter to the push of entering new people groups. As large teams emerged around the SC personnel, they often found themselves pulled into the role of administering personnel. Having to spend increasing time and energy supervising growing teams, SC personnel expectedly had less time and energy to devote on pushing toward the edge.

Further, although the writing down of the guiding principles effectively defined the ethos for CSI personnel, in Stroope's own words, "These statements codified what CSI was about."[168] The codification of the ethos also seemed to have the effect of reducing mission as defined by these principles. CSI, through these written guiding principles, was beginning to define mission rather than continuing to allow mission to continually define and change CSI.

---

[163] Guder, *Conversion of the Church,* 187,

[164] Stroope, *CSI Guiding Principles.*

[165] Stroope, *CSI Guiding Principles.*

[166] Stroope, interview by author, 4.

[167] Bosch, *Transforming Mission,* 53.

[168] Stroope, interview by author, 4.

As Guder says, "Reductionism does not mean that what remains is wrong: it means that what remains is too little."[169]

The struggle for survival within the Board as a whole, also contributed to the loss of dynamism. In a document prepared for Willis in 1995, Stroope sought to respond to the following question asked him by Willis, "If we were starting all over again, what would we do differently?"[170] In replying to this question, Stroope asked, "Just because CSI is the focus of organizational friction, does this mean it is the only point at which things need to be fixed?"[171] The disruption at the Board over the SC paradigm and CSI consumed an enormous amount of Stroope's energy as he struggled on behalf of CSI for its survival. Many others within CSI were also drawn into this struggle. This struggle for survival by CSI can be compared to Guder's observation of the early church as "it began to be concerned with itself, with its identity, structure and survival."[172] Bosch stated, "Their survival as a separate religious group…began to preoccupy them."[173] Just as the early church was preoccupied by the struggle for recognition in a hostile world, so CSI was preoccupied by its struggle within an increasingly inhospitable environment at the Board.

All of these factors contributed to CSI moving away from its vision of pushing the edge, losing some of its distinctive vivaciousness and exuberance. All of these factors were the effect of the shift to institution. Thus, the "Re-dreaming the Dream" conference in February 1996 had as its purpose the "defining/redefining what it will take to see the vision of CSI and purposes of our Lord become reality."[174] The objectives of the conference were as follows:

1. To ***pray*** for a "defining moment," in which we hear what God will say to us through His Word and His Spirit.
2. To ***evaluate*** (assess, critique, inquire into) the present reality of the unreached world and our organization.

---

[169] Guder, *Conversion of the Church,* 189. Guder (189-91) talks about the effect of reductionism on the institutional church. He stresses that reduction of the gospel message by the church has always been a temptation. The issue is manageability of the gospel by the church. The effect of this reductionism is that the church begins to shape the gospel message rather than allowing the gospel to shape the church.

[170] Stroope, *Perspective and Prospects,* 1.

[171] Stroope, *Perspective and Prospects,* 1. The entire document is a proposal by Stroope suggesting some possible solutions to the tension between CSI and other parts of the Board. He offers three different solutions, pointing out the strengths and weaknesses of each. The document affirms that CSI was in a battle for its survival within the Board.

[172] Guder, *Conversion of the Church,* 189.

[173] Bosch, *Transforming Mission,* 50.

[174] *Redreaming the Dream* (Chiang Mai, Thailand: Cooperative Services International, February 1996), 1.

3. To ***imagine*** (create, design, form) needed organizational procedures, structures, ethos, system, etc. in order to accomplish the vision.
4. To ***project*** change for CSIers, teams and the organization.[175]

Stroope knew that continual change was integral to the ethos of the SC paradigm and CSI. Although the paradigm had become institutionalized, the paradigm did not have to lose its vitality. As long as the paradigm was willing to change to the realities of the world around it, it would survive. In fact, the survival of the paradigm depended upon its ability to change. Even though the SC paradigm had demonstrated success in reaching into World A, it could not allow itself to codify its ethos, solidify its structures or institute its methods as canon. To not change would mean retreating from the edge, and the edge was where CSI belonged.

Postmodern Elements of the SC Paradigm[176]

According to Bosch, Christian mission at the end of the twentieth century was moving away from an Enlightenment missiological paradigm into a postmodern missiological paradigm.[177] Several of the key elements of Bosch's emerging paradigm are evident in the SC paradigm, which in turn was having a significant impact on other areas of the Board. Sherrill, in writing about Rankin's tenure as president of the Board, sought to highlight several of the postmodern paradigm components in Rankin's missiology.[178] However, some

---

[175] *Redreaming the Dream,* 1.

[176] I will utilize Bosch's nomenclature for this comparison between the SC paradigm and the elements of the postmodern ecumenical paradigm put forward by Bosch.

[177] See Bosch, *Transforming Mission,* 349-510. In the later part of his book, Bosch sought to show how the Enlightenment paradigm was beginning to break up and then described what he perceived were the elements of the emerging postmodern paradigm. Although I do not agree with some of the theological and missiological convictions of Bosch, I do believe that he has correctly identified a number of significant elements of an emerging missiological paradigm, of which the SC paradigm is a part and is helping to shape. Even Bosch himself concluded that what he perceived was a paradigm in the making and it remained to be seen what shape the paradigm would take.

[178] See Jon D. Sherrill, "Jerry Rankin: Ideology of a Postmodern Paradigm," *Faith and Mission* 16, no. 1 (Fall 1998), 25-43. Sherrill seeks to point out several areas where Rankin's thinking converges with the postmodern paradigm such as *missio Dei*, mission as contextualization and mission as common witness. For a related study, see Lester David Mills, "An Analysis of the Cooperative Baptist Fellowship's Missiological Paradigm," (Ph.D. dissertation, Wake Forest: Southeastern Baptist Theological Seminary, 2004). The Cooperative Baptist Fellowship (CBF) was a group that emerged during the Southern Baptist Convention's (SBC)controversy from 1979-90 when conservatives within the convention intentionally sought and gained control over the SBC and its various schools and agencies. While CBF leaders do not claim to have

of these same elements emerged in Parks' thinking and in the NRM/SC paradigm before Rankin's tenure as president, suggesting that perhaps, even amidst the tension and disruption caused by CSI, Rankin and other leaders at the Board were attentive to and shaped by the SC paradigm. What clearly is evident is that both the SC paradigm and Rankin's thinking show some of the key elements of the postmodern (ecumenical) paradigm posited by Bosch. As these elements emerged in the SC paradigm and the Board as a whole, they began to shift the direction of the Board even further toward World A.

Mission as missio Dei

The concept of *missio Dei*[179] was prevalent in the missiology of both Stroope and Rankin, and it became a central idea of the SC paradigm. In his first report to the Board in 1993, Stroope asserted that the formation of the SC paradigm at the Board was an expression of "the commitment of Southern Baptists to be a part of what God will do to bring the nations to himself."[180] This would be a recurring theme in almost every report that Stroope presented to the Board, especially in reference to God's mission among the World A peoples. For example, Stroope believed that "participation with God in His redemptive activity means we are at the Edge."[181] *Missio Dei*, for Stroope and for CSI, was a call to join God in World A:

---

started a new denomination, the group operates like a separate denomination, mimicking, in many ways, the structure of the SBC. The CBF has its own mission agency. After resigning as president of the Foreign Mission Board, Keith Parks became the president of the new CBF mission agency, taking with him the emphasis on unreached people groups and much of the NRM/SC paradigm. Mills presents an extensive analysis of the missiological paradigm of this new group, using Bosch's paradigm as his interpretive grid. The CBF missiological paradigm, like the SC paradigm of the IMB, converges in various places with Bosch's postmodern paradigm.

179 *Missio Dei* is used here to refer to the belief that mission fundamentally begins with God. Mission is an attribute of God, that is, God is a missionary God. *Missio Dei* indicates all that God does for the purpose of establishing His kingdom in the world and reconciling a lost world to Himself in order that God might receive the glory and honour due Him. Missions, then, is the participation of God's people in His mission, the practical expression of God's mission in the world. Therefore, authentic missions only occurs when it fulfils God's mission.

180 Stroope, *Report to the Board,* December 08, 1993.

181 Stroope, *Taking the Edge.*

> What I want to underline…is that God is at work. We're seeing Him at work. We're seeing that it is His desire that those who live in these World A countries among these people groups be reached. We can praise God that He is at work.[182]

If "mission" was defined as *missio Dei*, then, for CSI, "missions" was the effort to join God where He was at work in World A. The 1995 priority goal for CSI reflects this differentiation, stating that CSI must "acknowledge where God is working in World A and join Him in what He is already doing."[183] The guiding principles exhorted CSI personnel to "continually remember that we are participants in World A only at our Lord's gracious invitation."[184] Stroope summarized the calling of CSI to preach the gospel to those in World A who had never heard, stating, "We feel that in doing this we participate with him in establishing 'his glory among the nations, his marvellous deeds among all peoples.'"[185] Although not specifically referring to World A, Rankin expressed a similar understanding, stating, "God has His own strategy for redeeming a lost world….fulfilling His mission and simply gives us the privilege of joining Him in that mission."[186]

As Board leaders began to incorporate *missio Dei* into their missiology, they found it difficult to justify neglecting World A at the expense of investing the majority of their resources in the so-called "harvest fields." Rankin signifies this shift in thinking, stating, "We could concentrate all our missionaries in seven or eight countries and report baptisms far in excess of what we are now reporting, but to neglect taking the gospel to other nations, to all nations, would be a distortion of our missions task and incompatible with the mission of God."[187] Willis also signified this growing emphasis on World A when he shared with trustees in 1995 about the Board's new effort, "Being on Mission with God to the Last Frontier."[188] Willis related that the goal of this effort was

---

[182] Michael W. Stroope, *Report to the Board: Cooperative Services International* (Huntsville: Southern Baptist Foreign Mission Board, Accession Number 1787, April 27, 1995).

[183] *Vision, Objectives, Goals and Principles* (London: Cooperative Services International, 1995), 1.

[184] Stroope, *CSI Guiding Principles.*

[185] Stroope, *One Day…Is Today!*

[186] Jerry A. Rankin, "From the Rankin File: A Kingdom Task," *The Commission* (January-February 1995), 103.

[187] Jerry A. Rankin, *Report to the Board* (Gape Girardeau: Southern Baptist Foreign Mission Board, Accession Number 2338, April 18, 1996).

[188] Willis, *Report to the Board,* August 14, 1995. In 1995, the Board began a shift from using Barrett's World A, World B and World C taxonomies. The Board began using the term "Last Frontier." The "Last Frontier," as outlined in the *Strategic Directions-21 Evaluation Report of the International Mission Board* (Richmond: Southern Baptist International Mission Board, September 30, 2003), 38, has two levels. Level 0 is a Last

to make some adjustments in the Board's overseas efforts, asserting that the "number one critical issue right now is World A that does not have access to the Gospel."[189] According to Willis, the Board could not remain content just investing 13.5 percent of its resources in World A, stating, "There's got to be a radical shift to say how can we continue what God has already led us on, but go farther with that to reach what God has in mind."[190] While some questioned the change in taxonomy as a widening of the definition of the "edge" concept utilized by the SC paradigm, there is still evidence that the Board leadership had accepted the reality that to be on mission with God must include a deeper push into World A.[191] From its inception, the SC paradigm had championed this cause.

Mission as Common Witness

As discussed earlier, a trend started under Parks' administration and incorporated as a central component of the early NRM program was the pursuit of partnerships with the wider GCC community. The evangelical ecumenical movement influenced Board leadership as it began to implement its global strategy. Bosch asserted that the evangelical community pursued these partnerships primarily out of a "concern for pragmatic unity, involving

---

Frontier people group with no evangelical Christians or churches and no access to evangelical print, audio, visual or human resources. Level 1 is a Last Frontier people group less than 2 percent evangelized with some evangelical resources, but no church planting within the last two years. The term "unreached" people group included Levels 0 and 1, but also included two other levels – Levels 2 and 3. Level 2 is a people group less than 2 percent evangelized, but with some initial church planting within the past two years. Level 3 is a people group less than 2 percent evangelized with widespread church planting within the past two years.

[189] Willis, *Report to the Board,* August 14, 1995.

[190] Willis, *Report to the Board,* August 14, 1995.

[191] See Eitel, *Paradigm Wars,* 100-5. The effort "Being on Mission with God to the Last Frontier" was a prelude to wide-scale changes Rankin would later institute in 1997 called "New Directions." Eitel viewed these changes suspiciously, as did a number of others. Eitel especially questioned what he perceived as a dilution of the term "unreached." Eitel noted that Rankin, in response to an inquiry about this matter, confirmed that he was lessening the distinction between World A people groups and other people groups identified as unevangelized because all groups represented people who were lost. In "The Southern Baptists Restructure to Reach the Unreached Peoples: An Interview with Jerry Rankin, IMB President and Avery Willis, Senior Vice President for Overseas Operations," *Mission Frontiers Online* (July-October 1997); available from http://www.missionfrontiers.org/1997/0710/jo976.html. Rankin and Willis express this shift in thinking. Nevertheless, the emphasis on the "Last Frontier" was a continued emphasis on World A. See "Board of Trustees Minutes," (Knoxville: Southern Baptist Foreign Mission Board, Accession Number 2162, February 12, 1996).

planning, mutual encouragement, and the sharing of resources and experiences."[192] This was the emphasis built into the initial NRM training as these NRM personnel sought to mobilize resources from the wider GCC community for impact within their targeted people group.

This expanded within CSI under the leadership of Stroope. The environment of empowerment, which was a part of the CSI ethos, contributed to this expansion of GCC partnerships. According to Smith, "By authorizing SCs to mobilize Great Commission Christian (GCC) resources and apply those to approved action plans, SCs were empowered to build working relationships with not only agencies such as Campus Crusade Jesus Film Project and radio broadcasters, but also any other evangelical Christians that shared similar goals."[193] In his 1992/93 review, Stroope reported, "A reoccurring theme…is the increasing amount of involvement from GCC sending agencies, broadcast groups, translation teams, and prayer groups in CSI assignments."[194] By 1995, Stroope would have this to say about the SC paradigm's success in building partnerships with the wider GCC community:

> Witness in World A has been strengthened by the joining of hands with individuals and agencies of the Great Commission community. The list of those with whom CSI partners reads like the 'Who's Who' of the evangelical mission world: Operation Mobilization, Youth With A Mission, People International, World Evangelism Crusade, Pacific Resources International, The Evangelical Alliance Mission, Action Partners, Frontiers, and a myriad of other evangelical groups.[195]

As the SC paradigm expanded the Board's involvement with the wider GCC community, there did arise some tensions over maintaining Baptist distinctives while, at the same time, building cooperative relationships with other evangelical groups.[196] What emerged within the SC paradigm was partnership

---

[192] Bosch, *Transforming Mission,* 461.

[193] Smith, "Thoughts for Bruce."

[194] Stroope, *1992/93 Statistical Report,* 10.

[195] Stroope, *Perspective and Prospects,* 6.

[196] See Section 2.4.2, note 102. In the dialogue with Rankin and the Board, Eitel raised the issue of maintaining Baptist doctrinal distinctives in the midst of partnership with other GCC groups, especially as related to the issue of church planting. Eitel also believed there was a direct relationship between the partnership issue and the lessening of seminary requirements for career personnel. Eitel expressed concern over what he believed to be the lack of a mechanism whereby field personnel could evaluate the multitude of evangelical agencies, many with whom these field personnel were developing partnerships. Of particular concern to Eitel was the large number of charismatic groups. In Eitel and Hadaway, "Points of Discussion," a possible solution as requiring all groups that field personnel cooperated with in church planting to be in

with other groups in a functional manner, cooperating because of a common vision to evangelize a specific people group. At times, tension did arise as some GCC groups wanted to limit CSI personnel from starting Baptist churches in lieu of starting churches that reflected a more ecumenical pattern.[197] On the one hand, Stroope stressed CSI should seek to hold on to its Baptist distinctives; while, on the other hand, Stroope also stressed, "I think our fallacy…has been that we have put our heritage and our tradition in front of the biblical mandate and also we've made that a test case for our cooperation."[198] It is inevitable when forming partnerships with the wider GCC community that CSI and the Board would experience some tension and conflict. Bosch stated the reality of tension that comes with mission as common witness as follows:

> …holding onto both mission and unity and to both truth and unity *presupposes tension* [emphasis Bosch]. It does not presume uniformity. The aim is not a leveling out of differences, a shallow reductionism, a kind of ecumenical broth. Our differences are genuine and have to be treated as such.[199]

Just as the SC paradigm under Stroope's leadership expanded partnership with other GCC groups, so Rankin continued and expanded Parks' vision of the Board working in cooperation with the wider GCC community. After Willis and Rankin attended the Global Consultation on World Evangelization in Korea in May 1995, Rankin, marvelling on the multitude of networks within the GCC community, remarked, "These expanding networks make it clear that those…who chose to work alone will find themselves left far behind and isolated."[200] After attending this meeting, Rankin publicly acknowledged the extensive experience of CSI in developing networks and partnerships with GCC groups.[201] It is clear that the SC paradigm, in particular, and the Board, in general, were embracing partnership as an integral part of their missiology. The tension and conflict inherent in this aspect of the emerging postmodern missiological paradigm continues within Southern Baptist circles to this day.[202]

---

agreement with the *Baptist Faith and Message 2000* (See http://www.sbc.net/bfm/default.asp).

[197] Stroope, Interview by Eitel: 26.

[198] Stroope, Interview by Eitel: 25.

[199] Bosch, *Transforming Mission,* 464.

[200] Don Martin, "Evangelical Groups Seek an End Run to End Times," (Richmond: Southern Baptist Foreign Mission Board, May 31, 1995); available from https://solomon.imb.org; Stories database.

[201] Don Martin, "Evangelical Groups Seek an End Run to End Times."

[202] See *Something New Under the Sun: New Directions at the International Mission Board* (Richmond: Southern Baptist International Mission Board, January 1999), 36. In seeking to deal with some of the tension and conflict that the partnership issue created, the Board sought to clarify the various levels at which its field personnel could enter

Mission as Church-With-Others

Sweet, who has written extensively on postmodern culture and the church in the United States, claims that there are four key phrases that describe the postmodern person: experience, participatory, image-drive, and connected.[203] The SC paradigm was maturing in an age of transition from a modern cultural paradigm toward a postmodern cultural paradigm. This transition toward postmodern culture had an influence on Southern Baptist churches. Emerging on to the scene was a new generation of Southern Baptists. This generation was no longer willing just to give of their financial resources through the convention's Cooperative Program and the Board's Lottie Moon Christmas Offering to faceless missionaries serving in distant lands.[204] This generation and the churches to which they belonged were keen for experience, hands-on participation in cross-cultural work and personal connectedness to missionaries

---

into partnership with other GCC groups as well as providing a guiding principle at each level. Although this was beneficial in providing guidance to field personnel, it did not resolve the tension between the Board and others within Southern Baptist circles. See Chapter 3, note 195.

[203] Leonard Sweet, *Post-Modern Pilgrims* (Nashville: Broadman and Holman, 2000), 27-138. Sweet seeks to describe key aspects of the post-modern cultural paradigm and the impact these aspects have on the church in the United States (or any church seeking to witness in a post-modern world). Sweet has written extensively on this issue, seeking to help the U.S. church, the large majority of which is still operating with an Enlightenment paradigm, minister in a world that is rapidly transitioning from modern to post-modern. Other key works by Sweet include: *Quantum Spirituality: A Postmodern Apologetic* (Dayton: Whaleprints, 1991); *SoulTsunami: Sink or Swim in New Millennium Culture* (Grand Rapids: Zondervan, 1999); *AquaChurch: Essential Leadership Arts for Piloting Your Church in Today's Fluid Culture* (Loveland, Co.: Group, 1999); and *SoulSalsa* (Grand Rapids: Zondervan, 2000).

[204] In 1925, the Southern Baptist Convention founded the Cooperative Program whereby individual Southern Baptist churches could support the various mission and ministry efforts of the various state conventions and the national convention. Each Southern Baptist church decides how much of their financial resources they desire to contribute. The church then sends this agreed upon percentage to the respective state convention of which the church is a member. The state convention decides what percentage of the total gifts it receives from the local churches will stay for missions and ministries within the state with the remaining percentage then forwarded on to the national convention. At its annual meeting, the national convention then decides how to distribute the funds it receives from the various state conventions. These funds support the North American Mission Board, the International Mission Board, the seminaries of the convention and other ministries under the direction of the Southern Baptist Convention. The Lottie Moon Christmas Offering is an annual offering taken in Southern Baptist Convention churches entirely for use by the International Mission Board. The overwhelming majority of the Board's annual budget is comprised of funds received from Cooperative Program gifts and the Lottie Moon Christmas offering.

on the field. Because of the environment within CSI that encouraged innovation and risk-taking, the SC paradigm demonstrated its ability to adjust to the changing scene in a much more rapid manner than the traditional mission structures around the world.

As noted above, one of the results of the empowerment given to SC personnel was that they were able to go directly to Southern Baptist churches and mobilize resources for work among their targeted World A population segment. The SC paradigm provided an avenue for Southern Baptist churches to rediscover their missionary nature.[205] Further, through the development of World A people group advocacy materials and extensive prayer mobilization, SC personnel began to tap into the massive resources available within Southern Baptist churches.[206] By 1992, the Board was able to identify through its International Prayer Strategy Office over 900 different Southern Baptist churches, mobilized by SC personnel, who had adopted various World A people groups.[207] As Southern Baptists churches began to pray for World A peoples, an ever-increasing number of missionary volunteers began to appear. By June 1993, CSI reported 367 missionary volunteers, the bulk of which came from Southern Baptist churches.[208] The figure of missionary volunteers from churches in the United States nearly doubled the next year, jumping to 723 volunteers.[209] By the end of 1995, CSI reported 1,061 volunteers in World A efforts.[210] The SC paradigm was demonstrating its ability to adjust to the changing world by effectively mobilizing Southern Baptist churches that were realizing their responsibility in world missions.[211] In Bosch's emerging missionary paradigm, the church rediscovering its missionary nature is one aspect of mission as church-with-others. A second aspect is what Bosch described as the "the rediscovery of the local church as the primary agent of mission."[212] He went on to add that this rediscovery "has led to a fundamentally new interpretation of the purpose and role of missionaries and mission

[205] See Bosch, *Transforming Mission,* 372-3. Bosch asserts that in the emerging postmodern ecclesiology, the church is missionary in its very nature. The church is not the sender of missionaries, but actually is the one sent into the world to be missionary. See also Willem A. Saayman, "Missionary By Its Very Nature: A Time to Take Stock," *Missionalia* 28, No. 1 (April 2000): 4-22.

[206] See Chapter 2, Prayer as Strategy.

[207] Williard, "World A: Out of the Shadows."

[208] Stroope, *1992/93 Statistical Report,* 9.

[209] Stroope, *1993/94 Statistical Report,* 9.

[210] Stroope, *One Day...Is Today!*

[211] The following chapter will explore this element of the postmodern paradigm further as various efforts developed within the Board to mobilize and train local churches to serve as strategy coordinators.

[212] Bosch, *Transforming Mission,* 380.

agencies."[213] The SC paradigm within the Board was the primary catalyst for leading the Board to accept this reality. The SC role, as already explained, was primarily a catalytic role. SC personnel were adept at leveraging the resources readily available in Southern Baptist churches and the wider GCC community.

However, not only was the SC paradigm a shift in the missionary role, it facilitated a shift in the manner in which the Board viewed itself as an agency within the Southern Baptist Convention. Over the years, conventional thinking had developed among Southern Baptists that its Foreign Mission Board was the agency that carried out cross-cultural missions on behalf of Southern Baptists. This new vision statement implied a significant shift in the way the Board envisioned its role within the convention: "We will lead Southern Baptists to be on mission with God to bring all peoples of the world to saving faith in Jesus Christ."[214] Not only did this vision reflect the concept of *missio Dei*, but in stating that the Board's vision was to lead Southern Baptists indicated a shift in the role of the Board in terms of its historical relationship with its constituency. In explaining this shift, Rankin commented:

> The board does not exist to fulfil the Great Commission on behalf of Southern Baptists. Being on mission with God to reach the world is the task of every believer, every church, every convention entity and program. Our vision is to be that agency that leads Southern Baptists in being obedient to the Great Commission. We will seek to mobilize Southern Baptists, facilitate involvement, enlist personnel and channel resources so that we might be obedient to God's mission, and all the world might know Him.[215]

Rankin's comments indicate that he was keenly aware that churches were realizing their inherent missionary nature and that the local church can be a primary agent of mission.

One significant change that occurred because of this paradigm shift was the establishment of the Creative Access Network at the Board, an effort to begin to personalize cross-cultural missions for Southern Baptist churches.[216] The Board enlisted the help of a group called Global Focus as it embarked on seeking to help local Southern Baptist churches become personally involved in the world mission endeavour.[217] Through the Creative Access Network with the

---

213 Bosch, *Transforming Mission,* 380.

214 "Board of Trustees Minutes," December 12, 1994.

215 Jerry A. Rankin, "Compelled by a Vision," *The Commission* (March-April 1995), 103.

216 "Board of Trustees Minutes," (Richmond: Southern Baptist Foreign Mission Board, Accession Number 1961, October 9, 1995).

217 "Board of Trustees Minutes," October 9, 1995; Mary E. Speidel, "Personalizing Missions is Focus of FMB Conference," (Richmond: Southern Baptist Foreign Mission Board, October 19, 1995); available from https://solomon,imb.org; Stories database.

help of Global Focus, the Board sought to enlist churches to adopt people groups and build personalized partnerships with field personnel. Since the adoption of its Bold Mission Thrusts in 1976, the Board strove to increase volunteer participation in its world mission efforts.[218] With the development of the Creative Access Network, the Board would accelerate this effort.[219] The following comment by a Southern Baptist pastor, whose church was involved with the Creative Access Network, reveals how churches were acknowledging this trend of the church rediscovering its inherent missionary nature and the local church's importance in the world mission effort:

> It has given a new vitality to our (church body),...People are coming to understand that missions isn't an attachment to the body (of Christ). It's what we're all about.[220]

The SC paradigm was instrumental in facilitating church-planting movements among various World A people groups. Inherent in these movements are these two key aspects of mission as church-with-others described by Bosch. As later defined by Garrison, when there is a swift, proliferation of churches throughout a people group fuelled by churches planting churches, then a church-planting movement is in process.[221] As Bosch described the emerging paradigm, he observed, "It has become impossible to talk about the church without at the same time talking about mission."[222] As the church-planting movement phenomenon captured the attention of CSI and the Board as a whole, it became clear that fundamental to a rapid, exponential growth of the church was the local church's understanding and fulfilling of its missionary nature.

Further, within the church-planting movement context no outside entity, such as a mission, exercises authority or control over the local churches. Stroope, in reporting to the Board of Trustees about the beginning movement in Cambodia, stressed the significant fact "that none of these churches have ever been pastored by a missionary, nor have they even been under the patronage of a mission."[223] The autonomy of the local church in the context of these church-

---

[218] See Appendix B, Number 4.

[219] See *Strategic Directions-21 Evaluation Report of the International Mission Board* (Richmond: Southern Baptist International Mission Board, September 30, 2003), 85. By 2001, the Board reported 33,963 short-term volunteers from Southern Baptist churches, more than double the number reported in 1995.

[220] Speidel, "Personalizing Missions."

[221] Garrison, *Church Planting Movements,* 7.

[222] Bosch, *Transforming Mission,* 372.

[223] Stroope, *One Day...Is Today!* See also R. Bruce Carlton, *Amazing Grace: Lessons on Church-Planting Movements from Cambodia,* 2nd edition (Singapore: by the author, 2004). As the first representatives of the Board to live and work inside of Cambodia, my

planting movements is paramount.[224] Further, in church-planting movements, the local church in its context is the principal agent of mission.

As local Southern Baptist churches in the United States began to demand a more direct involvement in world mission, the SC paradigm was in a unique position to facilitate this involvement. As the SC paradigm fostered an increase in the personal involvement of Southern Baptist churches overseas, the Board as a whole had to respond as well. Further, the emergence of church-planting movements began to alter the manner in which Board personnel related to the local churches overseas. New Directions, launched in 1997 under Rankin's leadership, would acknowledge these trends and incorporate them into its missiology for the 21st century.

Mission as Ministry by the Whole People of God

Another aspect of what Bosch identified as part of his emerging postmodern paradigm, which also began to emerge within the SC paradigm, was a "movement away from ministry as the monopoly of ordained men to ministry as the responsibility of the whole people of God."[225] Again, this manifested itself in both the Southern Baptist churches mobilized for mission by SC personnel and in the local churches overseas that began to emerge.

The SC paradigm's development of creative means to access World A peoples opened the door for a wide variety of Southern Baptist and GCC laity, who otherwise might not have considered cross-cultural missionary work, to serve in strategic ministry among World A peoples. Throughout most of its

---

wife Gloria and I were able to witness the beginning of this church-planting movement. Like Stroope, I can attest to the fact that no outsider controlled the churches planted through our ministry in Cambodia (1990-6).

[224] It is interesting that one of the key beliefs of Southern Baptists has always been the autonomy of the local church. However, in its overseas work, the Board often violated this key principle. Although the Board would verbally uphold the autonomy of the local church as paramount, in reality, many missionary personnel served as pastors of congregations and held positions of authority in the denominational institutions, which the Board helped to create. Further, the dependency created by extensive financing of these institutions and so-called "younger" churches allowed the Board to exercise control over the local church in many places. Throughout the Parks and Rankin eras, the Board has struggled with turning over work to local churches, particularly turning over the various institutions that our Board helped to create. See Roland Allen, *Missionary Methods: St. Paul's or Ours?* American edition. (Grand Rapids: Eerdmans Publishing, 1962). Allen's classic work vividly points out the differences between the methodology of Paul and the methodology of the majority of mission agencies from the West. Allen loathed the idea that a mission agency would exert control over the local churches. Originally published in 1912, Allen was a prophetic voice in a world of Western mission agencies and churches who, for the most part refused to listen.

[225] Bosch, *Transforming Mission,* 467.

history, the Board had emphasized the need for seminary training and two years of full-time ministry experience as a prerequisite for its missionaries. Although the Board did appoint missionaries with secular training, the pattern was for these missionaries to serve primarily in support roles within the mission settings. With the emergence of the SC paradigm, this began to change. As SC personnel developed platforms to penetrate World A, people with training in business and other secular fields found themselves in front-line evangelism, discipleship and even church-planting roles. For some within Southern Baptist circles, this created much concern.[226] Although this issue spurred some controversy, nevertheless, the mobilization of large numbers of lay people, spearheaded by the SC paradigm, was a significant shift in the Board's missiology.

Within the church-planting movements occurring within World A, the concept of the entire body of Christ being involved in mission emerged.[227] Garrison would later encapsulate this trend in his presentation of the ten universal principles found in church-planting movements.[228] Within these church-planting movements, leaders were often lay people and local believers were the primary agents in "winning the lost and planting new cell churches themselves."[229] In these church-planting movements, although leadership was present, the distinction between clergy and laity was not as pronounced as within the Western church model.

Points of Divergence from Bosch's Postmodern Paradigm

While there are various points where the SC paradigm converges with Bosch's postmodern paradigm, there also are some key points of divergence. These points of divergence are reflective of the evangelical soil out of which the SC paradigm grew. Specifically, three areas warrant comparison: (1) mission as

---

[226] See Chapter 1, note 102. In Eitel, *Vision Assessment,* 4, Eitel stressed that neither did he seek to demean those missionaries with secular backgrounds nor did he advocate for a cease or a limit to the involvement of laypersons in missions. Yet, he expresses concern that a lack of theological training was resulting in a number of churches lacking a solid biblical ecclesiology. By helping laypersons develop greater theological expertise, they then would have a frame of reference to guide them in the church-planting process. See also Jerry A. Rankin, "Reply to Eitel," Electronic Letter to Keith Eitel, October 30, 2003. In his reply to Eitel, Rankin argued that Eitel's interpretation of the Great Commission, as indicated in a communication to another leader at the Board, demonstrated a false dichotomy between laity and clergy.

[227] Bosch, *Transforming Mission,* 470-4. Bosch refers to this emerging concept as the "apostolate of the laity."

[228] See Garrison, *Church Planting Movements,* 33-6.

[229] Garrison, *Church Planting Movements,* 36.

mediating salvation; (2) mission as evangelism; and (3) mission as witness to people of other living faiths.

Mission as Mediating Salvation

In Bosch's postmodern paradigm, he advocates for a reinterpretation of salvation. He appeals for a holistic view of salvation, one that incorporates physical, social and spiritual needs.[230] In this holistic understanding of salvation, both the horizontal (social dynamics) and vertical (individual conversion) are equal. Bosch does not dismiss the need of individual repentance and faith in Jesus Christ, but does assert that this view of salvation is not comprehensive in that it excludes the ethical and social dimensions.[231] In forging his postmodern paradigm, Bosch dismisses a dualistic view of salvation as inadequate to address the issues of the world.

At this point, Southern Baptists, in general, and the SC paradigm, in particular, would significantly deviate from Bosch's paradigm. With its emphasis on fulfilling the Great Commission through the evangelization of World A people groups, the SC paradigm presupposes the need for a conversion experience or new birth for salvation. *The Baptist Faith and Message* is a guiding document for all IMB personnel, defining the theological parameters within which they must work. This document affirms the Baptist belief that salvation involves regeneration, and one experiences this new birth through repentance and personal faith in Jesus Christ.[232] This view of salvation was inherent in the development of the NRM role, a role with the goal of evangelizing an unreached people group. Believing that those who had not heard the gospel and separated from God faced an eternal judgment, NRM and SC personnel were motivated to find ways to penetrate the barriers of taking the gospel message to these peoples who had not yet had an opportunity to hear and respond to the Gospel. Stroope summarized this belief, stating, "Every day, every hour thousands spill over the Edge into eternity and judgment without the chance to say 'Yes' or 'No' to Jesus Christ."[233] He further adds that these unreached peoples have "no one to warn them or to turn them from the eternal abyss which awaits them."[234] Rankin affirmed this view of salvation as core to the Board's missiology, indicating that one of the basic principles was that personal belief in Christ is the only way to salvation and, without this salvation, people faced a destiny in hell.[235]

---

230 Bosch, *Transforming Mission,* 399-400.
231 Bosch, *Transforming Mission,* 399-400.
232 *The Baptist Faith and Message* (Nashville: Southern Baptist Convention, 2005), 4.
233 Stroope, *Taking The Edge.*
234 Stroope, *Taking The Edge*
235 Jerry A. Rankin, *Report to the Board* (Wake Forest: Southern Baptist Foreign Mission Board, Accession Number 1743, February 13, 1995).

A component of the NRM role as delineated by Barrett was the need to integrate evangelism and social concern in the strategy implementation, yet this is not the same as Bosch's view.[236] Bosch would decry the view that evangelism and social concern need integrating because such a view "tends to suggest that evangelism *a priori* lacks a social dimension and social action an evangelistic dimension."[237] Nonetheless, the conversionist view of salvation does not dismiss the responsibility of Christians for ministry to the physical, social or emotional needs of others. To the contrary, because of the experience of new birth, one can effectively have a Christ-like impact on society. *The Baptist Faith and Message* expresses it in this way:

> All Christians are under obligation to seek to make the will of Christ supreme in our own lives and in human society. Means and methods used for the improvement of society and the establishment of righteousness among men can be truly and permanently helpful only when they are rooted in the regeneration of the individual by the saving grace of God in Jesus Christ.[238]

Many SC personnel in CSI established platforms that not only facilitated access to the targeted people group, but also allowed them to minister to physical or social needs. Yet, the overall goal was, and continues to be today, the presenting of the gospel message with the intent that those hearing are born again into God's kingdom through faith in Jesus Christ. The following statement by Rankin encapsulates this belief:

> Even as we engage in holistic ministries in response to the needs of a hurting world, we must never lose sight that our missions task is one of proclamation. As we use secular platforms to gain entry into closed places, we must lift up Jesus Christ in a bold, positive witness and enable the Word of God to speak spiritual truth to hearts that are empty and searching.[239]

Mission as Evangelism

During Parks' tenure as president of the Board and continuing through the early years of Rankin's tenure, the primary emphasis for missionary personnel was evangelism that would result in churches. In 1992, Parks stated this as one of

---

[236] Barrett and Reapsome, *Seven Hundred Plans,* 36.
[237] David J. Bosch, "Evangelism: An Holistic Approach," *Journal of Theology for Southern Africa* 36 (September 1981): 48.
[238] *Baptist Faith,* 9.
[239] Jerry A. Rankin, "The 21st-Century World May Look Dismal, but the Future of Missions is Bright," (Richmond: Southern Baptist International Mission Board, May 10, 2001); available from: https://solomon.imb.org; stories database.

the seven key principles around which the Board structured its mission effort.[240] Five years later, Rankin asked the Board of Trustees to reaffirm this principle as one of the cornerstones of the Board's missiology.[241] Within the SC paradigm, the result of mission activity was facilitating a church-planting movement among every people group (See Appendix E).

On the one hand, the Board understood mission at its core as *missio Dei*; on the other hand, the goal of mission was evangelism leading to conversion and resulting in the establishment of the church. Stroope clearly demonstrated this view when he expressed that the Board created CSI specifically "to be a part of what God will do to bring the nations to himself…a medium which opens the possibility of witness and the planting of churches in World A."[242] While Board missionaries may have been involved in numerous roles such as church development or human needs ministry, the goal of their missionary activity remained the same – the evangelization of the people among whom they lived and worked. Within the SC paradigm and the Board as a whole, the goal of *missio Dei* was the evangelization of all people in the world and Christians joined God in His mission through involvement in evangelism that resulted in the planting of His church.

This view of mission deviates somewhat from Bosch's postmodern paradigm. Bosch asserted that mission is broader than evangelism or church planting.[243] Evangelism and church planting are simply one aspect of mission. At the same time, Bosch defined evangelism in much broader terms than traditional evangelicals such as Southern Baptists did. To illustrate the differences between what he saw as the emerging ecumenical, postmodern paradigm and the traditional evangelical paradigm, Bosch compared the Melbourne and Pattaya conferences regarding their views of mission and evangelism (See Table 1).[244] Bosch would accept the Melbourne conference view of mission as more acceptable; whereas, the SC paradigm would fall more in line with the views expressed by the Pattaya conference.

Bosch's alignment with the ecumenical perspective of mission and

---

[240] R. Keith Parks, *Controlling Principles in Southern Baptist Foreign Missions* (Clemson: Southern Baptist Foreign Mission Board, Accession Number 1029, April 06, 1992).

[241] Rankin, *Report to the Board,* February 13, 1995.

[242] Stroope, *Report to the Board,* December 08, 1993.

[243] Bosch, *Transforming Mission,* 411; Bosch, "Evangelism," 47.

[244] The 1980 Melbourne conference stressed the role of the poor and oppressed in God's mission, underlining the radical aspects of the gospel message and challenging the power present in political, church and mission life. The church as defined by the Melbourne conference was a healing community. The 1980 Pattaya conference, held within a month of the Melbourne conference, focused on the evangelization of the unreached peoples. The comparison between these two conferences highlights the significant differences between the ecumenical and evangelical approaches to mission.

evangelism is evident in his construction of his view of evangelism in *Transforming Mission.* According to Bosch: (1) mission is more extensive than evangelism as mission is the complete task of God given to the church, while evangelism simply is one aspect of that task; (2) mission and evangelism are not identical; (3) evangelism is fundamental to the task of the church; (4) evangelism is witness to the work of God in the past, present and future, but cannot be defined as occurring only when there are results or converts; (5) evangelism does seek for a decision; (6) evangelism is an invitation to turn to God because of His love not out of fear of hell; (7) we are witnesses not judges; thus, it is too simplistic to divide the world between saved and lost; (8) evangelism is not optional, but must always be carried out in humility; (9) effective evangelism occurs when the church models its message; (10) evangelism is the offer of salvation, a salvation that begins in the present with the promise of eternal fulfilment; (11) evangelism cannot be equated with proselytism; (12) evangelism cannot be reduced to church growth; (13) evangelism and church growth, while different, are connected; (14) evangelism is aimed at people because only people, not nations, groups or families can respond; (15) genuine evangelism requires contextualization; (16) evangelism and social justice are intertwined; (17) evangelism is not a tool to employ for ushering in the second coming of Christ; and (18) evangelism is both word and deed.[245]

There are several points of divergence between Bosch's view as expressed above and the SC missiological paradigm. As noted above, the belief that God's desire and aim is to His church among all people was fundamental to CSI. Further, there is an eschatological expectation couched within this vision of seeing God's church planted among all peoples. For example, the 1994 vision statement of CSI states that its mandate is "to use all appropriate means to bring salvation to Jesus Christ to the unreached peoples and cities of the world; and to establish indigenous churches among every tribe, tongue, and nation as we anticipate the imminent return of Christ."[246] Stroope adds that because "a church for every people group and the knowledge of his name among all peoples are the chief items on our Lord's agenda before he returns, we believe this should be our aim as well."[247]

Within CSI and the IMB, there are eschatological overtones when talking about global evangelization. The missiological eschatology expressed in Matthew 24:14 was a strong motivation for Board leadership; therefore it initiated efforts to reach every people group with the message of salvation. Rankin viewed this as a movement toward the fulfilment of this missiological

---

[245] Bosch, *Transforming Mission,* 411-20.
[246] Stroope, *One Day...Is Today!*
[247] Stroope, *One Day...Is Today!*

eschatology.[248] By accelerating efforts to evangelize every people group, Rankin implies that the church could "hasten" the day of the Lord (2 Peter 3:12). Stroope expresses the same theology and explicitly linked taking the "Edge" with the second coming of Christ in the following statement:

> The Edge is the Goal of God's Redemptive History. Our Lord defines the goal of history in terms of the Edge. He states that "this gospel of the Kingdom will be preached as a witness to all nations [peoples], and then the end will come" (Matthew 24: 14). Once the Edge has been taken, time and history as we know it will come to an end.[249]

Bosch views the dichotomy of people between the saved and the lost as overly simplistic. Yet, within the evangelical tradition of Southern Baptists, this of people is the fundamental motivation for their mission enterprise. Rankin expressed as one of the basic cornerstones of the Board's missiology that those without faith in Christ are lost.[250] This view, in turn, reflects why the Board, including CSI, measures the effectiveness and success of evangelism in terms of decisions, baptisms, church membership and numbers of churches planted. The annual reports of CSI and the other areas of the Board reflect this pragmatic approach in measuring effectiveness in the mission enterprise.

Just as there is a significant difference between Bosch and the SC paradigm regarding salvation, so there is a significant difference in how they define mission and evangelism. While the SC paradigm has willingly assimilated some aspects of the postmodern paradigm, its deep, evangelical roots will not allow for divergence away from the core belief that mission is the proclamation of the gospel message to a world that is lost, separated from God and destined to an eternity in hell.

Mission as Witness to People of Other Living Faiths

Bosch's postmodern paradigm views the modern-day, evangelical attitude toward other religions as exclusivist, asserting that one cannot simply view Christianity as having the absolute truth.[251] Bosch also dismisses the view that asserts Christianity is the fulfilment of all religions, while, at the same time rejecting relativism that would hold the claims of other religions as equally valid with the truth claims of Christianity.[252] At the same time, Bosch concludes that Christians must hold fast to the belief "that God, in sending

[248] Rankin, *Report to the Board,* February 13, 1995.

[249] Stroope, *Taking the Edge.* Stroope referred to World A as the "Edge," and the mandate of CSI was to take the "Edge."

[250] Rankin, *Report to the Board,* February 13, 1995.

[251] Bosch, *Transforming Mission,* 478-9.

[252] Bosch, *Transforming Mission,* 479-83.

Jesus Christ into our midst has taken a definitive and eschatological course of action and is extending to human beings forgiveness, justification, and a new life of joy and servanthood, which, in turn calls for a human response in the form of conversion."[253] At the same time, holding fast to this conviction does not, for Bosch, sanction the continued promulgation of the traditional, evangelical view of salvation.[254] There is an obvious tension between missionary activity and the need for dialogue with other religions within Bosch's postmodern paradigm, a tension the church cannot resolve yet one calling for the adoption of a position of humility and dialogue with competing world religions, acknowledging that it does not have the definitive answers.[255] Clearly, within the SC paradigm and the missiological paradigm of the Board, this is a point of divergence from Bosch. The belief that Jesus Christ is the only provision for salvation propelled Parks to support the non-residential missionary approach in an effort to lead the Board to complete the task of world evangelization by taking this message to those who had never heard. It was not a matter of dialogue nor of questioning whether those carrying the gospel message have the definitive answer, but one of presenting the claims of Christ, seeking to evoke a response of either acceptance or rejection of the truth of the gospel. The missiological issue within the SC paradigm simply was one of providing every people group access to the gospel message. Because salvation comes only through faith in Christ, it is imperative that every people group receives the opportunity to hear and respond to this offer of salvation. Stroope eloquently expressed the issue as follows:

> People in the accessible places of the world repeatedly hear the claims of Christ and either decide against Christ or to ignore him. These pass into eternity having had the opportunity to decide. However, there are approximately 1,700,000,000 men, women and children who are at risk. They are at risk not because they have decided or chosen to ignore Christ, but because they have NO WAY WHATSOEVER of knowing Christ.[256]

---

[253] Bosch, *Transforming Mission*, 488.
[254] Bosch, *Transforming Mission,* 488.
[255] Bosch, *Transforming Mission*, 489.
[256] Stroope, *Taking the Edge*.

Table 1: Comparison between the Melbourne and Pattaya conferences[257]

Melbourne	***Pattaya***
Showed a preference for the "Jesus language" of the Gospels.	Showed a preference for the language of Paul's epistles.
Began with "man's disorder."	Began with "God's design."
Stressed unity (at the expense of truth?)	Stressed truth (at the expense of unity?)
Believed that God reveals Himself also through contemporary experience.	Believed that God reveals Himself only through Jesus Christ (and in Scripture/the Church).
Emphasized the deed (orthopraxis).	Emphasized the word (orthodoxy).
Regarded social involvement as part and parcel (or all?) of the Christian mission.	Regarded social involvement as separate from mission, or as a result of conversion.
Judged societal ethics to be of prime importance.	Judged personal ethics to be of importance.
Viewed sin as having a corporate dimension.	Viewed sin as exclusively individual.
Tended to equate mission with humanization or social change.	Tended to equate mission with a call to conversion or church planting.
Viewed proclamation as *rendering support* to fellowship and service.	Viewed proclamation as primary; it *gives birth* to fellowship and service.
Emphasized liberation.	Emphasized justification and redemption.
Heard the cry of the poor and oppressed.	Heard the cry of the lost.
Considered man from the perspective of creation.	Considered man from the perspective of the Fall.
Judged humanity positively.	Judged humanity negatively.
Denied the existence of clear boundaries between the Church and the world.	Affirmed the existence of clear boundaries between the Church and the world.
Regarded the world as the main arena of God's activity.	Regarded the Church as the main arena of God's activity.
Underscored the Church's credibility.	Underscored the Church's opportunities.
Was concerned about witnessing where the Church *is*.	Was concerned about witnessing where the Church is *not*.
Divided the world into rich and poor, oppressor and oppressed.	Divided the world into "people groups."
Revealed a proclivity towards Socialism.	Revealed a proclivity towards Capitalism.
Highlighted Jesus' human nature.	Highlighted Jesus' divine nature.
Focused attention on the universality of Christ.	Focused attention on the uniqueness of Christ.

[257] Taken from David J. Bosch, "Evangelism: An Holistic Approach," *Journal of Theology for Southern Africa* 36 (September 1981): 44.

The SC paradigm reflects an exclusivist position toward other religions. Ebbie Smith describes the exclusivist position as affirming (1) the Bible reveals the truth of God and Christ and is essential for guiding humankind toward salvation; (2) salvation is only available through Christ and not possible through general revelation; (3) salvation is only available for the living; (4) because of their own choice, the unsaved face eternal separation from God; and (5) no other religions offer the possibility of salvation.[258] Specifically, the theological position expressed within the SC paradigm would be what Smith refers to as realistic exclusivist, the belief that there is "no genuine salvation apart from explicit faith in Christ."[259]

While those working out of the SC missiological paradigm would agree with Bosch that the gospel message interacts differently as it encounters the various world religions, they would not dispute the absolute truth of the message. Whether one is Muslim, Buddhist, Hindu or another faith, the claims of Christ remain unchanged. Within the SC paradigm, those without Christ are lost and the message of salvation through Jesus Christ is the only answer. The tension between the missionary task and the need for dialogue with other world religions has not been an issue in the history of Southern Baptist mission efforts neither is it an issue within this emerging paradigm of the Board. Within this theological framework, there is no doubt as to the lostness of human beings who do not express a saving faith in Jesus Christ.

Panta ta ethnē

One of the key missiological emphases for the Board resulting from the influence of the NRM/SC paradigm was one away from geopolitical entities toward a people group focus, specifically those people groups considered unreached and unevangelized. The following chapter will discuss in more detail how this emphasis eventually led the Board to shift toward a people group emphasis worldwide. This people group emphasis evolved out of a specific interpretation of the Biblical phrase *panta ta ethnē*, which Board leaders understood to indicate ethnic people groups. Crawley summarized this interpretation held by Board leaders as follows:

> In New Testament times, modern "nations" (composed of many people groups) did not exist. Therefore, biblical references to nations actually refer to ethnic or

[258] Ebbie Smith "Contemporary Theology of Religions," in *Missiology: An Introduction to the Foundations, History, and Strategies of World Missions,* ed. John Mark Terry, Ebbie Smith and Justice Anderson (Nashville: Broadman and Holman, 1998), 428-9.
[259] E. Smith, "Contemporary Theology of Religions," 429.

> people groups. *The Gentiles* is a term roughly synonymous with *the nations* and refers collectively to all the non-Jewish people groups.[260]

This interpretation follows closely that of other evangelical missiologists. According to Piper, the phrase *panta ta ethnē* occurs in the Septuagint nearly one hundred times, and he asserts that the meaning consistently carries the sense of all non-Jewish people groups.[261] Piper adds that in the Greek New Testament, the phrase or variations of it occur eighteen times and at least half of these references clearly indicate people groups.[262] Barrett's bases his extensive research presented in his *World Christian Encyclopaedia* on a similar interpretation. He cites several passages in the book of Revelation (5:9; 7:9; 10:11; 11:9; 13:7; 14:6; 17:15), which he asserts affirm the ethnic, cultural and linguistic diversity of peoples.[263] Barrett asserts, "The Bible can thus be said to be fully aware of the vast ethno linguistic diversity of the world and of its importance for the Christian world mission."[264]

It is evident that McGavran constructs his homogenous unit principle on this interpretation.[265] The primary emphasis in the church growth missiology developed by McGavran is on the homogenous principle, which asserts that "people like to become Christians without crossing racial, linguistic, or class barriers."[266] In a further explanation of this principle, McGavran adds:

> The principle is also readily discerned when it comes to pronounced class and racial barriers. It takes no great acumen to see that when differences of color, stature, income, cleanliness, and education are present, unbelievers understand the

---

[260] Crawley, *Global Mission,* 245. Emphasis is Crawley's.

[261] John Piper, *Let the Nations Be Glad! The Supremacy of God in Missions.* (Grand Rapids: Baker Books, 1993), 181.

[262] Piper, *Let the Nations Be Glad!* 180. According to Piper, Matthew 25:32 is the only reference that carries the meaning of individual Gentiles. Further, he adds that eight passages refer to either people groups or Gentiles. The nine passages that Piper asserts refer specifically to people groups are Mark 11:17; Luke 21:24; Acts 2:5; 10:35; 15:17; 17:26; Galatians 3:8; Revelation 12:5; 15:4.

[263] David Barrett, George T. Kurian, and Todd M. Johnson, *World Christian Encyclopaedia: A Comparative survey of churches and religions in the modern world,* 2nd edition. (New York: Oxford University Press, 2001), 15.

[264] Barrett, Kurian and Johnson, *World Christian Encyclopaedia,* 15.

[265] Donald A. McGavran, *Understanding Church Growth,* 3rd edition, revised and edited by C. Peter Wagner (Grand Rapids: William B. Eerdmans, 1990), 45. McGavran interpreted *panta ta ethnē* as including all classes, tribes, castes, ethnic groups and economic groupings in the world.

[266] McGavran, *Understanding Church Growth*, 163.

> gospel better when expounded by their own kind of people. They prefer to join churches whose members look, talk, and act like themselves.[267]

Bosch, a critic of the Church Growth movement, viewed the term *ethnē* as "completely unrelated to the question of homogenous units."[268] Bosch asserts that the term primarily has a religious meaning rather than a designation of ethnicity, a term that distinguishes the pagan Gentiles from the Jews, God's chosen people.[269] Therefore, the term *ethnē* must be understood from a theological perspective not a sociological one. Such a rendering of *ethnē* invalidates the key theological foundation of the homogenous unit principle. Regarding the phrase *panta ta ethnē* as seen in Matthew 28:19, Bosch explains it as follows:

> Within the context the emphasis is clearly on the entire world of humanity; the expression is used "in view of the worldwide mission." An unbiased reading of Matthew 28:19 can therefore not take it to imply that the Christian mission is to be carried out "people by people," but that it is to reach far beyond the confines that existed up to that time.[270]

Further, Bosch attacks the predominant evangelical view that the Great Commission is a command that the church must obey. He argues that no place in the New Testament do the apostles reference these words of Jesus to explain their mission, and neither did the church engage in "mission to Jews and Gentiles simply because it had been told to do so."[271] For Bosch, to view mission as mandatory based on this one passage of Scripture is nothing short of legalism.[272]

Clearly there are variations in the interpretation of *panta ta ethnē* among Biblical scholars. Bosch accepts the reality of differences in interpretation. What Bosch is unwilling to accept is the Church Growth movement's reasoning that *panta ta ethnē* affirms the homogenous unit principle. He explains his position in this way:

> Undoubtedly there is validity in the Church Growth movement's honoring of the homogenous unit principle as a communications guideline. We may, however, not take a communications principle and make it an ecclesiological norm by

[267] McGavran, *Understanding Church Growth*, 167.

[268] David J. Bosch, "The Structure of Mission: An Exposition of Matthew 28:16-20, in *Exploring Church Growth,* ed. Wilbert R. Shenk (Grand Rapids: William B. Eerdmans, 1983), 237.

[269] Bosch, "Structure of Mission," 236.

[270] Bosch, "Structure of Mission," 236.

[271] Bosch, "Structure of Mission," 219.

[272] Bosch, "Structure of Mission," 219.

> reasoning that (1) homogenous churches grow more rapidly than others; (2) all churches should grow more rapidly; and (3) therefore all churches should be culturally and socially homogenous. This reasoning cannot but lead to a wrong view of the church.[273]

Saayman criticizes the homogenous unit principle on two grounds. First, he states that this principle can create "the dangerous possibility of including ethnic elements as revelatory principles next to Scripture in church formation."[274] Second, Saayman warns that this principle could lead to large numbers of churches composed solely of homogenous groups, which could undermine the unity and universal nature of the church.[275] In comparing the homogenous unit principle with events within the Dutch Reformed Church of South Africa, Saayman further warns "of the dangers which are inherent in adopting an approach aimed specifically at a certain group, and excluding others, although at the time they may seem nothing more than a practical aid in facilitating evangelism."[276]

While missiologists should heed both Bosch's and Saayman's warnings, the homogenous unit principle is not simply a phenomenological approach to mission. As noted above, this principle is based on a theological interpretation of the phrase *panta ta ethnē* as referring to all nations, tribes, castes, classes and ethnic groups. Clearly, there is validity in utilizing this interpretation as a communications guideline in the global evangelization effort. At the same time, there is no validity, as both Bosch and Saayman emphatically warn, in the church maintaining class or ethnic distinctions as Biblical imperatives.

The understanding of *ethnē* as referring to people groups coupled with the belief that the Great Commission was a command to the church of Jesus Christ led the Board to begin moving toward a global strategy that had within its scope the evangelization of every people group. The NRM/SC paradigm's emphasis on unreached or World A people groups served as a way of pragmatically measuring the progress toward sharing the gospel with all the people of the world. The Board was beginning to understand that looking at the world solely through geo-political lenses resulted in the neglect of numerous people groups who had yet to hear the gospel. The segmentation of the world according to ethno linguistic people groups was a more effective way of gauging the Board's progress toward the fulfilment of global evangelization. Seeking to explain the emerging emphasis on ethno linguistic people groups,

---

273 Bosch, "Structure of Mission," 239.

274 Willem A. Saayman, "The Church Growth Movement: An Appropriate Challenge? A Response to Chris de Wit," *Missionalia* 14, No. 2 (August 1986): 101.

275 Saayman, "Church Growth Movement," 101.

276 Willem A. Saayman, "The Case of South Africa: Practice, Context, and Ideology," in *Exploring Church Growth,* ed. Wilbert R. Shenk (Grand Rapids: William B. Eerdmans, 1983), 142.

Crawley explained that "this emphasis picks up a biblical concept and places it in a current sociological frame of reference."[277]

At the same time, the influence of the Church Growth movement's homogenous unit principle is evident. In delineating the guiding principles of CSI, Stroope affirms that "an indigenous church-planting movement among every people must be the point of all we do."[278] Implied in this statement is the belief that homogenous churches among every people group is the most effective way to complete global evangelization. The Board must face the reality of the danger that can arise if these churches remain homogenous, thus effectively hindering their ability to be salt and light to other peoples around them. The challenge this presents to the church is formidable. Local churches always must understand that they do not exist in isolation from one another. Each local church is an extension of God's universal church, a beautiful mosaic of peoples from different tribes, languages and people groups. McGavran summarizes the challenge facing these churches as follows:

> Becoming Christian should never enhance animosities or the arrogance common to all human associations. As members of one class, tribe, or society come to Christ, the church will seek to moderate their ethnocentrism in many ways. It will teach them that persons from other segments of society are also God's children.[279]

Conclusion

The new missiological paradigm conceived by Barrett, encouraged by Parks and nurtured under Garrison, quickly expanded and matured under the skilful, visionary leadership of Stroope. The decision by the Board to merge the former NRM program with the CSI-China office into CSI and to elevate the new entity to the status of an official administrative area within the Board, created, at least for a while, the necessary shield of protection for the new paradigm's growth. At the same time, this decision to elevate CSI to area status, equal to the other administrative areas of the Board, began the process of shift from movement to institution. The tension and controversy continued to swirl around this new paradigm. At times, this was distracting, but did little to halt its influence within the Board. The change of leadership from Parks to Rankin, seen by some as a possible threat to this new paradigm, did not diminish the Board's emphasis on World A. To the contrary, spurred by the rapid growth of CSI in terms of personnel and new World A people groups targeted by SC personnel, the Board journeyed even further into the world of unreached and unevangelized peoples. As Rankin sought to lead the Board toward a relevant

---

277 Crawley, *Global Mission,* 245.
278 Stroope, *CSI Guiding Principles.* (See Appendix E, Guiding Principle #1).
279 McGavran, *Understanding Church Growth,* 177.

missiology for the 21st century, evidence shows that this new paradigm influenced his thinking and planning in a number of areas. The SC paradigm was firmly rooted within the Board.

At the same time that CSI was expanding and maturing, it had to battle against the inertia that often accompanies a shift from movement to institution. Stroope sought to counter this possibility through the careful development of a unique ethos within CSI. The vision to continually push the edge of extending its work into every World A people group was the core of this unique ethos. Refusing to allow the new paradigm to stagnate, Stroope navigated CSI through the stormy process of institutionalization. At one point, CSI seemed as if it was sacrificing its vision on the altar of its own ethos, embodied in its ten guiding principles. Whether the cause was arrogance over its success or its fierce struggle for survival within the Board, CSI was in danger of losing its verve. Stroope sought to overcome this inertia by calling CSI to re-dream its dream.

As the SC paradigm matured, evidence suggests that a number of elements of the emerging postmodern, ecumenical paradigm as posited by Bosch appeared. Although these elements may not have emerged as fully envisioned by Bosch, it is clear that the SC paradigm shared many of these same characteristics. At the same time, the SC paradigm did not pull away from its strong, evangelical roots. One might claim this was the emergence of a postmodern, evangelical paradigm. Nonetheless, this was truly a new missiological paradigm for Southern Baptists, and it was exerting a significant impact far beyond the boundaries of CSI into many other areas of the Board.

Stroope fought vigorously to preserve CSI as an entity within the Board's administrative structure. He strove diligently to keep the fires of the new paradigm burning hot. However, the tension of two paradigms, two philosophies operating under one Board would eventually lead the Board to search for resolution. Would the new paradigm survive?

CHAPTER 4

From Maverick to Mainstream

Introduction

During Stroope's tenure as the leader of Cooperative Services International (CSI), the strategy coordinator (SC) paradigm emerged from its childhood into maturity. At the same time, the tension between CSI and other administrative areas of the Foreign Mission Board (FMB) would inevitably lead to changes of the Board's structure in an effort to resolve this tension. Before his presidency, Rankin had served as an Area Director with the Board, and during that time, he expressed disagreement with the position CSI held within the Board. Upon becoming president of the FMB in 1993, Rankin made clear that changes within the administrative structure of the Board's overseas operations would be forthcoming.

Initially, although Rankin's uneasiness with CSI was evident, it was unclear what changes he would implement that would affect CSI and, subsequently, the SC paradigm with its emphasis on engaging the unreached peoples of the world. However, by 1997, there was little doubt that Rankin placed the responsibility of conflict and friction between the Board's various areas onto CSI's existence as an administrative area. Rankin viewed this as the major reason for a lack of unity within the organization, and he was unwilling to live with the tension any longer.[1] In a report to the Board, Rankin expressed his goal, stating, "I believe we can have an organization which works together in unity and in which every entity works together in cooperation with mutual respect and support of others, a structure in which there is no internal competitiveness, turf protection and jealousy, an organization that would facilitate a mobility of personnel flowing freely between units to priority areas of need."[2]

---

[1] Jerry A. Rankin, *Report to the Board* (Winston-Salem: Southern Baptist International Mission Board, Accession Number 2509, February 10, 1997). In his report to the Board, Rankin affirmed Parks' decision to lead the Board to begin focusing on restricted-access countries and unevangelized people groups; however, he clearly blamed the decision to make CSI an administrative area as the source of conflict and tension within the Board.

[2] Rankin, *Report to the Board,* February 10, 1997.

The primary thrust of this chapter will be to demonstrate the impact of the SC paradigm on the Board's reorganization in 1997 called New Directions. As a prelude to demonstrating the paradigm's impact, this chapter will outline some of the critical issues and primary emphasis of Rankin's reorganization. Then a comparison between the SC paradigm and New Directions will show the influence of the paradigm.

Stroope's Analysis and Suggestions

It is important to precede the discussion about New Directions with a brief explanation of Stroope's analysis of the situation within the Board and his suggestions for resolving the conflict and tension. Stroope, as the area director for CSI, was keenly aware that Rankin and other leaders at the Board were seriously considering a major reorganization of the Board's overseas administrative structure, a change that would have a significant impact on CSI. In fact, the existence of CSI was at stake. As early as 1995, Willis approached Stroope for recommendations regarding a possible administrative reorganization. Stroope responded to Willis' request with a document in which he outlined three possible options. As noted in the previous chapter, the way Willis approached the issue indicated that Board leadership saw CSI as the problem.[3] Stroope, in his response to Willis, acknowledged that the tension within the Board centred on CSI, and attributed this tension to a competition over resources and unresolved missiological differences.[4] At the same time, Stroope asserted that the tension could be resolved if leaders at the Board would take a public stance in support of CSI, stating, "It seems we have become the whipping boy for whatever is wrong in the organization, and this will continue, until someone with authority decrees it as inappropriate."[5]

Stroope presented three possible options along with his personal assessment of each. Stroope's three options were (1) to fuse CSI with the other nine geographical areas to create uniformity across all regions; (2) to allow the dichotomous paradigms to co-exist, affirming both as appropriate and encouraging cross-fertilization; or (3) to initiate a major organizational paradigm shift in order to accommodate the missiological paradigm shift that already had occurred.[6]

For Stroope, the first option was the least desirable. He believed that folding CSI into the other regions to create uniformity would be a decision favouring the status quo, eventually halting the Board's progress in penetrating World A.

---

[3] See notes 167 and 168 in Chapter 3.

[4] Stroope, *Perspective and Prospects,* 7.

[5] Stroope, *Perspective and Prospects*, 12.

[6] Stroope, *Perspective and Prospects*, 8-15.

Stroope saw this option as merely putting new wine into old wineskins.[7] The second option was more favourable, but a decision to allow the divergent paradigms to coexist, in Stroope's opinion, would require a move by Board leadership to openly support paradox within the organization as something beneficial to the overall mission effort.[8] Stroope favoured the third option and saw that as the most gallant direction in which to move. The major organization paradigm shift that Stroope advocated was a separation of CSI from the Board, enabling CSI to function as a semi-independent, ancillary unit of the Board with accountability back to the larger organization in the areas of finances and reporting.[9]

There was little support for Stroope's ideas presented in his proposal. In fact, Stroope acknowledged that in a subsequent meeting with Willis, Willis expressed his dissatisfaction with Stroope's ideas.[10] However, what emerged in Rankin's New Directions, although not as Stroope envisioned, was a significant organizational paradigm shift. Perhaps Stroope's ideas did have an impact on what eventually emerged in the organizational restructure presented by Rankin nearly two years later.

Launching New Directions

In February 1997, Rankin reported on the formation of a task force consisting of trustees and members of the Senior Executive team "to explore a paradigm shift in our overseas organizational structure that will position us to accelerate our thrust into the 21st century."[11] Within two months, this task force presented to the Board of Trustees a detailed plan of organizational and strategic restructuring known as New Directions.[12] New Directions abolished CSI as a separate administrative area of the Board's overseas operations and sought to co-opt some of the innovative methodologies of the new paradigm in order to revivify the more traditional areas of the Board in an effort to resolve the conflict between CSI and other administrative areas. The rationales for the reorganization and the resulting organizational and strategic changes clearly indicate the influence of the SC paradigm.

---

[7] Stroope, *Perspective and Prospects*, 8-10.
[8] Stroope, *Perspective and Prospects*, 12.
[9] Stroope, *Perspective and Prospects*, 13.
[10] Stroope, interview by author, 4.
[11] Rankin, *Report to the Board,* February 10, 1997.
[12] "Board of Trustees Minutes," April 07, 1997. At this meeting, the Board of Trustees officially approved a name change from "Foreign Mission Board" to "International Mission Board." Henceforth, I will use the name "International Mission Board" (IMB).

Rationales and Recommendations

At the April 1997 Board meeting, Rankin presented the underlying rationales for the proposed organizational changes. The key rationales of New Directions asserted (1) that in order to remain in step with God's work in the world to fulfil the Great Commission, the Board must do whatever it takes and make necessary changes; (2) the progress of the IMB is not accelerating at the same rate as what God appears to be accomplishing through others; (3) the organizational structure of the IMB must respond appropriately and timely to the rapid changes occurring in the world; (4) an atmosphere must be developed whereby individual missionaries are empowered to make the most of their abilities; and (5) there is a need to develop an administrative structure that develops leaders who are strategic as opposed to being managers of personnel.[13] In elaborating on the rationales in his report, Rankin's comments demonstrate the impact of the new paradigm and CSI on New Directions. He reported the following:

> We must nurture innovation and risk-taking, encourage mobility and absolutely eliminate any vestige of provincialism if we are to make a global impact....We should expect accountability and recognize the demands for equity among missions, missionaries and areas contradict the ability to be responsive to strategic priorities. We cannot stay on the cutting edge if we continue to succumb to parallelism that would hold all needs and the entitlement of all personnel to be equal....Obviously, changing the structure and roles of leadership will not bring about this new paradigm, but it can create an ethos that is liberating and empowering.[14]

These words from Rankin reflect some of the key aspects encapsulated in the CSI guiding principles. If one did not know the source of these words, one just as easily might attribute them to Stroope as to Rankin.

The recommendations that flowed out of these rationales significantly altered the overseas administrative structure of the Board's work. These included (1) the restructuring of the Board's overseas work into fourteen regions along both geographical and cultural affinity; (2) dissolving CSI as its own administrative area and developing CSI-like components for work among unreached people groups in each respective region; (3) separating leadership roles within each region into those that focus on strategic leadership and those that would focus more on administrative responsibilities; and (4) the creation of the office of Associate Vice-President for Strategy Coordination and Mobilization.[15]

---

[13] "Board of Trustees Minutes," April 07, 1997.
[14] Rankin, *Report to the Board,* April 07, 1997.
[15] "Board of Trustees Minutes," April 07, 1997.

Although New Directions led to the dissolution of CSI as an administrative area, the creation of the office of Associate Vice-President for Strategy Coordination and Mobilization did emphasize several key elements of the SC paradigm. Three key responsibilities of this new role were (1) to ensure that every IMB missionary receive adequate training in methodologies for work among the unreached people groups; (2) to network with other Great Commission Christian (GCC) organizations as well as assist the various regional leaders in developing an emphasis on extending God's kingdom through the development of strategic partnerships with other GCC groups; and (3) to lead the Board in identifying the restricted-access countries and people groups that might open to mission efforts, developing plans for rapidly deploying missionary personnel into these areas.[16]

Evidence does seems to suggest that one of the key rationales behind New Directions, although not overtly stated by Rankin, was the harvest philosophy of the church growth movement, a philosophy that advocated for a primary emphasis on the so-called responsive peoples as opposed to those considered resistant. This philosophy is evident in the job description drafted for the Associate Vice-President for Strategy Coordination and Mobilization. One of this role's key responsibilities was to work with the various regions in helping them develop strategies that focused on the unreached peoples and the so-called harvest fields.[17]

It does seem evident that in launching New Directions, Rankin sought to maintain an effort to target World A people group, but not at the cost of advance and growth in the more traditional mission fields of the Board. The realignment of the Board's overseas structure into fourteen new regions sought to provide a balance in the number of missionaries across all regions in order to

---

[16] "Board of Trustees Minutes," April 07, 1997. In June 1997, the Board approved David Garrison, the first director of the Non-residential Missionary Program, for this position. See "Board of Trustees Minutes," (Richmond: Southern Baptist International Mission Board, Accession Number 2556, June 02, 1997). The third key responsibility of the Associate Vice-President for Strategy Coordination and Mobilization reflected an attitude of Rankin evident from his tenure as an Area Director in Southeast Asia under Parks' administration. See Smith, "Response to Your Questions about the SC Paradigm vs. Church Growth," September 14, 2005. Smith, who was a field supervisor of CSI personnel serving in Southeast Asia, recalled a conversation with Rankin in which Rankin advocated sending missionaries into areas and people groups discovered to be responsive by CSI personnel. According to Smith, as reports indicating response to the Gospel among the Khmer people of Cambodia emerged, Rankin sought to transfer this work under his region's administration. As the CSI strategy coordinator for the Khmer people of Cambodia, I was aware of this dialogue in the early 1990s. The attitude projected was that CSI personnel were not real missionaries.

[17] "Board of Trustees Minutes," April 07, 1997.

position each region for growth in terms of personnel.[18] At the same time, Rankin challenged the Board to place a strong emphasis on China and India as well as other major unreached people groups around the world "without diminishing our deployment and advance in other areas of the world."[19]

Even though Rankin sought to maintain this dual emphasis, he intentionally lessened the distinction between World A people groups and other people groups identified as unevangelized. Perhaps the need to validate the appropriateness of this dual strategy led to this lessening of the distinction. Eitel notes that he perceived this dilution of the term 'unreached' in Rankin and Willis' comments regarding New Directions, and when he contacted Rankin for clarification, Rankin confirmed he was lessening the distinction.[20] This lessening of the distinction between World A and other people groups by widening the definition of 'unreached' did not take into consideration a people group's access to the gospel to be an important criterion regarding deployment of missionaries.[21] The primary issue for Rankin and Willis was not whether a people group was World A, but was on the lostness of people. Willis stated it in this way:

> The territory is lostness. Above everything else that we are dealing with in terms of strategy, we are talking about the lost that Jesus came to seek and to save. Wherever they are, whatever their names....We must address lostness.[22]

With the onset of New Directions, the Board developed a new model for understanding the status of evangelization for various people groups. What the Board previously identified as World A would now become the Last Frontier. The Last Frontier people groups would be identified as those with less than 2 percent evangelical Christians with little or no access to the gospel.[23] Unreached people groups would include the Last Frontier peoples, but also include any people group less than two percent evangelical, regardless of their access to the gospel.[24]

On the one hand, Rankin admitted that the SC paradigm was successful in opening doors for mission among previously unreached people groups, while,

---

[18] Jerry A. Rankin, "From the Rankin File: Organizing for Global Impact," *The Commission* (September 1999), 53.

[19] Jerry A. Rankin, "From the Rankin File: Vision 2001," *The Commission* (January 1998), 53.

[20] Eitel, *Paradigm Wars,* 102, 110.

[21] Eitel, *Paradigm Wars,* 102, 110.

[22] Avery T. Willis, Jr. *Report to the Board* (Del City: Southern Baptist International Mission Board, Accession Number 2616, March 19, 1998).

[23] *Status of Global Evangelization* (Richmond: Southern Baptist International Mission Board, July 2004), 1.

[24] *Status of Global Evangelization,* 1.

on the other hand, he believed there was an acceleration of response and harvest in the traditional fields where Southern Baptist missionaries had served for many years.[25] From the inception of the non-residential missionary (NRM) program throughout Stroope's tenure as area director for CSI, the Board increasingly deployed more resources for World A people groups perceived as resistant to the gospel. For those who held to the harvest philosophy, the annual increase of resources, financial and human, deployed to World A via CSI ran counter to this missiological philosophy. By dissolving CSI as an administrative area, New Directions did eliminate the struggle for Board resources that had developed, thus freeing up more resources for traditional fields. This also would help to eliminate what some saw as the increasing inequity of resource distribution to so-called resistant peoples of World A.

Although evidence suggests that this harvest philosophy was behind the changes brought about by New Directions as well as behind the lessening of a distinction between World A and other unevangelized people groups, it must be pointed out that New Directions did continue a strong emphasis on World A people groups. As mentioned previously, the effort "Being on Mission with God to the Last Frontier" was an indication that Rankin sought to continue an emphasis on World A people groups. In launching New Directions, Rankin, in an interview with Board journalists, stated this continued emphasis on what would now be the Last Frontier as follows:

> CSI is not ceasing to exist. It has continued to grow and expand as that cutting-edge part of our organization to reach the Last Frontier. As with other areas, we had to ask how much it could continue to grow until it began to lose its effectiveness. We are very strongly affirming CSI, but it will be configured in regional components rather than a global entity. Nothing will cease in terms of continuing to focus on those Last Frontier people groups.[26]

In one sense, CSI did cease to exist as an official administrative area within the Board's overseas operations. In another sense, Rankin was correct in saying that CSI would not cease to exist because the SC paradigm, set in motion by the Global Strategy group and nurtured within CSI, was not dependent upon any specific organizational structure for its survival. Further, some of the decisions implemented through New Directions intentionally sought to inject key principles and methodologies of the new paradigm throughout the entire organization.

---

[25] Mark Kelly, "New Directions," (Richmond: Southern Baptist International Mission Board, June 01, 1997); available from https://solomon.imb.org; stories database.

[26] Kelly, "New Directions."

It is clear that New Directions sought to co-opt the key methodologies of the SC paradigm in an effort to rejuvenate the work in many of the traditional fields. Willis summed it up in this way:

> Any missionary can do what CSI is doing. The CSI methodology focuses on getting a witness out, working with Great Commission Christians, starting churches. All the ways CSI workers get to unreached people can actually be used with any group of people.[27]

Not only did New Directions seek to co-opt key methodologies of the SC paradigm, but it also attempted to capture the ethos of CSI, seeking to perpetuate that ethos throughout each of the fourteen new regions created by the reorganization. The distinctives and unique elements of New Directions as expounded by Board leadership confirm this.

New Directions Distinctives: Repackaging the SC Paradigm

As New Directions unfolded, Rankin and Board leadership sought to clarify for missionary personnel and Southern Baptist constituent churches the unique elements and distinctives of this reorganization and realignment. Although New Directions would bring an indelible transformation to the IMB over the next several years, it is clear that most of the unique features and distinctives of New Directions essentially were a repackaging of the SC paradigm for the entire organization.

Realizing the need to interpret New Directions for missionary personnel along with a need to retrain and retool missionary personnel, the office of Global Strategy prepared an internal document to help guide the task force formed to address these issues.[28] This document dealt with fourteen key distinctives of New Directions, all of which directly or indirectly link to the SC paradigm and CSI (see Table 2). Some of the key distinctives that directly parallel the SC paradigm included (1) a focus on ethno linguistic people groups; (2) strategy coordinators assigned to one people group; (3) all peoples and nothing less; (4) networking and partnership with Great Commission Christians; (5) use of platforms for creative access into restricted areas and countries; (6) strategies designed around the specific worldview of the people group; (7) asking the question, "What will it take?"; (8) streamlined,

[27] Kelly, "New Directions."

[28] *Strategic Directions-21 Evaluation*, 28. This internal document was titled "Distinctives of the New Directions of the IMB." The document was not available to the author, but the *Strategic Directions-21 Evaluation* summarized the fourteen distinctives addressed in this internal document.

corporate-like structure for administration and accountability; and (9) a goal of church-planting movements.[29]

In an effort to communicate the essence of New Directions to missionary personnel and Southern Baptist constituent churches, the Board published *Something New Under the Sun.* In this small booklet, the Board described New Directions in terms of seven unique features. The seven features were (1) a need for organizational change to respond to new possibilities in missions offered by a rapidly, changing world; (2) a need to accelerate church planting efforts through a new aim of facilitating church-planting movements as opposed to just doing evangelism that results in churches; (3) a need to change the focus to ethno linguistic people groups rather than geopolitical entities; (4) a need to ask a different question (What will it take to complete the task?) that emphasizes the enormity of the task rather than what one can do personally; (5) a need to recognize the massive amount of Great Commission Christian resources beyond Southern Baptists available for the task of Global evangelization; (6) a need to develop new strategies in order to increase missionary effectiveness; and (7) a need to change the organizational structure of the Board as a response to the changing realities in missions.[30] While many missionary personnel and Southern Baptist churches may have understood these to be new ideas, the reality is that none of these seven features was unique. All of these ideas parallel key components of the SC paradigm and CSI (see Table 3). What was different was that these features no longer were inimitable to CSI, but now New Directions disseminated these throughout the entire organization.

To The Edge Workshops and Strategy Coordinator Training

New Directions sought to lead the entire IMB through an organizational-wide paradigm shift, borrowing heavily from key elements of the SC paradigm. The process of this missiological paradigm shift took several years to accomplish, and, in fact, is still in progress. How did the Board seek to disseminate this new paradigm into each of the fourteen new regions created by New Directions?

There were two training processes utilized by the Board to help missionary personnel understand the implications of New Directions. One was the training tool *To The Edge: A Planning Process for People Group Specific Strategy Development* developed by Lewis Myers and Jim Slack.[31] Subsequent to the launching of New Directions, Myers and Slack conducted forty-five workshops

---

[29] *Strategic Directions-21 Evaluation*, 28-9.

[30] *Something New Under the Sun,* 5-48.

[31] Under Parks, Myers served as the vice-president for CSI, and under Rankin, served as the vice-president for World A Strategies. Slack was a former missionary to the Philippines, and later served in the global research department for the Board.

throughout the various regions.[32] The stated purpose of these workshops was to "provide participants with a sufficient understanding of the people group planning process for them: to understand the UPG [unreached people group] process; to become a Strategy Coordinator; to become informed members of an SC-led team; and to develop a first draft of plans for cooperating with the Holy Spirit in initiating a church-planting movement among a specific people group."[33]

Myers and Slack integrated into their training manual a significant number of the methodologies of the SC paradigm as articulated within CSI. They examined and evaluated the work of effective strategy coordinators, and after identifying the characteristics these personnel shared in their work, developed the training manual.[34] The strategic planning process taught in these workshops was built around (1) a focus on ethno linguistic people groups; (2) a strategy coordinator who takes responsibility for one people group; (3) the development of prayer networks; (4) extensive worldview and cultural research; (5) the mobilization of team members; (6) envisioning that provides a picture of the end result of the evangelization process; (7) the development of a comprehensive strategy; (8) the building of partnerships with Great Commission Christians; and (9) the development of platforms for creative access to the people group.[35]

---

[32] *Strategic Directions-21 Evaluation,* 30.
[33] Myers and Slack, *To The Edge,* 1.3.
[34] Myers and Slack, *To The Edge*, 2.27.
[35] Myers and Slack, *To The Edge*, 2.27-8.

Table 2: Comparison between New Directions and SC Paradigm[36]

Distinctives of New Directions	Distinctives of SC Paradigm
1. Ethno linguistic people group focus	1. As individuals and as a group, we dare not draw back from the edge of World A.
2. Empowered Strategy Coordinator held responsible for one ethno linguistic people group.	2. Strategy Coordinator committed to one World A population segment.
3. Strategy Coordinator-led people group focused teams rather than geo-politically focused missions.	3. Strategy Coordinator-led World A people group focused teams rather than geo-politically focused missions.
4. Vision driven rather than resource driven. We do not ask, "What can we do with what we have?" but ask "What's it going to take under the Lordship of Jesus Christ to accomplish God's purposes?"	4. The edge (World A) is where we belong. The organization is not your god. Power does not lie in the organization's resources but in the One who created all things.
5. Goal of church-planting movements.	5. An indigenous church-planting movement among every people must be the point of all we do.
6. All peoples, nothing less. Our vision is one of every tribe and tongue standing before the throne of God.	6. All peoples, nothing less. We do what the Lord has asked of us, believing that He intends His church to exist among all peoples before He returns.
7. Use of multiple platforms. With more countries closed to traditional presence, we must explore other alternatives.	7. Use of multiple platforms. We will do whatever it takes to get to the destination.
8. Extensive, yet appropriate, relationships with GCC agencies and individuals. Asking the question, "What will it take?" forces us to look beyond our own limited resources.	8. Networking and partnership with GCC groups. Strategy Coordinator is a bridge between the people group and the world of GCC resources. Asking the question, "What will it take?" not "What can I do?"
9. Division of strategy design and implementation from strategy support functions. Free leadership to be vision-driven.	9. Strategy Coordinator responsible for development and implementation of comprehensive strategy for an unreached population segment.
10. Intensely incarnational. Approaches to evangelism developed for specific heart	10. Strategy Coordinator, based on worldview of targeted people group,

[36] Distinctives of New Directions taken from *the Strategic Directions-21 Evaluation of the International Mission Board* (Richmond: Southern Baptist International Mission Board, September 30, 2003). Distinctives of the SC Paradigm taken from *CSI Ten-Guiding Principles* and Garrison, *Non-residential Missionary.*

languages and worldviews.	develops appropriate strategies for reaching the people group. Each people group deserves its own Scripture, its own Christian witness and its own church.
11. Increase security concerns as we target those areas previously considered off-limits.	11. Security concerns and issues central to the Strategy Coordinator training.
12. Exit mentality. A people-group focused team strategizes with the end in mind, a time when outside missionary presence no longer required.	12. Exit mentality. We must continue to enter new people groups and cities rather than seeking only to consolidate the gains we have made.
13. Increased mobility. "Where is the best place for me to live to reach my people?"	13. Emphasis on finding a strategic place of residence that allows for maximum impact on people group.
14. Streamlined administrative approval and support. More time spent on "main thing" and less on committees.	14. All of us are accountable to someone in a corporate-like structure where individuals are empowered for appropriate decision-making and leadership.

Myers and Slack were quick to affirm the influence of the SC paradigm, calling the SC training developed by Garrison, Stroope and others as the classicist expression of the training, and the objective of the workshop was to introduce the major principles, concepts and methodologies of this classicist model in order to help participants apply them in their respective setting.[37] Further, Myers and Slack employed the term "skunkworks" to denote the role of CSI and the SC paradigm within the Board, described as follows:

> "Skunkworks" was a term invented by Al Capps, the famous cartoonist, which was used in the 1940s and later by the U.S. Government and later by large American corporations. The U.S. government, and media personnel, used the term "skunkworks" when referring to the Manhattan Project, which developed atomic energy and the atomic bomb. Corporate America later began to use the term to talk about a very secret part of their corporation commissioned to develop new technology. If their corporate skunkworks could invent new techniques, the skunkworks would be made public and the technology brought into the corporations as updates or totally new innovations that put them ahead of their rivals. "Skunkworks" is a description of CSI with the SBC's IMB.[38]

---

[37] Myers and Slack, *To The Edge*, 1.4.
[38] Myers and Slack, *To The Edge*, 1.6.

Table 3: Comparisons between Seven Unique Features of New Directions and the Strategy Coordinator Paradigm[39]

Seven Unique Features of New Directions	Strategy Coordinator Paradigm
1. New World of Possibilities – The pace of change in the world is accelerating and the IMB must change in order to take full advantage of the doors that are opening.	1. We must continually change. Our willingness to challenge and change the way we do things has been one of our strengths.
2. A New Goal – Church-planting movements among every people group.	2. An indigenous church-planting movement among every people must be the point of all we do.
3. A New Focus – People groups.	3. As individuals and as a group, we dare not draw back from the edge of World A. A Strategy Coordinator focuses on one unevangelized population segment.
4. A New Question – "What's it going to take to get the job done?"	4. We will do whatever it takes to get to the destination.
5. New Resources – Working with Great Commission partners to reach the world.	5. To get to this destination, we must move beyond restrictive thinking, work with Great Commission brothers and sisters, and believe He is working in every situation.
6. New Approaches – Comprehensive strategies to utilize the basic pillars of prayer, God's Word, evangelism and church planting, and mobilization.	6. A comprehensive strategy built on the pillars of prayer, Scripture, Media ministries, and Christian witnessing presence.
7. New Structures – Tightly knit teams, smaller than traditional missions, are able to penetrate individual people groups.	7. We are part of the organizational family, and yet we do not have to look or act exactly like our brothers and sisters. The context in which we work and the stewardship of resources demand that we operate in the most efficient, effective manner possible.

[39] Information on New Directions taken from *Something New Under the Sun: New Directions at the International Mission Board* (Richmond: Southern Baptist International Mission Board, January 1999), *CSI Ten Guiding Principles,* and Garrison *Non-residential Missionary*

By describing the SC paradigm in this fashion, Myers and Slack were inferring that the SC paradigm had successfully developed and employed new, innovative mission methodologies for reaching unreached people groups; therefore, the Board through New Directions was now taking these methodologies public to the entire organization.

Along with the *To The Edge* training, the Board also deployed the SC training team of Smith and Sergeant, both former strategy coordinators, to train personnel throughout most of the regions. During the first three years of New Directions, this team trained 444 personnel from thirteen of the Board's fourteen regions.[40] Having served as strategy coordinators within CSI, Smith and Sergeant's training essentially was the CSI-version of the SC training. Smith reports that during the initial years the training was not highly successful because most of those participating in the training were obdurate, yet mandated by their region to attend.[41] In a number of these training events conducted by Smith and Sergeant, participants openly expressed their dissatisfaction with the concepts, described by Smith in this way:

> In a training session hosted by one non-World A region, some IMB participants became so aggravated at the concepts being presented, that they got up and stomped out. In another…a training session degenerated into a shouting match in which one participant heatedly stated, "That may be what the Bible teaches, but that is not what we Baptists do in this country." In another non-World A region the SC training was almost halted and cancelled midway through when the majority of participants indicated they had no intention of implementing the concepts being presented.[42]

Although many trained appeared to be intractable, Smith affirmed that some individuals embraced the concepts and expressed a willingness to implement what they had learned.[43] Further, in subsequent years, the personnel trained shifted from those mandated to attend to more who volunteered, resulting in a higher percentage of those trained applying the methodologies and concepts in their work.[44] Smith also observed that while some who embraced the new paradigm began to witness significant results in their work, a number of others opted to transfer to roles where they could work among World A or Last Frontier peoples.[45]

---

[40] Smith, "Additional Document;" *Strategic Directions-21 Evaluation,* 40.

[41] Smith, "Thoughts for Bruce;" Smith, "Additional Document."

[42] Smith, "Thoughts for Bruce."

[43] Smith, "Thoughts for Bruce."

[44] Smith, "Additional Document."

[45] Smith, "Additional Document."

Smith's assessment of the problem with acceptance of the new paradigm may be somewhat short-sighted. Part of the problem may have centred on the translation of the new paradigm as it crossed from the CSI culture into the traditional mission culture of the Board. There are striking parallels between Guder's discussion on translation of the gospel in mission and New Directions' efforts through these training events to communicate the paradigm shift. Guder points out the challenges of translation and reductionism the church faces as it seeks to communicate the gospel message.[46] Every time the church takes the gospel message from one culture to another, it involves a translation of that message. According to Guder, the translation of that message unavoidably involves the risk of reductionism, as those communicating the message yield to the temptation that their interpretation of the message is the absolute truth.[47] Not only is there the risk of reductionism of the message, but the church also runs the risk of organizational reductionism, as those communicating the message impose the structure of the church within their home culture as normative for the new host culture.[48] Thus, for Guder there is the need for the continuing conversion of the church so that the church can avoid reductionism in its message and in its structure.

The major task of the *To The Edge* workshops and the SC training was communicating the distinctives of this organizational paradigm shift to personnel around the world. For over ten years, there were two missionary cultures within the Board. The majority culture was that of the traditional mission structures in every country where the Board had deployed personnel. The minority culture was that of CSI, which housed the SC paradigm. Through these training events, the Board sought to pull the SC paradigm out of its home culture and diffuse it into the traditional culture of the IMB. This involved a process of translation with its inherent risk of reductionism.

Guder, in talking about translating the gospel when crossing cultures, asserts that neither the culture of the one communicating the message nor the recipient culture is normative.[49] It is important that the one communicating the message not reject the culture of the one receiving the message. It is conceivable that part of the resistance met by Smith and Sergeant resulted in part because of the manner in which they translated the paradigm to those from the traditional mission settings. Myers and Slack presented the *To The Edge* training as the classicist model developed within CSI. Smith and Sergeant presented the CSI-version of the SC training. Initially, most of these training events were mandatory for personnel, and many may have felt the Board was imposing this new paradigm and rejecting the paradigm out of which they had laboured for

---

[46] Guder, *Conversion of the Church,* 73-141.

[47] Guder, *Conversion of the Church,* 100.

[48] Guder, *Conversion of the Church,* 147.

[49] Guder, *Conversion of the Church,* 85.

years. When the Board evaluated New Directions several years later, one of the glaring weaknesses revealed was that the terminology of the new paradigm was in use in almost every region of the Board; however, this did not necessarily result in a change of behaviour as many continued to do their work the same way they had always done it.[50] The evaluation further revealed that some of the new regions created by New Directions simply had no interest in learning about the new paradigm.[51] These revelations seem to confirm a translation problem in taking the SC paradigm out of its home culture and injecting it into the traditional mission culture of the Board.

Another factor contributing to the problem of translating the SC paradigm may have been the fact that neither Myers nor Slack had first-hand experience as a strategy coordinator. Thus, the New Directions training they conducted promulgated much of the jargon and taxonomy of the paradigm, but fell short in actually achieving the implementation of the SC paradigm in most places. According to Smith, one of the key reasons for the shortcomings of the *To The Edge* training was because "the manual was written by someone…who had a number of biases and projection onto CSI from his own agendas."[52] Smith also points out that most of the new regions formed as a result of New Directions had regional leadership with little or no SC experience, thus were either unable to guide their personnel in implementing the training or unwilling to empower those trained to apply the methodologies and principles of the new paradigm.[53]

Guder asserts that the continual translation of the gospel message through successive generations and across numerous cultures has led to a reductionism in the message, a reductionism "that has become pervasive in our traditions and churches."[54] According to Guder, reductionism is the result of our desire to control, a desire arising from our claim that our understanding of the truth is absolute.[55] According to Stroope, one of the reasons for dissolving CSI in New Directions stemmed from a perceived need on the part of Board leadership to control a part of the organization seemingly growing out of control.[56] Thus, while co-opting much of the SC paradigm and wanting to infuse it throughout the organization, there was also a need to exert control. This led to a reductionism of the SC paradigm within New Directions.

One reductionism centred on the concept of SC-led teams, a key component of the *To The Edge* training. One of the misinterpretations by New Directions was the belief that the key to the effectiveness of CSI was the concept of teams.

---

[50] *Strategic Directions-12 Evaluation,* 41.

[51] *Strategic Directions-12 Evaluation,* 41.

[52] Smith, "Additional Document."

[53] Smith, "Additional Document."

[54] Guder, *Conversion of the Church,* 72.

[55] Guder, *Conversion of the Church,*, 100.

[56] Stroope, Interview by Keith E. Eitel: 22.

Thus, with New Directions there was an effort to dissolve the bureaucratic mission entities and reconfigure personnel into smaller teams. The effort to simply transition from mission structures to teams did not effectively create the desired paradigm shift. What was missing? Teams were a natural expression within the SC paradigm. However, within CSI, the SC paradigm shaped the structure that emerged; the structure did not fashion the paradigm. Smith assesses the dilemma of New Directions in this area as follows:

> Some regions, and Richmond administrators, recognizing that the bureaucratic logjam of traditional decision-making had slowed down effectiveness, decided that part of the genius of CSI effectiveness was "teams." Therefore, they unilaterally assigned all personnel in traditional areas to a team and then set about vigorously training personnel in how to function as teams. Generally, there was no consensus of a team vision, extremely weak leadership since teaming was often portrayed as decision-making by consensus of the group, and the results were fiascos. Very few of those teams in the 1997-1999 time frame became effective work units.[57]

Smith may have overstated the case, yet he does point out the faulty thinking that changing structure inevitably will lead to the desired paradigm shift. This further illustrates the reductionism that can result from inaccurate translation coupled with the desire to control.

The evaluation of New Directions by the Board in 2003 revealed that the shift to teams did not necessarily lead to the desired paradigm shift. The evaluation found that some strategy coordinators developed large teams, focused their energies on managing those teams, and continued to look to the IMB as the sole provided of the resources for their team's mission work.[58] Another shortcoming revealed in the evaluation process was that in some regions of the world there was a lack of supervision and accountability in the shift from mission to team structure.[59]

As New Directions sought to translate key elements of the SC paradigm throughout the entire organization, it not only reduced the paradigm structurally, but also reduced the paradigm to specific methodologies. Myers and Slack built their training manual around the methodologies of what they perceived to be successful strategy coordinators. However, what made the SC paradigm unique was not just its methodologies, but it ethos. The ethos of CSI breathed life and energy into the SC paradigm. Despite the Board's intense and sincere efforts to propagate the methodologies of the new paradigm throughout

---

57 Smith, "Thoughts for Bruce."

58 *Strategic Directions-21 Evaluation,* 41.

59 *Strategic Directions-21 Evaluation,* 41.

every region, during the early years of New Directions it failed to effectively capture the unique ethos surrounding the paradigm.

Another significant element of the *To The Edge* training warrants mentioning. Although these workshops served to disseminate key elements of the SC paradigm to the wider organization, the workshops also propagated the redefinition of unreached peoples as delineated by New Directions. Myers and Slack acknowledged the original definition of unreached as referring to those people groups with minimal or no access to the gospel, but also affirmed that the term referred "to those ethno linguistic peoples…who may have lived in and around Christianity and Gospel presentations but for whatever reason or reasons, have been left out or overlooked or unresponsive."[60]

While there may have been some shortcomings during the initial attempts to translate the new paradigm for the entire organization, the training efforts were not entirely a failure. First, these training events did establish the SC role as the stack pole for building people group- focused teams. The SC role would no longer be unique to CSI. Over the next, several years as the Board evaluated the progress of New Directions, it would affirm the SC role as the primary missionary role for developing and implementing people group-focused mission strategies throughout every region.[61]

Further, these training events did propagate key elements of the SC paradigm beyond CSI to a wider audience, helping many within the organization to gain a clearer understanding of the role and the missiological paradigm surrounding it. Guder contends that as the church seeks to translate the message, "each translation reveals dimensions of the gospel that had not fully been seen before."[62] This is true for both the translators and the receivers of the message. As already noted, outside of CSI there were a number of misperceptions regarding the SC paradigm. Much of these misperceptions of the paradigm resulted from the fact that CSI, in a large part, functioned separate from the rest of the organization while being a part of the organization. These training events hammered away at the walls of ignorance as they sought to explain and clarify the SC paradigm to missionary personnel around the world. Further, despite the translation problems during the initial years, it became clear through the emergence of various CSI-type components in several regions that the paradigm was applicable for work outside of World A. Along with a concerted effort by Board leadership to communicate the new paradigm across the whole spectrum of the organization, these training events played a significant role in guiding the IMB through a major missiological paradigm

---

[60] Myers and Slack, *To The Edge,* 2.5.

[61] "Board of Trustees Minutes," (Richmond: Southern Baptist International Mission Board, Accession Number 2685, May 18, 2000); "Board of Trustees Minutes," November 10, 1993.

[62] Guder, *Conversion of the Church,* 87.

shift. The following section will seek to show how core elements of the SC paradigm remained intact, while various innovative dimensions of the paradigm emerged.

Significant Influences of the SC Paradigm in New Directions

Despite some of the problems and difficulties encountered in seeking to spread the new paradigm throughout the Board's fourteen regions, the SC paradigm did exert a significant influence on the overall missiology of the Board. There were some noticeable changes in various regions and with the overall missiological direction of the Board as the result of New Directions. Three years subsequent to the launching of its organizational restructure, the Board announced that New Directions would become Strategic Directions for the 21st Century, completing the process of institutionalizing this missiological paradigm as the paradigm for the IMB for the first part of the 21st century.[63]

When the Board formally validated New Directions as its missiological paradigm for the early part of the 21st century, it acknowledged six initial outcomes from 1997 to 2000. These outcomes were that (1) the focus of missionary personnel had shifted from geopolitical entities to people groups; (2) the goal was planting churches that would plant churches; (3) the question being asked had changed from "What can we do?" to "What will it take?"; (4) the Board recognized the need for continual change; (5) missionary personnel must be willing to innovate and take risks; and (6) SC-led teams had replaced traditional mission structures.[64] These outcomes, although significant, do not reflect the full extent of the SC paradigm's influence as repackaged and propagated under the banner of New Directions or Strategic Directions for the 21st Century.

People Group Focus

Willis, in an interview with *Mission Frontiers,* acknowledged that one of the most important contributions of the SC paradigm was shifting the Board to view the world through the same set of lenses that God views the world – people groups as opposed to geopolitical entities.[65] Winter had brought to the attention of missiologists the concept of people groups, more specifically the 'hidden' people groups, in the early 1970s. The concept of focusing on these 'hidden' or World A ethno linguistic people groups was the cornerstone upon

63 "Board of Trustees Minutes," May 18, 2000.

64 "Board of Trustees Minutes," May 18, 2000.

65 "The Southern Baptists Restructure." The belief that God viewed the world as peoples not countries emerged as Board leaders, influenced by CSI and other evangelical missiologists, began to understand that the Greek phrase *panta ta ethnē* (Matthew 28:19), often translated 'nations,' referred to ethnic people groups.

which Barrett, Parks and others developed the non-residential missionary (NRM) paradigm, and subsequently the SC paradigm as expressed within CSI. The Board had begun to become keenly aware of ethno linguistic people groups through the efforts of CSI, but it took nearly ten more years before the IMB as a whole awoke from what Winter called 'people blindness.'[66]

Nevertheless, the Board, through New Directions, did awaken from its people group blindness. The research begun by Barrett and carried on in later years by Board researchers initially had identified nearly 13,000 people groups. In 1997, the Board counted 83 strategy coordinators focusing on specific ethno linguistic people groups; however, within three years, there were 1, 118 teams throughout the fourteen regions engaging specific ethno linguistic people groups or population segments.[67] By 2003, Board personnel across the fourteen regions were working among 1,371 different people groups.[68]

Although not all of these groups engaged by Board personnel were World A or Last Frontier peoples, the shift toward ethno linguistic people groups clearly was evident. At the same time, there was a slight increase in the percentages of Board personnel working among Last Frontier people groups. In 1999, twenty percent of Board personnel were working among these peoples. Rankin's following words appear to express this as one of the key achievements of New Directions:

> For the first time, every nation and every people group is within the mission focus and responsibility of IMB regional strategies. In order to reach the whole world, almost 20 percent of IMB personnel are in sensitive assignments where they cannot be identified as missionaries....They focus on 'The Last Frontier' of the Great Commission. Others are expanding their witness through people-group teams focused on starting church-planting movements to reach all nations.[69]

This is a significant increase from the two percent of IMB personnel working among World A people in 1989; however, while CSI was an overseas administrative area of the Board, the number of personnel working among

[66] Ralph D. Winter, "The New Macedonia: A Revolutionary New Era in Mission Begins," in *Perspectives on the World Christian Movement,* ed. Ralph Winter and Stephen Hawthorne (Pasadena: William Carey Library, 1981), 302. In using the term 'people blindness,' Winter was referring to the inability of missionaries and mission agencies to see the distinct communities of people groups within countries. Missionaries, particularly those from the West, had focused on geopolitical entities throughout their history, thus leading them to become blind to the multitude of ethno linguistic communities, which resided within those geopolitical boundaries.

[67] "Board of Trustees Minutes," May 18, 2000.

[68] *Strategic Directions-21 Evaluation,* 37.

[69] Jerry A. Rankin, "Rankin File: Into all the World," *The Commission* (April 1999), 29.

World A people groups had grown to at least fourteen percent.[70] Therefore, New Directions cannot take the entire credit for the twenty percent of Board personnel working among Last Frontier people as the overwhelming majority of these personnel in all probability were former CSI personnel reassigned to one of the fourteen new regions formed through New Directions. While twenty percent signified growth in the percentage of IMB personnel working among Last Frontier people groups, the fact remained that New Directions, with its dual focus on the Last Frontier and harvest fields, had not, in its initial years, facilitated a significant increase in work among these Last Frontier peoples.

Some feared that New Directions would seriously dilute the Board's emphasis on evangelizing the Last Frontier people groups, especially with the redefining and broadening of the term 'unreached.' In some regions where SC personnel in CSI had previously focused, the engagement of these Last Frontier peoples did not diminish. This was true for at least three of the fourteen new regions created by the reorganization – North Africa and the Middle East, Central and South Asia and East Asia. In 1997, these three regions reported personnel working among 201 people groups, most of whom were Last Frontier peoples.[71] By 2000, the number of people groups engaged by personnel in these three regions increased to 353.[72] In at least one other region a significant shift toward engaging Last Frontier people groups occurred. Bill Phillips reported that within a year of transitioning from a geopolitical to a people group focus, 95% of the personnel in his region of West Africa were working among Last Frontier people groups.[73]

Evidence also suggests that while some feared a dilution of the Board's efforts to engage Last Frontier people groups because of New Directions, others feared that the emphasis on people groups would lead to an increasing emphasis on the Last Frontier at the expense of traditional areas considered the harvest fields. As early as 1998, upon hearing various reports from different regions regarding their efforts to focus on people groups, Cal Guy, a noted Southern Baptist missiologist and trustee member, expressed concern that the Board might penalize the work in the harvest fields for the sake of reaching into

---

[70] Myers, *Roads Less Traveled.* In 1994, Myers reported that fourteen percent of Board personnel were working in World A. CSI continued to grow in the period 1995-97, and during that same period, a few other areas of the Board assigned personnel to work among World A people groups. Thus, the twenty percent reported by Rankin in 1999 can be misleading.

[71] *Strategic Directions-21 Evaluation,* 37.

[72] *Strategic Directions-21 Evaluation,* 37.

[73] Bill Phillips, *Report to the Board* (Fort Lauderdale: Southern Baptist International Mission Board, Accession Number 2656, November 18, 1998).

the Last Frontier.[74] Robin Hadaway, the regional leader for Eastern South America, expressed a similar concern:

> When I was interviewed in April 1997 for a Regional Leader position, I was asked hypothetically how I would distribute IMB personnel. I replied that I would place 25% in the least reached part of the world and 75% in those places where [we] are reaping a harvest....I believe we should have a '"probing presence" in the "rocky soil" places and a reaping force in the responsive locations.[75]

The concerns expressed by both men indicate that perhaps New Directions did not de-emphasize the Last Frontier, but, to the contrary, put a strong emphasis on these people groups. By directing the entire organization toward a people group focus while seeking to lead the Board to take seriously *missio Dei* and the challenge of engaging all of these people groups, it would be inevitable that over time the Last Frontier people groups would elicit an increasing amount of attention by Southern Baptists.

The shift to a people group focus did begin to focus the effort and energies of the majority of missionaries away from some traditional missionary roles toward a more active role in planting churches among peoples and population segments where little, if any, church planting efforts had occurred. For many years, a number of IMB missionaries had assumed roles of support to and ministries within the local Baptist denominations in their respective countries. However, the shift to a people group focus altered those relationships and moved a number of IMB personnel out of denominational building roles. For example, in Western South America, as missionaries began to focus on nearly three hundred different people groups within the five countries of this region, the relationship with Baptist denominational groups shifted from one of assistance in denominational building toward cooperation in evangelizing those

---

[74] "Board of Trustees Minutes," (Fort Lauderdale: Southern Baptist International Mission Board, Accession Number 2656, November 18, 1998).

[75] *Strategic Directions-21 Evaluation,* 178. See Robin Hadaway, "Balancing the Biblical Perspectives: A Missiological Analysis," *Journal of Evangelism and Missions*, 2 (Spring 2003): 103-14. In this article, Hadaway advocated for the harvest theology popularized by McGavran, Wagner and others, arguing that the IMB had a responsibility to evangelize unreached peoples as well as continuing to work in the harvest fields. Hadaway criticized the Board's priority of population size of a people group in determining deployment of its resources. Besides population size, Hadaway argued that two other factors needed to be taken into consideration: (1) the percentage of 'lost' people among the people group and (2) the percentage of people within the group who would respond to the Gospel.

identified people groups.[76] Phil Templin, the regional leader for Middle America, explained the shift in his region:

> In the past, we talked about -- we are going to plant a church; we are going to reach some people; or we are going to go to a city. The light that came on was the idea that we are no longer talking about a church or a city, we are talking about everyone.[77]

Evidence does suggest that the shift away from geopolitical entities toward a people group focus was a catalyst in helping IMB missionaries around the world catch the same vision that had motivated personnel within CSI – all peoples, nothing less!

In launching New Directions, Rankin and Willis had stressed that the emphasis of the Board would be about reaching lost people, wherever they were located. While New Directions did help steer the entire organization toward an unreached people group focus, as newly defined by the Board, it initially did not correct the imbalance of personnel and finances deployed to those major unevangelized peoples and areas. The Global Analysis Project (GAP), initiated by the Board to guide the Board in tracking the status of global evangelization, revealed this deficiency of New Directions. Using China and India, where over half of the world's population resided, as examples, Garrison reported that neither the Board's personnel nor its distribution of financial resources was adequate to address the massive population of unevangelized peoples in these two countries.[78] The Board would need to address this structural imbalance of personnel and finances.

After the Global Analysis Project demonstrated that New Directions had not significantly led the Board to penetrate the part of the world where half of the world's population lived, there was a strategic shift in Rankin's thinking. Originally, the emphasis was on the lost, wherever they were. However, in Rankin's report to the Board in May 2001, the issue had changed. Rankin expressed the issue in this way:

> There are those who make no distinction between evangelism and missions; they would see missions as just evangelism done apart from our own geographic and cultural context. But missions is not an effort to win as many people as possible to the Lord and bring them into the Kingdom. If this were true we could probably deploy all our missionary personnel to just seven countries and double our

---

[76] Larry Gay, *Report to the Board* (Shreveport: Southern Baptist International Mission Board, Accession Number 2698, March 08, 2001).

[77] Phil Templin, *Report to the Board* (Louisville: Southern Baptist International Mission Board, Accession Number 2635, September 14, 1998).

[78] V. David Garrison, *Global Analysis Project Report* (Shreveport: Southern Baptist International Mission Board, Accession Number 2698, March 08, 2001).

> number of reported baptisms. But these responsive harvest fields would represent less than 20% of the peoples of the world. Not only that, it would mean duplicating efforts in countries where there are already over thousands of Baptist churches. Is there no responsibility for penetrating the darkness represented by those still waiting for a witness? By what criteria should any people be denied an opportunity to hear, understand and respond to the gospel in their own cultural context? Hence, the command to disciple the nations is reflected in our vision, 'to be on mission with God to bring all the peoples of the world to saving faith in Jesus Christ.'[79]

Eventually, the Board did address this imbalance in the deployment of its resources, both human and financial. From 1997 to 2003, the Board financially was able to deploy missionaries anywhere in the world based on the priorities of the individual regions without much regard to the overall global strategic needs. In 2003, an economic crisis emerged that forced the board to stem the flow of missionaries.[80] This economic crisis, as expressed by Rankin, was a challenge to the Board to "use limited resources and remain focused on our vision of leading Southern Baptists to be on mission with God to bring all the peoples of the world to saving faith in Him."[81]

One response to this crisis was a global summit of all the regional leaders from the fourteen administrative regions in August 2003. During this summit, regional leaders intensely sought to examine the Board's deployment of resources in light of the economic crisis and in light of the Board's overall strategy. At the meeting, the global research department provided an enormous amount of information that illustrated the imbalance in the Board's resource deployment across the world and revealed the reality that the traditional so-called harvest fields were showing less growth than many of the Last Frontier peoples who had been deemed as unresponsive.[82]

The major result of this regional leaders' summit was a decision to reconfigure the Board's deployment of its resources, focusing on those people groups and areas of the world that were now being viewed as harvest fields, but where large percentages of lost people still resided.[83] Before this historic meeting of regional leaders, Board leadership already had set as one of its key strategy objectives to "implement a strategic staffing plan to ensure all overseas

---

[79] Jerry A. Rankin, *Report to the Board* (Richmond: Southern Baptist International Mission Board, Accession Number 2699, May 21, 2001).

[80] Mark Kelly, "Lost World Needs More, not Fewer Missionaries," (Richmond: Southern Baptist International Mission Board, August 13, 2003); available from https://solomon.imb.org; stories database.

[81] Kelly, "Lost World."

[82] William Smith, "Response to Bruce," Electronic letter to Bruce Carlton, November 30, 2004.

[83] Kelly, "Lost World."

personnel are deployed according to the most urgent needs and highest priority assignments by the end of 2004."[84] The regional leaders, after confronting the realities as displayed by the global research department, recognized the massive gaps in the Board's priority needs, recognized the significant numbers of personnel in low priority assignments and affirmed the importance of a base staffing plan for the entire organization.[85] The Board is now prioritizing its personnel deployment based on a global strategic perspective, a goal that Parks and others had sought to realize. One key result of this effort is a sharpening of the Board's focus on Last Frontier peoples.

The shift away from geopolitical deployment of missionaries toward a focus on ethno linguistic people groups increasingly heightened awareness of these 'hidden' peoples throughout the entire organization. Over time, this heightened awareness coupled with massive data showing the imbalance of resource deployment and the threat of a financial crisis shifted the Board even further toward engaging the Last Frontier people groups. The generation of non-residential missionaries and strategy coordinators who championed the people group approach and Rankin's institutionalization of the concept throughout the entire organization have left an ineffaceable impact on the missiology of the IMB.

Working with Great Commission Christians

One of the key features of New Directions was the recognition of the need to network and partner with other GCC organizations. Under Parks' leadership, the Board began to explore the possibility of networking and partnering with these groups as Parks believed such partnership to be indispensable to the effort of global evangelization. A significant component of the NRM role, and later the SC role, was the idea of serving as a bridge between an unreached people group and the world of Great Commission resources needed to evangelize that people group. Strategy coordinators had recognized the unique diversity within the wider body of Christ and had demonstrated the effectiveness of partnerships with a number of these GCC groups such as Youth With A Mission, Campus Crusade, TransWorld Radio, The *Jesus Film* Project and Wycliffe Bible translators.

Like the focus on ethno linguistic people groups, Rankin sought to diffuse this component throughout the entire organization, positioning it as one of the cornerstones of the Board's global strategy. Rankin, aware of the success of CSI in building partnerships, not only sought to diffuse this idea into every

[84] "Board of Trustees Minutes," (Framingham: Southern Baptist International Mission Board, Accession Number 2376, May 6, 2003).

[85] R. Bruce Carlton, "Notes from the November 2003 Global Regional Leadership Team Forum," (Rome, GA: Southern Baptist International Mission Board, 2003) [electronic document]; available from the author, 16.

region, but also assiduously led the IMB to pursue key partnerships on an organization-to-organization level. Starting in 1994, Rankin, in cooperation with Wycliffe Bible translators, began hosting an informal, annual retreat where leaders of some of the largest evangelical mission organizations in the United States would dialogue about cooperation in global evangelization efforts.[86] Like Parks, Rankin was looking to build functional partnerships that allowed for cross-fertilization of ideas and resources without sacrificing the Board's autonomy or the autonomy of the other organizations. At the same time, Rankin wholeheartedly believed that global evangelization would accelerate as GCC organizations laboured together within an atmosphere of foregoing concerns over which organization was in control or which organization would receive the credit.[87]

These partnerships with other organizations also revealed that the Rankin and Board leadership had not disengaged entirely from the emphasis on Last Frontier peoples. For example, in 1999 and 2000, IMB leadership convened "Accelerating World Evangelization" conferences, which brought together various GCC mission agencies in the United States and Baptist partners around the world to discuss how to engage the remaining unreached peoples of the world with the Gospel.[88] The most significant partnership into which Rankin has led the IMB is the 'Table 71' partnership.[89] The organizations that formed the 'Table 71' partnership committed to working cooperatively together to

---

[86] Jerry A. Rankin, "Rankin File: Great Commission Partners," *The Commission* (March 1998), 53.

[87] Rankin, "Great Commission Partners," 53.

[88] Mark Kelly, "Mission Leaders Discuss Ways to Speed Outreach," (Richmond: Southern Baptist International Mission Board, July 01, 1999); available from https://solomon.imb.org; stories database; and *Strategic-Directions-21 Evaluation,* 9. The "Accelerating World Evangelization" conferences sought to explain New Directions to these Baptist partners as well as to enlist them as partners with the IMB in the global evangelization effort. See also Eitel, *Paradigm Wars,* 102-3. Eitel points out that Board leadership did not consult with Baptist partners before the New Directions restructuring, a restructuring that radically altered the relationship between the IMB and many of these denominational structures with whom the Board had related for many years.

[89] See Steve Steele and Jim Montgomery, "'Table 71' Creates Most Significant Missiological Advance Since 1974," *Mission Frontiers* (November-December 2002): 9-12; and "Mission Leaders Respond to the Dawn Report Assessment of 'Table 71,'" *Mission Frontiers* (November-December, 2002): 13-6. 'Table 71' was named after the number of the table at a round table discussion in the Strategy Coordinators Task Group, Amsterdam 2000 evangelism conference sponsored by the Billy Graham Association. Present at this table were representatives from the IMB, Campus Crusade for Christ, The Jesus Film Project, Wycliffe Bible Translators, The Seed Company, Discipling a Whole Nation, World Teach (Walk Through the Bible) and Youth With A Mission. Willis and Garrison represented the IMB at the original meeting of 'Table 71' in Amsterdam.

initiate work among the remaining, unengaged, unreached people groups. Willis, in reporting about this meeting stated, "It is a blight on the name of Christ that there is anybody in this world who does not have access to the gospel."[90] Steele and Montgomery hailed 'Table 71' as "the most significant missiological advance since the original Lausanne Congress on World Evangelization in 1974."[91]

Rankin also has led the IMB into other noteworthy organization-to-organization partnerships. One such partnership is with Wycliffe Bible Translators where the IMB has appointed and deployed five missionaries with Scripture translation skills and seconded them to Wycliffe.[92] Two other such partnerships have led to the development of the Harvest Information System, a global missions database maintained by a consortium of agencies, and the Missions Atlas Project, a massive multi-agency effort to map all inhabited villages and cities and evangelical churches throughout the world.[93]

The establishment of these multi-agency, multi-dimensional partnerships seems paradoxical to the vision of Rankin as delineated during his initial years at the helm of the IMB and with New Directions. Upon succeeding Parks, Rankin stated that he wanted to move away from strategy being driven by a central group at the home office and push the strategic planning as close to the field structures as possible. The dissolution of the Global Strategy Group and the creation of fourteen new regions empowered with strategic decision-making for their respective regions signified Rankin's antipathy toward centralized strategy development and implementation. At the same time, Rankin's desire to establish a number of organization-to-organization partnerships reflects to some degree a shift back toward centralized strategy. Is Rankin leading the Board more toward a centralized global strategy, developed and implemented from its home office rather than from its field-based teams? Do these organization-to-organization partnerships dovetail with the various regional strategies? In what ways do the organizational partnerships serve the SC-led, people-group focused teams on the field?

What is notable is the fact that Rankin has led the Board, at least at the central level, to pursue enthusiastically and intentionally major partnerships with a variety of like-minded evangelical mission agencies. Non-residential missionaries and strategy coordinators had begun to lead the Board to broader relationships with other GCC groups as they developed partnerships for work among specific people groups. Rankin has skilfully exploited this key component of the SC paradigm to lead the Board organizationally into

---

[90] Avery T. Willis, Jr., *Report to the Board* (Portland: Southern Baptist International Mission Board, Accession Number 2696, November 06, 2000).

[91] Steele and Montgomery, "Table 71," 10.

[92] *Strategic-Directions-21 Evaluation,* 91-2.

[93] *Strategic-Directions-21 Evaluation*, 92-3.

partnerships with other GCC agencies unparalleled in the history of the Board.

In New Directions, Rankin also sought to persuade Board missionaries around the world of the need to look beyond their own denomination and agency and look toward the massive resources available within the wider GCC community. For many of the Board's missionaries, working with non-Baptist entities was uncharted territory. One critical issue would focus around working with GCC partners without compromising the Board's mandate to plant indigenous Baptist churches. In an effort to help its missionaries in the process, the Board developed five levels of possible partnership as a guide for traversing the vast territory of partnership between IMB personnel and non-IMB groups (see Appendix F).[94] At each level of relationship with non-IMB partners, the goals and needs changed. The levels moved from access to the people group (level one), to mobilizing prayer and ministry to physical needs (level two), to evangelism (level three), to church-planting (level four) and finally to church development and maturation (level five).[95] As partnerships moved from level one to level five, the scope of potential partners would, as defined by the Board, narrow considerably. These boundaries, while not addressing every theological or doctrinal issue that might arise in partnership with non-IMB entities, did serve as an important compass for field personnel.

Rankin did implement some significant organizational-level partnerships, but New Directions failed to effectively stimulate a notable increase in catalytic, multinational partnerships with GCC groups at the field level. The 2003 *Strategic Directions-21 Evaluation* noted that few field-based teams consisted of Baptist or GCC partners, an indication that the majority of these teams remained IMB-centric in their work.[96] Noting this weakness, the evaluation task force recommended that Board leadership communicate with field-based teams the need for a stronger emphasis in this area.[97]

Through New Directions, Rankin successfully led the Board to embrace, at least on the organizational-level, this changing reality within the global mission community. In November 2003, the Board affirmed the nurturing of appropriate partnerships with GCC entities as one of the four key components of its global strategy.[98] This affirmation of the Board was more than an affirmation of New Directions, it also served as an affirmation of a key component of the SC paradigm. The path, which the NRM program and CSI blazed, was now the path the entire organization would travel.

---

[94] See Chapter 3, notes 192 and 198.

[95] *Something New Under the Sun*, 29-35.

[96] *Strategic Directions-21 Evaluation,* 15.

[97] "Board of Trustees Minutes," November 10, 2003.

[98] "Board of Trustees Minutes," November 10, 2003.

Prayer as Strategy

As non-residential missionaries and strategy coordinators began to focus on World A people groups, who often lived in some of the most restricted-access countries, they discovered the effectiveness in utilizing prayer strategically. Not only did these networks provide a critical base of prayer support for the work, but out of these networks directly flowed a large majority of the resources – human and material – needed to penetrate their specific people group. These extensive prayer networks were an indispensable part of the comprehensive strategy developed by SC personnel.

Not only was the concept of strategic prayer networks incorporated into the *To The Edge* training, but Rankin also expanded strategic prayer initiatives at the broader organizational level. Utilizing the information technology of the internet and worldwide web, Rankin has led the Board to develop various websites such as CompassionNet, a site promoting prayer for the Board's work and personnel around the world, and PeopleTeams, a site that allows the people group-focused teams of the IMB mobilize prayer support for their work.[99] Through its CompassionNet website, individuals can be linked to a variety of intercessory prayer emphases and resources. For example, through this website churches can become Prayer*plus* partners, specifically adopting an unengaged, unreached people group and committing long-term to pray for the evangelization of that specific group.[100] Various other resources available through the IMB include information on prayer walking, daily prayer updates from around the world and urgent prayer requests from the field.[101] The development and wide dissemination of these prayer resources has mobilized hundreds of Southern Baptist churches and thousands of individual Christians to strategically pray for global evangelization. Before New Directions, individual SC personnel and their teams had very limited organizational resources upon which to draw in developing their prayer networks. However, as Rankin embraced a key element of the SC paradigm and skilfully incorporated it into the Board's overall organizational structure, the result was the provision of a much-needed service to the thousands of IMB missionaries serving around the world.

---

[99] "CompassionNet," (Richmond: Southern Baptist International Mission Board, 2005); available at http://imb.org/CompassionNet; and "PeopleTeams," (Richmond: Southern Baptist International Mission Board, 2005); available at http://PeopleTeams.org.

[100] "Prayer*plus* Partnership," (Richmond: Southern Baptist International Mission Board, 2005); available at http://imb.org/CompassionNet/prayerplus.asp.

[101] *Strategic Directions-21 Evaluation,* 43-4.

Personnel Growth

Within CSI, strategy coordinators were encouraged and empowered to relate directly to Southern Baptist constituent churches, which enabled them to personally mobilize needed personnel for work among their targeted people group. One of the keys to the growth of personnel in CSI during Stroope's tenure as its area director was the strategic utilization of short-term, two-year International Service Corps (ISC) and Journeymen personnel. CSI viewed these two-year personnel as full-fledged missionaries, often utilizing them to open up new, frontier areas. Through its influence, CSI also was able to convince the Board to allow the terms of these ISC and Journeymen personnel to qualify for the two-year, full-time ministry experience required for appointment as a career missionary. Further, because of the need to find creative ways to access World A people groups, SC personnel opened the door for a wide variety of laypersons, many of whom might not have considered serving as missionaries, to serve in strategic ministry among these World A peoples. The net result was that from 1992-1995, CSI experienced a 264 percent growth in the number of personnel from 156 to 412 with 47 percent of the total as short-term, two-year personnel.

Under New Directions, the Board shifted from large mission structures with a geopolitical focus to smaller SC-lead teams focusing on specific people groups. As a result, in many of the traditional mission fields of the Board, missionary personnel began to focus on the neglected people groups within their countries. As these teams sought to engage these previously neglected people groups, they discovered the need for creative means to access these peoples. Further, many of these newly formed teams were empowered to relate directly to constituent churches back in the United States. While CSI was an administrative area (1992-97), there were forty-two strategy coordinators appointed, annually averaging 3.3 percent of the total of all career appointments by the Board.[102] Under New Directions from 1998-2002, the annual average of long-term missionaries appointed by the Board to serve as strategy coordinators grew to 6.5 percent as the Board appointed 115 new strategy coordinators during this five-year period.[103] The overall growth of missionary personnel during the first five years of New Directions was 29 percent.[104]

The *Strategic Directions-21 Evaluation* conducted in 2003 cited four key reasons to explain this growth in strategy coordinator appointments and in the overall missionary force. The reasons presented to explain this growth were (1) SC-led teams were doing a more effective job in recruiting new personnel; (2) the focus on unreached people groups opened up more positions for laypersons;

[102] *Strategic Directions-21 Evaluation*, 72.

[103] *Strategic Directions-21 Evaluation*, 72.

[104] *Strategic Directions-21 Evaluation*, 74.

(3) the largest numerical growth in personnel were short-term, two-year personnel; and (4) 41 percent of all long-term missionaries appointed previously had served as short-term personnel.[105] Table 4 shows the parallels between the growth of CSI (1992-97) and New Directions (1998-2002).

As the Board began to diffuse the SC paradigm throughout each of the fourteen regions, missionaries trained began to adopt the methodologies and the attitude of CSI, which were a core reason for its explosive growth under Stroope. As the Board sought to implement New Directions, Willis asserted that any missionary could do what CSI personnel were doing. In this area, at least, Willis' words rang true. As the Board sought to empower its missionaries to actively recruit for their teams and as many missionaries discovered the strategic role many of the ISC/ Journeymen personnel and laypersons could fill on their teams, the number of personnel across the entire organization began to increase more rapidly.

CSI-like Components in Various Regions

Rankin, in announcing New Directions, asserted that the Board was not eradicating CSI; rather the Board was going to reconfigure CSI in such a way that various regions would have CSI-like components. In other words, as regions sought to engage the unengaged people groups identified within their respective areas, the Board would empower that region to apply CSI-type strategies to effectively penetrate those people groups. Several regions developed such programs, particularly aimed at mobilizing ISC, Journeymen and volunteer teams from constituent churches in the United States. One region developed strategy coordinator training aimed at mobilizing and equipping local Christians to initiate mission work among unengaged, unreached people groups within their countries.

Within a few short months subsequent to the implementation of New Directions, the newly formed Central and Southern Asia region initiated an effort to rapidly mobilize, train and deploy strategy coordinators who would focus on specific unengaged, unreached people groups in two major restricted-access countries within the region. 'Rapid Advance' was the name given to this unique effort. At about the same time, the East Asia region began its 'Rapid Advance' program. The original thrust of these 'Rapid Advance' efforts was to mobilize and train short-term ISC and Journeyman personnel who would develop a strategy aimed at facilitating church-planting efforts among these unreached peoples.[106]

---

105 *Strategic Directions-21 Evaluation*, 74.

106 Erich Bridges, "RapAdvance: How Rapid?" (Richmond: Southern Baptist International Mission Board, October 01, 1999); available from https://solomon.imb.org; stories database.

In 2000, one of the 'Rapid Advance' efforts in the Central and Southern Asia region shifted away from training IMB personnel and began to mobilize and equip local Christians. This 'Rapid Advance' effort focused on the countries within South Asia. This team set its objective as seeing every unreached people group and city engaged with a strategy aimed at catalyzing movements of churches within ten years.[107] The team developed the *Acts 29 Training*, which sought to equip local, South Asian missionaries and church planters in the principles and concepts of strategy coordination.[108] Since January 2000, the 'Rapid Advance' team has trained over one thousand South Asian Christians, resulting in thousands of new churches planted among different unreached people groups. The 'Rapid Advance' team also trained a number of these strategy coordinators to be trainers, most of whom are replicating the training throughout South Asia.

---

[107] R. Bruce Carlton, *Rapid Advance of South Asia Team Scorecard* (Singapore: Rapid Advance of South Asia, 2000) [electronic document]; available from the author.

[108] See R. Bruce Carlton, *Acts 29: Practical Training In Facilitating Church-Planting Movements Among The Neglected Harvest Fields* (Singapore: by the author, 2003). The training materials are now available in fifteen different languages, and various regions of the Board are utilizing the materials in their strategy coordinator training efforts. A few of these regions have also shifted toward training local Christians within their respective areas as strategy coordinators. The Board divided Central and Southern Asia into two regions on December 31, 2001. Neither 'Rapid Advance' effort within Central Asia and South Asia remain. The only continuing 'Rapid Advance' effort is in the East Asia region.

Table 4: Parallels between personnel growth under New Directions (1997-2003) and CSI (1992-97)[109]

New Directions	CSI
1. More mobilization of new personnel by Strategy Coordinator-led teams resulted in personnel increase.	1. Strategy Coordinators encouraged to go directly to churches and individuals to recruit for their teams.
2. The focus on unreached people groups in restricted-access countries opened up more personnel requests for laypersons; whereas, previously the majority of personnel requests were for seminary-trained clergy.	2. Strategy Coordinators developed creative ways to access World A people. This opened the door for a wide variety of laypersons many of which might not have considered cross-cultural missionary work, to serve in strategic ministry among World A peoples.
3. Greatest growth in personnel was in short-term, two-year personnel. This reflected an attitude change on the part of many career missionaries. Short-term personnel, once thought to be support helpers, now seen as real missionaries.	3. Within CSI, the attitude was that 'everyone wears long pants.' Short-term personnel treated as real missionaries, often sent to open up work in difficult, hazardous, front-line areas.
4. Process of growing long-term missionaries from short-term personnel accelerated. In 2002-3, forty-one percent of career appointments were personnel who had previously served as short-term, two-year personnel.	4. CSI utilized short-term, two-year personnel as a personnel farm system, allowing these personnel to hone their skills and gifts in preparation for career missionary service.
5. Process developed allowing for a quick 'turnaround' for short-term, two-year personnel. They no longer have to start all over again in the appointment process.	5. CSI influenced the Board to allow the short-term, two-year term overseas to qualify as the two years of full-time ministry experience needed for career appointment.
6. Organization-wide personnel growth from 1998-2002 was 29 percent.	6. In a four-year period (1992-95), CSI personnel growth was 264 percent.

109 Information from *Strategic Directions-21 Evaluation,* Stroope, interview by author, Williard, "Shaping New Strategies," Stroope, Interview by Keith E. Eitel, and Smith, "Thoughts for Bruce."

Other regions also began to implement unique strategies for engaging the unreached peoples in their respective regions. In Western South America, the region developed the 'Rapid Entry and Advance Plan' (REAP).[110] The region identified various unengaged micro people groups (less than twenty-five thousand in population), and sought to mobilize and equip Southern Baptist churches to serve as strategy coordinators for that specific group.[111] Many Southern Baptist churches were active in sending volunteer mission teams each year, but the large majority of these churches would send teams to many different areas. The uniqueness of REAP was the emphasis on churches repeatedly sending their volunteer teams to the same micro people group in order to establish continuity and consistency in the evangelization effort, and challenging the church to send someone from their own congregation to serve as the field strategy coordinator, becoming a link between the church and the people group.[112] An additional CSI-type strategy deployed in South America is the 'Xtreme Team' effort. 'Xtreme Team' seeks to mobilize and equip short-term, two-year personnel to work among some of the most isolated peoples living within the Amazon jungle and Andes mountains.[113]

One of the results emerging from the 'Table 71' partnership is the formation of Epic Partners, a joint project of the IMB, Wycliffe Bible Translators, Campus Crusade for Christ, TransWorld Radio and Youth With A Mission. Realizing that the majority of the remaining unengaged, unreached people groups were oral communicators with sizeable non-literate populations, these various agencies united to recruit teams who would penetrate these people groups and help to compile a set of oral Bible stories in the group's heart language.[114] With 2700 languages without a Bible and the majority of people speaking these languages being non-literate, the effort to develop an oral Bible is a critical step in communicating the Gospel to these people groups. While Epic Partners emerged from an organization-to-organization partnership, several regions such as West Africa, South Asia and North Africa and Middle

---

[110] Larry Gay, *Report to the Board* (Sacramento: Southern Baptist International Mission Board, Accession Number 2676, November 15, 1999). In 2004, the Western South America region and Eastern South America region merged to become the South America Region.

[111] Gay, *Report to the Board,* November 15, 1999.

[112] Gay, *Report to the Board,* November 15, 1999.

[113] "The Xtreme Team," (Richmond: Southern Baptist International Mission Board, 2004); available from http://www.thextremeteam.org.

[114] "Board of Trustees Minutes," (Charlotte: Southern Baptist International Mission Board, Accession Number 2810, March 14, 2005); "Board of Trustees Minutes," (Midland: Southern Baptist International Mission Board, Accession Number 2812, May 19, 2005).

East have deployed teams through this partnership effort.[115] This provides a positive example of how an organization-to-organization partnership is effectively supplementing the strategies of various regions.

The above examples reveal that creative methodologies built upon many of the key concepts of the SC paradigm indeed did begin to emerge. As New Directions consistently reinforced the vision of reaching all peoples, empowered the regions to find innovative ways to engage the unreached peoples in their respective areas and disseminated widely key concepts of the SC paradigm, various regions responded. The translation of the paradigm spawned new and innovative dimensions of the paradigm. The dissolution of CSI as an administrative area was not its death, but, in a way, it experienced a metamorphosis and surfaced with a new face in these various innovative efforts.

Strategic Utilization of New Technologies

The NRM/SC paradigm emerged at a time of escalating technological advance in the world. Within the IMB, these new missionaries pioneered the use of various emerging technologies as they sought to penetrate the world of unreached people groups. Through the emerging technology of Internet communications, strategy coordinators were able to build networks of partners among Southern Baptist churches and the wider GCC community. These SC personnel and their teams passionately embraced media technologies such as radio and the *Jesus Film* as viable tools for evangelizing these people groups.

By 1997, when the Board unveiled New Directions, the advances of technology had expanded at an exponential rate. McConnell and Esler accurately point out that these new technologies "are as normal for a missionary as they are for a business executive."[116] New Directions, like the SC paradigm, embraced these technological advances and sought to exploit them for the Board's global mission effort. Through the strategic development and utilization of a variety of these technologies, missionary personnel are now able to connect instantly with each other, with constituent churches as well as avail themselves of continual learning opportunities.

Besides the extensive prayer website resources mentioned previously,

---

[115] "Board of Trustees Minutes," March 14, 2005; "Board of Trustees Minutes," May 19, 2005.

[116] Douglas McConnell and J. Tedd Esler, "The Impact of New Technologies: Life in the Virtual World and Beyond," in *The Changing Face of World Missions: Engaging Contemporary Issues and Trends,* eds. Michael Pocock, Gailyn Van Rheenen and Douglas McConnell, Encountering Mission Series, ed. A. Scott Moreau, (Grand Rapids: Baker Academic, 2005), 299. In their article, McConnell and Esler seek to demonstrate how the technological advances of the later part of the 20th century influence and shape the global mission enterprise.

various websites developed by the Board offer information ranging from information about people groups and teams around the world to training resources for missionary field personnel. The *PeopleTeams.org* website enables Christians to instantly access information, prayer requests and other needs generated by the people group-focused teams deployed by the Board around the world. The *newWway.org* website offers extensive resources at the touch of the keyboard to enhance the work of field personnel. The *peoplegroups.org* website enables individuals to access information from the Board's global research department on people groups within nearly every country in the world as well as information tracking the status of global evangelization.[117] Another significant media tool developed by the Board in the past few years has been the *Following Jesus* series on CD-Rom technology. This series seeks to help missionaries and others effectively evangelize, disciple and train leaders among oral learners through four hundred Bible storytelling sessions.[118]

Personalizing Missions for Local Churches

One of the unique contributions of the SC paradigm was that strategy coordinators were empowered to directly connect with constituent Southern Baptist churches. Strategy coordinators recognized a trend within the Christian world, a trend of local churches shying away from blind support of denominational institutions toward a more personal, intimate involvement in the global mission effort. Recognizing this trend, many strategy coordinators were able to mobilize Southern Baptist churches for work among their specific targeted people group.

Rankin was also keenly aware of this trend among churches, and in 1992 led the Board to develop the Creative Access Network with the purpose of mobilizing Southern Baptist churches for global evangelization. As churches adopted an unreached people group overseas they became Global Priority Churches, and by 1999, there were 370 of these churches.[119] Since the beginning of New Directions, the Board has expanded its service to constituent Southern Baptist churches as they seek personal involvement in the global mission effort.

In 1999, Rankin published a small book *Mobilizing for Missions in the New Millennium*, challenging Board missionaries to awaken to the realities of the changing attitudes among local Baptist churches in the United States. Rankin challenged field personnel to view the massive resources within Southern

---

[117] See http://PeopleTeams.org; http://all.PeopleTeams.org; http://newWway.org and www.peoplegroups.org.

[118] *Strategic Directions-21 Evaluation,* 95.

[119] Mary E. Speidel, "Churches in Touch with God Can Reach a Lost World," (Richmond: Southern Baptist International Mission Board, June 09, 1999); available from https://solomon.imb.org; stories database.

Baptist churches not as pipelines for funding their work, but rather as valuable partners needed to evangelize the unreached peoples of the world. Rankin called for an attitude change among missionaries, one that recognized that the Board "cannot afford to be a funnel, restricting the resources and involvement of others, doing only what we ourselves can do, but we must have a vision of inclusive strategies, facilitating God's people to be on mission."[120]

In 2002, Rankin formed a personalization discovery team to interview a sample of Southern Baptist churches with the intent to develop a "proto-type model for personalizing relationships with churches."[121] Through this process, the team developed five distinct classifications of churches based on the church's involvement in missions, ranging on a continuum from those churches with no personal involvement beyond giving and praying for missions to those churches actively involved globally and enlisting other churches for the same.[122] Based on the findings of this study, Rankin then put together a team of staff members who would tailor mobilization efforts to churches in each category.[123]

As the Board reorganized away from the traditional bureaucratic mission structure to smaller SC-led, people-group focused teams and as these teams were trained and empowered to develop innovative strategies to evangelize their targeted people group, many of these teams and regions began to realize the potential within Southern Baptist churches. One result, as already noted, was the significant increase in the deployment of short-term, two-year ISC and Journeymen personnel. Another noted increase was in the area of short-term volunteers. In 1992, the number of volunteers from Southern Baptist churches was 10,239, which grew to 33,963 by 2001.[124] The mobilization of Southern Baptist churches led several regions to develop innovative approaches, asking churches to work among people groups independent of IMB missionaries. Through the innovative approaches regions challenged churches to function as strategy coordinators, taking responsibility for the evangelization of a people group, city or population segment.

As previously mentioned, the Western South America region developed the 'Rapid Entry and Advance Plan' (REAP) whereby churches adopt a micro people group and serve as the strategy coordinator for that group. In the East Asia region, the leadership launched an effort to mobilize Southern Baptist

---

[120] Jerry A. Rankin, *Mobilizing for Missions in the New Millennium: A Great Commission Vision for Southern Baptists in the 21st Century* (Richmond: Southern Baptist International Mission Board, 1999), 7.

[121] Jerry A. Rankin, *Report to the Board* (Knoxville: Southern Baptist International Mission Board, Accession Number 2732, March 13, 2003).

[122] Rankin, *Report to the Board,* May 13, 2003.

[123] Rankin, *Report to the Board,* May 13, 2003.

[124] *Strategic Directions-21 Evaluation,* 85.

churches to implement a church-planting strategy in a specific city less than one million in population.[125] The Middle America region began two training programs for Southern Baptist churches – 'Frontliners' conferences and SC Training.[126] 'Frontliners' conferences introduce the New Directions missiological paradigm to Southern Baptist volunteers serving in Middle America, while the SC training aims at equipping churches in developing and implementing a volunteer-based, evangelization strategy for an area in the region where IMB personnel are not working.[127] The South Asia region developed 'Project Thessalonica' as a vehicle for mobilizing churches to serve as a SC for an unevangelized city in the region, seeking to empower "the church to engage the mission process by delivering the same principles and tools passed on to hundreds of South Asian leaders and full-time foreign workers through the *Acts 29* training."[128]

In a world where numerous local churches were awakening to the reality that the mission task was a core characteristic of their identity as the church, mobilizing and equipping such churches to serve as strategy coordinators is a predictable progression in the growth of the SC paradigm under New Directions. The desire of churches for personalized involvement in the global mission task closely parallels a trend that Garrison noted was occurring within the global economic market – the trend of disintermediation or the exclusion of the middleman.[129] As Rankin noted, the Board would need to adjust in light of this trend, moving beyond the narrow mindset that the IMB did missions on behalf of Southern Baptist churches toward becoming a facilitator of Southern Baptist churches enabling them to fulfil their missionary responsibility. In addition, because of the strong catalytic component of the SC paradigm, churches functionally can step into the SC role. These churches function from a non-residential posture, much like those early NRM missionaries within the IMB. However, just as those initial NRM personnel demonstrated, churches from their non-residential base also can effectively leverage the needed evangelization resources from outside and within the targeted population segment.

Postmodern Elements Remain

As New Directions sought to instil the SC paradigm as the Board's primary missiological paradigm for the 21st century, it retained all the key postmodern

[125] Bill Fudge, *Report to the Board* (Sacramento: Southern Baptist International Mission Board, Accession Number 2676, November 19, 1999).

[126] Ken Sorrell, "SC Survey," Electronic letter to R. Bruce Carlton, March 29, 2005.

[127] Sorrell, "SC Survey."

[128] R. Bruce Carlton, *Project Thessalonica: Acts 29 Training for Churches* (Singapore: by the author, 2003), 8.

[129] Garrison, *Global Analysis.*

elements discussed in the previous chapter. Just like the SC paradigm, New Directions did not forsake its evangelical roots. This evangelical, postmodern paradigm emerged within CSI, and New Directions simply incorporated these postmodern elements into the overall missiology of the entire organization.

Missio Dei remained a fundamental concept within New Directions. The vision statement of the Board during Rankin's tenure asserted that Southern Baptists, in their efforts to pursue the evangelization of every people group, simply were joining God in His mission. Reflecting back on the early years of New Directions, Rankin commented, "It's awesome to be involved in missions not only as we transcend to a new millennium, but at a time when God is at work in unprecedented ways."[130]

The numerous organizational-level partnerships that Rankin led the Board to develop indicate his acceptance of mission as common witness. Rankin, like Parks and CSI, shied away from the ecumenical movement, and sought to lead the Board and its missionary personnel to "recognize that spiritual unity and cooperation can result in a stronger combination of synergistic evangelistic outreach than organizational ecumenical efforts."[131] By adapting to this trend in the global mission movement, Rankin led the Board to develop networks and partnerships unprecedented since its inception in the 19th century.

New Directions also embraced the postmodern concept of mission as church-with-others. Further, recognizing the trend of churches taking the initiative to implement their own global mission strategies, Rankin began to refocus the mobilization efforts of the Board toward facilitating the mission involvement of these churches into the Board's overall global strategy. Mobilization no longer simply focused on channelling material and human resources through the IMB to the field, but shifted toward "awakening and equipping of the whole body of Christ to participate in the whole mission of God to reach the whole world with the good news of Jesus Christ."[132]

The above examples further illustrate the pervading influence of the SC paradigm in New Directions. As CSI thrust a generation of missionaries into a new missiological paradigm, so New Directions would thrust an entire organization into the same paradigm. As the Board enters the 21st century, it

---

[130] Jerry A. Rankin, "Missions in the New Millennium – A Conversation with Jerry Rankin," (Richmond: Southern Baptist International Mission Board, January 01, 2000); available from https://solomon.imb.org; stories database.

[131] Jerry A. Rankin, "The Present Situation in Missions," in *Missiology: An Introduction to the Foundations, History, and Strategies of World Missions,* ed. John Mark Terry, Ebbie Smith and Justice Anderson (Nashville: Broadman and Holman Publishers, 1998), 46. Rankin believed the ecumenical movement had compromised the gospel message for the sake of unity. Thus, for Rankin, the ecumenical movement was obsolete.

[132] Erich Bridges, "Mobilization: The World Connection," (Richmond: Southern Baptist International Mission Board, July 01, 1999); available from https://solomon.imb.org; stories database.

has affirmed this emergent evangelical, postmodern paradigm as a key for accelerating its efforts toward global evangelization.

Conclusion

From the beginning of his presidency of the IMB, Rankin did not attempt to disguise the fact that he sought for a restructuring of the organization. Rankin was cognizant of the conflicts between CSI and the traditional areas of the Board, and he viewed the existence of CSI as a separate administrative area as the primary reason behind the tension. Despite his uneasiness with CSI, Rankin would allow it to remain and grow during the first five years of his tenure. Could various parts of the Board with two different missiological paradigms coexist within the same organization as Stroope recommended? Would Rankin simply dissolve CSI, as some may have desired? As he began to finalize what would become New Directions, Rankin expressed a desire for a unified organization, indicating that he did not believe the existence of divergent paradigms would best serve the interests of the Board's global mission effort.

New Directions may have dissolved CSI as an administrative area of the Board, yet it did not eradicate the missiological paradigm. To the contrary, evidence clearly demonstrates that New Directions was an effort by Rankin and other Board leaders to repackage the SC paradigm and infuse it throughout the entire organization. Every distinctive and characteristic of New Directions defined by Rankin and Board leadership can be traced directly back to the SC paradigm. New Directions, in reality, simply was the SC paradigm in new clothes tailored to fit the entire organization.

For Rankin, New Directions was his vision to position the Board for a more effective global mission thrust as it entered the 21st century. At the same time, the restructuring of the organization through New Directions was an attempt to infuse vitality into the traditional mission fields of the Board by injecting these fields with the SC paradigm. As with any major organizational restructure, Board leadership faced some difficulties and barriers in communicating this paradigm shift. Nonetheless, over time, evidence of the SC paradigm's influence emerged. After a few years, the Board of Trustees signified their approval of the paradigm shift by changing the name New Directions to Strategic Directions for the 21st Century. The shift from maverick to mainstream was complete.

CHAPTER 5

A Second Shift: Church-Planting Movements

Introduction

At about the same time that Rankin was launching New Directions, the strategy coordinator (SC) paradigm upon which most of New Directions was built began to experience some significant shifts. The primary catalyst for these shifts in the paradigm was the church-planting movement (CPM) phenomenon. Cooperative Services International (CSI) embraced the vision of church-planting movements among all World A people groups, yet there was scant knowledge of such movements. However, as several strategy coordinators began to witness the rapid growth and multiplication of indigenous churches among their targeted people group, CSI and the Board began to gain a better understanding of these movements. New Directions also sought to embrace the vision of church-planting movements throughout the world. The Board's overseas leadership team adopted a vision statement in 1998, stating, "We will facilitate the lost coming to saving faith in Jesus Christ by beginning and nurturing Church Planting Movements among all peoples."[1]

Initially, the non-residential missionary's (NRM) objective was to mobilize Great Commission resources for mission among the targeted people group so that everyone in that people group might have an opportunity to hear and respond to the gospel message, anticipating the planting of a beachhead church.[2] This objective was congruent with the Board's emphasis on evangelism resulting in churches. With the emergence of the CPM phenomenon, the overall objective shifted. The Board still defined the SC as one responsible for mobilizing Great Commission Christians (GCC) to evangelize a people group, yet the objective was to accomplish this through the planting of reproducing churches or a church-planting movement.[3] The planting of multiple reproducing churches replaced the emphasis on evangelism

[1] *Strategic Directions-21 Evaluation,* 32. See Glossary for one definition of church-planting movements.

[2] Garrison, *Non-residential Missionary,* 14. See Glossary for definition of a beachhead church.

[3] Erich Bridges, "ANALYSIS: Strategy Coordinator Role sets off Missions Revolution," (Richmond: Southern Baptist International Mission Board, September 28, 1999); available from https://solomon.imb.org; stories database.

that results in churches, a subtle, yet significant shift. With the shift of emphasis toward church-planting movements, other aspects of the SC paradigm also changed.

This chapter will define a CPM and explore the key characteristics of this phenomenon as expounded by the Board in its efforts to understand it. Further, this chapter will analyze some critical issues surrounding the Board's efforts to effectively describe the phenomenon. The Board's adoption of the church-planting movements as its primary thrust entering the 21st century warrants such an analysis. An examination of the major shifts within the SC paradigm resulting from the CPM emphasis will follow.

Church-planting Movements

As non-residential missionaries and strategy coordinators began to discover ways to penetrate the restricted countries and areas where World A peoples resided, in some situations they found people extraordinarily responsive to the gospel message. As indigenous churches took root, they began reproducing and multiplying rapidly. CSI missionaries encountered this phenomenon in places like China, India, North Africa and Cambodia. At the same time, there were other such movements identified in other areas of the world. In 1998, various region leaders presented ten case studies of where the church was growing and multiplying rapidly, five of those case studies were from World A people groups. Garrison cited four CPM case studies in the Board's publication *Church Planting Movements*, all of which emerged either among World A people groups or restricted-access countries.[4]

By 2001, the IMB was tracking thirty-five church-planting movements or near movements occurring around the world.[5] Two years later, the Board reported that it had assessed and confirmed seven church-planting movements and tracking forty-two other reported movements, revealing that such movements "among previously unreached people groups now are generating more new believers and new congregations than even traditional 'harvest field' countries like Nigeria and Brazil."[6] Driven by its vision to provide every person on earth an opportunity to hear and respond to the gospel, the Board embraced these movements as the most effective tool for fulfilling its vision. Rankin voiced this belief, stating, "We have recognized that the task of discipling the nations will be accomplished only as our methodology results in reproducing indigenous churches that are a local nucleus of worship, witness, teaching and

---

[4] Garrison, *Church Planting Movements,* 11-32.

[5] Garrison, *Global Analysis.*

[6] Mark Kelly, "IMB trustees evaluate strategy shift, adopt $258.9m budget, respond to criticism," (Richmond: Southern Baptist International Mission Board, November 18, 2003); available from https://solomon.imb.org; stories database.

ministry in a rapidly multiplying network that gives every person access to the gospel."[7]

Mission strategists at the Board sought to explain what they were witnessing in these movements. The Board assigned Garrison, Associate Vice-President for Strategy Coordination and Mobilization, to study these movements and delineate the key elements and characteristics.[8] What emerged from this extensive study were a concise definition, a list of unique characteristics, a list of potential barriers and obstacles and some prescriptive ideas on how to catalyze a CPM.

Defining the Phenomenon

In 1998, Willis stated that a CPM was "the rapid multiplication of churches to the extent that they can reach their whole people group and move out in missions to someone else."[9] Garrison, in an initial draft summarizing the findings from his study, defined it as "a rapid and exponential increase of indigenous churches planting churches within a given people group or population segment."[10] Later in the official Board publication on CPM, Garrison slightly altered the wording by referring to the growth as multiplicative rather than exponential.[11] Several years later, he would amend the definition once again, stating that a CPM was "a rapid multiplication of indigenous churches planting churches that sweeps through a people group or population segment."[12]

All of these definitions sound very similar to what Roland Allen described in 1927. Allen knew that more missionaries was not the answer to global evangelization, and he called for missionaries to labour in such a way as to facilitate the spontaneous expansion of the local church in places where missionaries served.[13] For Allen, the measurement of success of local churches in reaching their nation lay "not so much by the number of foreign missionaries employed, or by the number of converts, as by the growth of a native church in the power to expand."[14] In a sense, what mission strategists at the Board

---

[7] Rankin, *Report to the Board,* May 21, 2001.

[8] Rankin, *Report to the Board,* May 21, 2001..

[9] Willis, *Report to the Board,* March 19, 1998.

[10] V. David Garrison, *Church Planting Movement Profile* (Richmond: Southern Baptist International Mission Board, 1999) [electronic document], 1.

[11] Garrison, *Church Planting Movements,* 7.

[12] Garrison, *God Redeeming a Lost World,* 21.

[13] Roland Allen, *The Spontaneous Expansion of the Church,* American edition (Grand Rapids: Eerdmans, 1962; reprint, Eugene: Wipf and Stock, 1997), 18-42 (page citations are to the reprint edition).

[14] Allen, *The Spontaneous Expansion,* 19.

defined as a CPM was, in its simplest expression, a spontaneous expansion of the church.

There are some key components to this definition as put forth by Garrison. First, he states that within a CPM there is a rapid acceleration of new churches planted. In the 2000 booklet *Church Planting Movements*, the official Board publication on the phenomenon, Garrison does not explain what he means by rapid growth. However, in a video produced by the Board and in Garrison's second book on CPM, the explanation of rapid growth is growth that outpaces the population growth of a people group.[15]

A second significant component of the definition is multiplicative or exponential growth. Garrison points out that multiplicative growth is more than just multiple church starts, rather the number of church starts in a CPM doubles as one church plants another, the two then plant two more, and so on.[16] Like compounding interest in investment banking, compounding church starts are characteristic of these movements.

The simple explanation for this multiplicative growth is that churches within a CPM start new churches.[17] This, more than any other aspect, defines a church-planting movement. Churches within these movements typically fulfil their missionary nature, thus they do not delegate the task of church planting to the missionary, evangelist or church planter.

A fourth component is that churches within these movements are indigenous. Garrison simply states that the term indigenous within the context of this definition is a church planted by the local people as opposed to those from the outside.[18] Initial church starts within a CPM may have come from an

---

[15] *Like a Mighty Wave: Church Planting Movements,* produced by the Southern Baptist International Mission Board, 12 minutes, 2001, videocassette; Garrison, *God Redeeming a Lost World,* 22.

[16] Garrison, *Church Planting Movements,* 8.

[17] Garrison, *Church Planting Movements,* 8.

[18] Garrison, *Church Planting Movements,* 8; Garrison, *God Redeeming a Lost World,* 22. Garrison does not expound on the concept of indigenous churches, yet his simple explanation seems to imply that churches within church-planting movements follow the classical three-self understanding of an indigenous church as championed by Henry Venn, Rufus Anderson, and later by John Nevius in the nineteenth century. The three-self understanding of an indigenous church, simply stated, was that a church would be self-supporting, self-governing and self-propagating. A wider discussion on this issue is outside the scope of this research. However, for those interested in the thinking of these men, I recommend the following works. Venn (1796-1873) was the General Secretary of the Church Missionary Society. For a bibliography on Venn's writings, see William Shenk, *Bibliography of Henry Venn's Printed Writings* (Scottdale: Herald Press, 1975). Also, see Henry Venn, *To Apply the Gospel: Selections from the Writings of Henry Venn* (Grand Rapids: Eerdmans, 1971) and William Shenk, *Henry Venn – a Missionary Statesman*, American Society of Missiology Series (Maryknoll: Orbis, 1983). Anderson

outside missionary; however, "within a short time, the new believers coming to Christ…may not even know that a foreigner was ever involved in the work."[19]

Finally, according to Garrison's definition, a CPM typically occurs within a homogeneous population segment, people who share a common ethnicity, common languages and/or common culture. By including this in the definition, Garrison is not advocating for the homogeneous principle as expounded by McGavran, but rather is describing what seemingly is a natural process within a movement.[20] As strategy coordinators focused on the evangelization of a particular ethno linguistic people group or population segment and as churches began to emerge, the new churches, for the most part, naturally evangelized those from within their own people group. The majority of newly formed

---

(1796-1880) served as the Corresponding (Foreign) Secretary of the American Board of Commissioners for Foreign Missions (ABCFM). The official papers of Anderson are in the ABCFM archives at Harvard University. For a bibliography of Anderson's writings, see R. Pierce Beaver, *To Advance the Gospel: A Collection of the Writings of Rufus Anderson* (Grand Rapids: Eerdmans, 1967), 39-44. See also S.B. Treat, *Outline of Missionary Policy,* Missionary Tract No. 15 (Boston: ABCFM, 1856). This tract outlines Anderson's principles as stated policy for missionaries of ABCFM. Nevius (1829-1893) served as a Presbyterian missionary to China where he formulated his methods for missionary work, much in line with the thinking of Venn and Anderson. His classic work *The Planting and Development of Missionary Churches*, originally published by Presbyterian Press in Shanghai, 1886, delineates his methods. The most recent reprint of this work is by Monadnock Press, 2003.

[19] Garrison, *God Redeeming a Lost World,* 22.

[20] The homogeneous-unit principle is one of the foundational components of the Church Growth missiology as first delineated by Donald McGavran. This principle asserts that people desire to become Christians without having to cross social, class or language lines. Forcing people to cross such lines creates barriers and hinders the growth and expansion of the church. McGavran developed this principle from the people movements, which he encountered during his missionary work in India. In his book *Ethnic Realities and the Church: Lessons from India* (Pasadena: William Carey Library, 1979), McGavran provides an overview of nine different types of churches that have emerged within India. He asserts that the mono-ethnic churches are the most natural. Other books by McGavran that expound on this principle are *The Bridges of God* (London: World Dominion, 1955); *Understanding Church Growth* (Grand Rapids: Eerdmans, 1970) and *Momentous Decisions in Missions Today* (Grand Rapids: Baker Book House, 1984). See also Donald A. McGavran and Charles W. Arn, *How to Grow a Church* (Glendale: Regal Books, 1973) and *Ten Steps for Church Growth* (New York: Harper and Row, 1977). Garrison, in *God Redeeming a Lost Word,* 24-6, points out what he sees as a few significant differences between church-planting movements and the Church Growth movement.

churches were mono-ethnic. The various case studies presented in both of Garrison's books corroborate this dimension of church-planting movements.[21]

Describing the Phenomenon: Characteristics and Case Studies

Although the definition is not an exhaustive description, it does provide a succinct explanation of an emerging phenomenon. After collaboration with several missionaries experiencing first-hand involvement with a CPM, Garrison developed a list of characteristics as an attempt to provide a more thorough description of this phenomenon. Garrison divided his list of characteristics into two categories: (1) those always found in every movement and (2) those often found in a movement.

In the initial draft profile of church-planting movements, Garrison lists nine principal characteristics, which he asserts were included in every CPM investigated at that time. These universal characteristics are (1) massive sowing of the gospel message; (2) prayer; (3) church planting is deliberate; (4) leaders of churches are not outsiders, but from within the people group; (5) the majority of these leaders are not professional clergy, but typically lay persons; (6) the churches are small, normally meeting in homes or cell groups; (7) the churches are reproducing churches; (8) the authority of God's Word is paramount; and (9) the reproduction of new churches occurs rapidly.[22] By the time the Board published the small booklet *Church Planting Movements* in 2000, Garrison had added a tenth universal characteristic. He added that churches in these movements were healthy because they exhibited the five functions of worship, fellowship, ministry, evangelism and discipleship.[23]

About the same time of Garrison's initial draft but before the publication of the booklet by the Board, Sergeant and the Smiths, members of the Board's Global Resource Team, put together their version of a CPM profile.[24] In this version of the CPM profile, there is one distinct variation from Garrison. They list 'signs and wonders' as a characteristic discovered in every CPM studied.[25]

---

[21] Garrison, *Church Planting Movements,* 11-32; Garrison, *God Redeeming a Lost World,* 35-168. See also *Like a Mighty Wave* (videocassette), which gives an overview of several of the movements depicted in Garrison's books.

[22] Garrison, *Church Profile,* 2-3.

[23] Garrison, *Church Planting Movements,* 36.

[24] Curtis Sergeant, "Response: Questions about CPM Profile," electronic letter to R. Bruce Carlton, November 09, 2005. Sergeant, a strategy coordinator who was involved with a church-planting movement in Asia, and the Smiths were part of the Global Resource Team, responsible for providing strategy coordinator training on a global basis as part of New Directions. As Associate vice-President for Strategy Coordination and Mobilization, Garrison served as head of this team.

[25] Curtis Sergeant, William Smith and Susan Smith, *Characteristics of a CPM* (Richmond: by the authors, 1999) [electronic document], 10

While there is complete agreement with Garrison on the first nine characteristics, there is significant departure on the tenth. In Garrison's initial draft, there is no tenth characteristic and in the later booklet a tenth characteristic is listed, but one quite different from 'signs and wonders.' In Garrison's initial draft, he lists 'signs and wonders' as a characteristic often seen in a CPM, yet in the 2000 booklet 'signs and wonders' do not appear at all in the description of these movements. However, by 2004, 'signs and wonders' reappeared in Garrison's list of frequently found characteristics. Table 5 shows the comparison between the lists of universal characteristics developed by Garrison (1999, 2000 and 2004) and the list by Sergeant and the Smiths (1999).

Besides listing universal characteristics of a CPM, Garrison, Sergeant, and the Smiths described characteristics often found in these movements. Table 6 is a comparison of the characteristics often found in a CPM as described by Garrison, Sergeant, and the Smiths. There is some variation between these four CPM profiles, but such variations appear insignificant.

Table 5: Comparison chart of universal characteristics of CPM[26]

Garrison, 1999	Sergeant, Smith and Smith, 1999	Garrison, 2000	Garrison, 2004
Prayer	Prayer	Prayer	Extraordinary prayer
Abundant gospel sowing	Abundant gospel sowing	Abundant gospel sowing	Abundant evangelism
Intentional church planting	Intentional church planting	Intentional church planting	Intentional planting of reproducing churches
Scriptural authority	Scriptural authority	Scriptural authority	Authority of God's Word
Local leadership	Local leadership	Local leadership	Local leadership
Lay leadership	Lay leadership	Lay leadership	Lay leadership
Cell/house churches	Cell or house churches	Cell or house churches	House churches
Churches planting churches	Churches planting churches	Churches planting churches	Churches planting churches
Rapid reproduction	Rapid reproduction	Rapid reproduction	Rapid reproduction
	Signs and wonders	Healthy churches	Healthy churches

What emerged from these lists of universal and frequently found characteristics was a vivid picture of a phenomenon. Garrison, in both his 2000 and 2004 publications, sought to further develop the picture by presenting various case studies of actual movements.[27] While within each of these case studies, one can observe the characteristics of church-planting movements delineated by Garrison. Each movement also shows significant differences in how these characteristics manifested themselves. For example, house or cell

[26] Taken from Garrison, *Church Profile,* 2-3; Sergeant, Smith and Smith, *Characteristics of CPM,* 2-10; Garrison, *Church Planting Movements,* 33-6; Garrison, *God Redeeming a Lost World,* 171-98.

[27] Garrison, *Church Planting Movements,* 11-32; Garrison, *God Redeeming a Lost World,* 35-168.

churches are characteristic in each case study, yet the groups are not mirror images of each other from setting to setting.

Common Hindrances and Practical Handles

Not only did the Board seek to describe the phenomenon of a CPM via listing of the universal and frequently found characteristics, but it also sought to describe various hindrances that impede the emergence of a CPM. At the same time, the Board also presented some practical handles to help strategy coordinators and other missionaries overcome these hindrances. While the definition and characteristics were descriptive of a CPM, the listing of hindrances and handles were more prescriptive in nature.

The listing of hindrances intended to point out that while a CPM is foundationally God's work among a people group, there were things that human beings could do to hinder the emergence of a movement. Garrison asserts, "As with most of God's works among us, He allows us to actively cooperate with Him or become obstacles – consciously or unconsciously – to His desired purposes."[28] Sergeant, and the Smiths add, "Even though we cannot create a Church Planting Movement, we can certainly work to avoid blocking their emergence."[29] Later, Garrison would label those things that hinder a CPM from emerging as the "Seven Deadly Sins."[30] In introducing these seven obstacles or sins, Garrison adds:

> Over the past few years we've discovered more ways to obstruct a Church Planting Movement than we care to recall. But, we've also found a number of ways to overcome these barriers. When Jesus encountered a demon, he exposed it, calling it by name before casting it out. The first step in overcoming obstacles to Church Planting Movements is to name them, and then drag them into the light before casting them out.[31]

[28] Garrison, *Church Planting Movements,* 49.

[29] Sergeant, Smith and Smith, *Characteristics of CPM,* 18.

[30] Garrison, *God Redeeming a Lost World,* 239.

[31] Garrison, *God Redeeming a Lost World,* 239.

Table 6: Comparison chart of characteristics often found in a CPM.[32]

Garrison, 1999	Sergeant, Smith and Smith, 1999	Garrison, 2000	Garrison, 2004
Perceived crisis or vacuum of leadership or spirituality.	Societal crisis or turbulence.	Perceived leadership crisis or spiritual vacuum in society.	A climate of uncertainty in society.
Heart language used in worship.	Heart language used in worship.	Heart language used in worship.	Heart language used in worship.
Price to pay in society to become a Christian.	Persecution and suffering.	A price to pay to become a Christian.	High cost for following Christ.
On-the-job training for church leadership.	On-the-job training for church leadership.	On-the-job training for church leadership.	On-the-job leadership training.
Signs and wonders are evident.	Multiple or shared leadership in churches.	Decentralized leadership.	Divine signs and wonders.
Bi-vocational pastors.	Rapid incorporation of new converts into ministry of church.	Rapid incorporation of new converts into ministry of church.	Rapid incorporation of new believers.
Leadership from the common profile of the people.	Evangelism follows existing relationship lines.	Evangelism has communal implications	Family-based conversion patterns.
Small number of foreign missionaries in relation to local workers.	Outsiders keep a low profile.	Outsiders keep a low profile.	Insulation from outsiders.
Missionaries suffer.	Missionaries suffer.	Missionaries suffer.	Missionaries suffer.
	Passion and fearlessness.	Passion and fearlessness.	Bold fearless faith.

32 Taken from Garrison, *Church Profile,* 3-4; Sergeant, Smith and Smith, *Characteristics of CPM,* 11-8; Garrison, *Church Planting Movements,* 37-40; and Garrison, *God Redeeming a Lost World,* 221-38.

Table 7: Comparison chart of hindrances to CPM[33]

Garrison, 1999	Sergeant, Smith and Smith, 1999	Garrison, 2000	Garrison 2004
Extra-biblical definitions of and requirements for being a church.	Imposing extra-biblical requirements for being a church or a church leader.	Imposing extra-biblical requirements for being a church.	Improving the Bible - extra-biblical requirements for church and leaders.
When becoming a Christian results in the loss of a valued cultural identity.	Non-reproducible church models including subsidies or other support	Loss of a valued cultural identity.	Alien abduction – gospel perceived as foreign, injecting foreign elements.
Overcoming pre-existing patterns of Christianity.		Overcoming bad examples of Christianity.	Unsavoury salt – poor examples of Christianity.
Efforts to contain a CPM within a single denomination.		Planting churches that lack a zeal for pursuing the lost, but expect the lost to come to them. Frog vs. Lizard churches.	Blaming God – when prescriptive strategies do not work, blame God or disregarding where God is at work.
Planting churches that cannot be indigenously reproduced.		Non-reproducible church models	Blurred vision – no vision for a CPM, likely not to happen.
Money feeding into subsidies, pastors' salaries, some institutions, creating dependency.		Subsidies creating dependency.	Devil's Candy – subsidies, ministry as end in itself, and unity as a prerequisite for action.
	Linear, sequential thought and practice.	Linear, sequential thought and practice.	Sequentialism
		Imposing extra-biblical requirements for leadership.	
		Prefabricated methodologies.	

33 Taken from Garrison, *Church Profile,* 4-5; Sergeant, Smith and Smith, *Characteristics of CPM,* 18-21; Garrison, *Church Planting Movements,* 49-52; and Garrison, *God Redeeming a Lost World,* 239-56.

Table 7 is a comparison of the common hindrances found in Garrison's three profiles of a CPM and the profile developed by Sergeant, and the Smiths. Besides seeking to identify the attitudes and activities that missionaries should avoid, Garrison also proposed "practical things that missionaries can do to help initiate or nurture a Church Planting Movement."[34] While Garrison asserts that one cannot manufacture a CPM via the use of prefabricated techniques, he also asserts that there are some practical tools that missionaries can utilize to begin to facilitate a movement among their target population segment or people group.[35] In fact, in *Church Planting Movements,* Garrison stressed that if "missionaries enter a field with a pocket full of answers rather than a heart that is hungry to watch and learn where God is at work and what He is doing, they are limiting His ability to use them."[36] Garrison is also quick to point out that he is not advocating the complete abandonment of strategies, tools and methodologies, but rather is emphasizing the need for "humility and dependence upon God to reveal where and how He chooses to bring about a Church Planting Movement."[37] Table 8 compares the various compilations of these practical handles in Garrison's three profiles of a CPM.

Analysis

The effort to provide a vivid picture of church-planting movements is commendable and serves to help the church better understand this phenomenon. At the same time, the process of listing these characteristics reveals the inevitability of reductionism in translating these movements for those looking in from the outside. A few issues deserve attention.

First, the tenth characteristic described in Garrison's 2000 publication is strikingly similar to the five purposes of the church as described by Warren, pastor of one of the largest Southern Baptist churches in the United States and well-known author.[38] The issue for Warren is not church growth, but church health, and a healthy church is one that operates around the five purposes of worship, fellowship, ministry, evangelism and discipleship. In his 2004 book,

---

[34] Garrison, *Church Planting Movements,* 41.

[35] Garrison, *Church Planting Movements*, 52; Garrison, *God Redeeming a Lost World,* 273, 278.

[36] Garrison, *Church Planting Movements,* 52.

[37] Garrison, *Church Planting Movements,* 52.

[38] See Rick Warren, *The Purpose-Driven Church* (Grand Rapids: Zondervan, 1995), 85-110. Warren's purpose-driven church concept is very popular in the United States and gaining popularity worldwide. The website (www.purposedriven.com) reveals the global influence of this concept.

Garrison refers to Warren's contribution in reminding "the church of a more biblical standard for measuring church health."[39]

Table 8. Prescriptions and practical handles for CPM[40]

Garrison, 1999	Garrison, 2000	Garrison, 2004
A CPM mindset from the onset encapsulated in an end-vision.	Pursue a CPM orientation from the beginning.	A CPM mindset from the onset encapsulated in an end-vision.
Evaluation of every activity in terms of fulfilment of the end-vision.	Evaluation of every activity in terms of fulfilment of the end-vision.	WIGTake – What is it going to take to reach the people group?
No outsiders should be leaders in local churches.	Develop and implement comprehensive strategies.	Live and model the end vision yourself.
POUCH churches – participative Bible study, obedience-based discipleship, unpaid leaders, cell groups and/or house churches.	POUCH churches – participative Bible study, obedience-based discipleship, unpaid leaders, cell groups and/or house churches.	Do a GAP Analysis -Assess your people group according to the ten universal characteristics, ten common characteristics and seven deadly sins.
Passion and sense of urgency that stresses the value of conversion.	Use MAWL cycle for training – model, assist, watch and leave.	Develop strategies to bridge the gaps identified through the analysis.
Shorten the reproductive cycle of a CPM by remembering that discipleship and leadership development is an ongoing process not a stage in development.	Shorten the reproductive cycle of a CPM by remembering that discipleship and leadership development is an ongoing process not a stage in development.	Focus on key ingredients of vision, training, passion, developing co-labourers, and building a system of accountability that ensures all multiply.
Rapidly involve new Christians in ministry.	Gather them, then win them.	
Immediately encourage new believers to evangelize their family.	Employ filter to find those who have responded positively to the gospel.	
Prepare new Christians for persecution.	Prepare new Christians for persecution.	
OTJ training of workers.	OTJ training of workers	
Multiple leaders in churches.	Multiple leaders in churches	

[39] Garrison, *God Redeeming a Lost World,* 197.

[40] Taken from Garrison, *Church Profile,* 5-6; Garrison, *Church Planting Movements,* 41-4 and 53-6; and Garrison, *God Redeeming a Lost World,* 277-95.

Every house church leader given authority; no centralized church hierarchy.	Raise expectations and church planting responsibilities of new believers.	
Abundant evangelism.		
Fearlessness and boldness.		

In the 1999 profile draft, Garrison notes, "It is important at this point to remain as value-neutral as possible and faithfully describe what is seen in these works of God." By adding the tenth characteristic a year later, was Garrison remaining value-neutral and authentically describing a characteristic observed in every CPM or was he projecting a popular Western understanding of healthy church onto these movements? Garrison states that when news of these movements began to filter in from the field, various constituents – Board leaders, Board trustees, other Southern Baptists – questioned the validity of these reports, often assuming that rapid growth rate indicated unhealthy churches. The addition of this tenth characteristic was in response to those who questioned the legitimacy of the churches emerging in these movements.[41]

On the other hand, Warren claims to derive his five purposes from the New Testament (see Acts 2: 42-7). Therefore, was Garrison simply borrowing Warren's language to describe a New Testament-like church, which he observed in these movements? Garrison claims that all the missionaries involved in church-planting movements with whom he talked affirmed that churches within these movements expressed the five purposes.[42]

Second, the issue surrounding the appearance, disappearance and re-appearance of 'signs and wonders' warrants attention. In Garrison's 1999 draft, he lists 'signs and wonders' as a characteristic often found in these movements. Garrison describes what he means by 'signs and wonders' as follows:

> This is not the same as glossalalia or Pentecostalism. Typically, individuals involved in church-planting movements lived with a sense of expectancy that God was intimately involved in the work of His people and churches. This sense of God's activity overcomes the spiritual powers that plagued the worldview of the

[41] V. David Garrison, "Response: Healthy Churches," electronic letter to R. Bruce Carlton, November 09, 2005. In a conversation between Garrison, my wife Gloria and me in Bangkok, Thailand (2002), we asked him about this issue. He stated that in the official publication by the Board he needed to be sensitive to the constituency for which he was writing; i.e., Southern Baptists. I later wrote to Garrison seeking clarification. The email message cited is Garrison's reply to my inquiry. The rationale given for not including 'healthy churches' in the initial draft profile (1999) simply was that the profile was a work in progress, and the publication of the final version a year later was the result of a natural process in the development of a book.

[42] Garrison, "Response: Healthy Churches,"

> people prior to their salvation. Occasionally this divine involvement took the shape of vision, signs, healings, exorcisms, etc.[43]

In the 2000 Board publication, Garrison does not list 'signs and wonders.' However, in his 2004 book, not published by the Board, they reappear as characteristics often found in these movements.

As noted above the Smiths and Sergeant assert in their version of the CPM profile that 'signs and wonders' appeared in every movement studied. They state:

> In every Church Planting Movement which was examined, signs and wonders played a part. In some cases it was through dreams and visions, in some cases through healings, and in some other miscellaneous miracles or power encounters. In any case, the power of God was manifest in supernatural ways and people responded in faith and were incorporated into new churches.[44]

Sergeant claims that the larger Global Resource Team approved this version of the profile that provided the outline for Garrison's booklet.[45]

With 'signs and wonders' included in Garrison's 1999 profile and also in the latter version developed by the Smiths and Sergeant, why did they then disappear in the Board's 2000 *Church Planting Movements* publication? Were Garrison and the Board violating the claim of value-neutrality by such an omission? Does such an omission indicate a projection of a specific theological persuasion onto the CPM phenomenon rather than a simple description of the facts?[46]

The primary reason for asking these questions is to demonstrate the immense difficulty one faces when translating the fundamental nature of these movements to outsiders. Such a translation process does not take place within a vacuum, but rather within a distinct organizational and denominational culture.

---

[43] Garrison, *Church Profile,* 3.

[44] Sergeant, Smith and Smith, *Characteristics of CPM,* 10.

[45] Sergeant, "Response: Question about CPM Profile."

[46] In the same conversation my wife Gloria and I had with Garrison in Bangkok (2002), we raised this issue. We inquired as to why signs and wonders were not included in the Board's 2000 publication. Garrison's reply was that listing signs and wonders might not play too well with Southern Baptists. Further, he added, others had addressed the same issue to him. Sergeant in "Response: Question about CPM Profile," corroborates that he also questioned Garrison about the changes. According to Sergeant, Garrison responded that the Board likely would have not approved publication of the book if it included signs and wonders. Some Southern Baptists assert that signs and wonders are no longer relevant. Other Southern Baptists associate signs and wonders with the charismatic, Pentecostal movement. Thus, they might object to these being included in the Board's publication.

This culture of the Board, in particular, and Southern Baptists, in general, did influence this process of describing these movements.

Guder asserts that "the core of the church's missiological problem has always been the temptation to reduce the gospel to a manageable size."[47] The church, in seeking to translate the gospel, inevitably reduces the message in a variety of ways. The reduction of the gospel message stems from the desire of the church to control and manage the message, thus leading the church to shape the gospel into its mould rather than allowing it to continually convert the church.[48] One problem that emerges is this desire to control can lead the church to accept its reductions of the gospel as absolute truth.[49]

The CPM profile delineated by Garrison, endorsed and published by the Board, reduced these church-planting movements to a simple list of characteristics. Generating a list of universal characteristics, in a sense, led the Board to accept these reductions as absolute truth. For example, Garrison states, "Any missionary intent on seeing a Church Planting Movement should consider these 10 elements."[50] He goes on to add that the absence of some of these characteristics "may result in aborted movements."[51] Later, Garrison would assert that one should learn and apply the universal characteristics of a CPM because they "are invaluable to anyone wishing to align themselves with the way God is at work."[52] While Garrison claims that church-planting movements are not a mechanical process achieved through prefabricated techniques,[53] the implication in these statements is clear: these ten universal characteristics describe fully how God is at work through these church-planting movements, and the way to align one's life and ministry with God is through the application of these characteristics. To do otherwise is to be misaligned with the way God is working.

The issue is not that these descriptions are inaccurate, but that what remains is not enough. Although this reductionism is unavoidable, there is danger if the Board holds these characteristics as the only valid descriptions of these

---

47 Guder, *Conversion of the Church,* 188.

48 Guder, *Conversion of the Church,* 190.

49 Guder, *Conversion of the Church,* 100. Having served as a strategy coordinator and a trainer of strategy coordinators for the IMB, I personally have been involved in training aimed at equipping personnel with principles and tools aimed at facilitating a church-planting movement among their targeted population segment. I have utilized many of these characteristics of a CPM in the *Acts 29 Training: Practical Training In Facilitating Church-Planting Movements Among The Neglected Harvest Fields* (Singapore: by the author, 2003). Thus, I have contributed to this reductionism.

50 Garrison, *Church Planting Movements,* 33.

51 Garrison, *Church Planting Movements,* 53.

52 Garrison, *God Redeeming a Lost World,* 172.

53 Garrison, *God Redeeming a Lost World,* 273; Garrison, *Church Planting Movements,* 52.

movements. Further, this issue points to the probability that the organization, in the translation process, was seeking to shape the understanding of these movements according to the organization's and Southern Baptist's missiological assumptions as opposed to simply seeking to comprehensively describe the phenomenon regardless of whether or not such descriptions fit within the parameters of their missiology.

While the listing of universal and frequently found characteristics points to the inevitability of reductionism, the delineation of hindrances and practical handles demonstrates the temptation to move beyond objective description towards prescriptive methodologies. In Garrison's 1999 draft profile, he lists fourteen prescriptive strategies designed to help one stimulate and nurture a CPM.[54] These fourteen prescriptive strategies would emerge in the 2000 booklet as practical handles and suggested courses of action that could contribute to a CPM.[55] Both the avoidance of specific actions that could hinder a movement and the advocacy of specific actions that could foster a movement have strong prescriptive overtones. There is obvious tension between offering these prescriptive ideas and practical tools while, at the same time, warning against the danger of approaching the task with prefabricated methodologies.[56] The fact that Garrison warns against the danger of prefabricated techniques indicates an awareness of this tension.

There is strong evidence that indicates the acceptance within the Board of these characteristics as normative in assessing a missionary's work and progress toward the emergence of a CPM. Steve Evans, a missionary with the Board, developed a computer-based CPM assessment tool based on the universal characteristics, the frequently found characteristics and the

---

[54] Garrison, *Church Profile,* 5-6.

[55] Garrison, *Church Planting Movements,* 41-4 and 53-6.

[56] In the *Acts 29* training, which I implemented throughout South Asia and other parts of the world for the IMB from 2000-5, there are strong prescriptive overtones in the sessions on the characteristics and obstacles to church-planting movements. See Carlton, *Acts 29,* 223-51. These two sessions are designed to lead participants to evaluate their present work by identifying which characteristics and obstacles are present, implying that one can stimulate a church-planting movement by avoiding specific actions that hinder a movement and intentionally carrying out other specific actions based on the characteristics. Like Garrison, Sergeant and the Smiths, I, too, warned against the dangers of thinking that one could manufacture a CPM while, at the same time, advocating for specific prescriptive actions. In reality, I structured the entire training around these characteristics and obstacles. In reviewing the training materials, I now understand more clearly the delicate line between prescribing specific actions that might stimulate a movement and prefabricated techniques and methods designed to manufacture one.

obstacles.[57] The assessment tool allows one to rate the evidence of each of the characteristics on a scale of one to ten (one is the lowest and ten the highest) as well as the evidence of the obstacles (one being the highest and ten the lowest). After entering in the numbers for each characteristic, the program will then automatically generate a graph giving one a visual picture of the progress or lack of progress in stimulating a CPM.

Garrison offers a similar assessment process for missionary teams, which he asserts will assist them to "align your community with the ways God is at work in Church Planting Movements."[58] These tools seek to help missionaries analyze the gaps, which, according to Garrison, "lets *your community speak to you,* and tells you where change needs to occur in order to align with Church Planting Movement principles."[59] The Global Research Department of the Board developed a thorough guide for assessing reported church-planting movements.[60] As one scans through the assessment guide, the influence of Garrison's characteristics and obstacles is evident. All these tools, while having the potential to assist missionaries in their work, utilize a reductionist view of church-planting movements, and, therefore, one must understand this when employing such tools. Further, one must be careful in believing that simply filling in the gaps identified will result in the development of a church-planting movement. Just as having all the elements will not necessarily lead to a church-planting movement, so the absence of some elements does not automatically exclude a movement from being a church-planting movement. Misuse of these evaluative tools can easily lead to church-planting movements reduced to a mechanized process, the very danger Garrison and others warn against.

A New Church Model

The delineation of the characteristics of these movements coupled with the obstacles and practical handles helped to create a major missiological shift within the Board. This shift centred on the church-planting model. Having recognized that within church-planting movements the typical church model was a house or small group, the Board began to intentionally promote this model of church planting around the world. Within this house church model the emphasis is on unpaid, lay leadership, participative worship and Bible study, and obedience-based discipleship.[61] Missionaries involved with these

[57] See Appendix G. Evans stated that he developed this assessment while in residence at the home office, sometime between 2000 and 2003.

[58] Garrison, *God Redeeming a Lost World,* 283.

[59] Garrison, *God Redeeming a Lost World,* 285. Emphasis is Garrison's.

[60] See Appendix H.

[61] This model is the POUCH model, initially expounded by Sergeant and later described in Garrison, *Church Planting Movements,* 43. POUCH simply means participative Bible study, obedience-based discipleship, unpaid leaders, cell groups, and house churches.

movements recognized that the house model was easier to reproduce and did not require any outside funding, thus a much simpler model to emulate. This church model contrasts sharply with the traditional IMB and Southern Baptist model, which typically emphasized full-time, paid pastors and church buildings. The CPM emphasis considers full-time, paid pastors and buildings as extra-biblical and non-indigenous, thus a hindrance to the rapid multiplication of church. According to Rankin, "Subsidy propagates a Western model of a church that sees a building and a paid pastor as essential rather than encouraging a reproducible Biblical model of the church as gathered believers responsible to and for their own leadership and facilities."[62]

The house church model did stimulate a healthy return to a more Biblical understanding of church. The New Testament portrays the church as a community (organic) as opposed to an institution (cf. Rom. 12: 4-5; 1 Cor. 3: 9; 12: 12-27; 1 Tim. 3: 15; 1 Pet. 2: 4-10). Mays points out that the church in the West has held to a view of church moulded along the lines of Christendom, and through the years the church often has focused more on the institutionalization of the church, almost becoming blind to the concept of church-as-community.[63] In church-planting movements, not only did strategy coordinators discover they more easily and rapidly reproduced, but they also discovered that genuine community was more apt to develop in smaller, organic groups of disciples who centred their lives and community in Jesus Christ. Garrison states it in this way, "When the church left the home it left something vital behind: intimate contact with every facet of daily life."[64] The house church model does not necessarily lead to a lack of organization within the church, but it is a more natural organization in contrast with the institutional concept.[65]

During 2004-5, I have been involved in training new IMB missionaries during their orientation sessions held before their departure to the field. For several years, the missionary orientation process has emphasized this house church model. New missionaries gather in small groups to experience house church worship frequently during their seven-week orientation session. The style of worship is participative, and the new missionaries learn an obedience-based, inductive Bible study method for use in their house church experience. The strategy coordinator training led by the Smiths from their base in Singapore emphasizes this same model. The *Acts 29* training, which I have conducted over the past six years, also teaches a similar house church model called the "Open House Church." See Carlton, *Acts 29*, 25-7.

[62] Jerry A. Rankin, ""Rankin File: Help that hurts," *The Commission* (August 1997), 53.

[63] Patrick Mays, "After Christendom, What? Renewal and Discovery of Church and Mission in the West," *Missiology* 27, No. 2 (April 1999): 246.

[64] Garrison, *God Redeeming a Lost World*, 214.

[65] See Roland Allen, "The Family Rite," in *Reform of the Ministry: A Study in the Work of Roland Allen*, ed. David Paton (London: Lutterworth Press, 1968), 191-219. Allen's thinking about church altered over the years, and this article is a vivid description of his

However, what began as an effort to describe a model of church predominant within these movements and an effort to help missionaries develop a healthier, Biblical understanding of church quickly shifted to a prescriptive methodology for church planting. The prescribing of the house church model as normative for IMB missionaries demonstrates reductionism in much the same way as reducing the CPM phenomenon to a list of characteristics, hindrances and practical handles. Guder warns, "We need to accept the fact that the maintenance of particular organizational expressions of the mission community is not the priority of our vocation to be Christ's witness."[66] Further, he reminds the church "that a diversity of institutional and organizational forms of mission community is both biblically and historically validated."[67] Whether an institutional model (building and full-time pastor) or house church model, the danger lies in projecting a specific model or structure as the normative expression of the church. While Guder is challenging the large, institutional ecclesiastical structures so predominant in Western culture, his warning is just as valid for those who advocate for the house model as normative. The house church can become just as institutionalized as any other organizational form of church.

The Board recognized church-planting movements as the multiple, reproduction of indigenous churches sweeping through a population segment or area, a spontaneous expansion occurring "when God unleashes His Spirit through the power of the gospel."[68] These movements are genuine expressions of the growth of God's kingdom. While it is important to recognize and learn from what is happening in these movements, there is the danger of quenching this spontaneous expression by becoming overly prescriptive with specific methodologies and church models. If the Board and its missionaries do not recognize this danger, these church-planting movements may easily lose their dynamism as missionaries and others exert control, intentionally or not, over the church-planting model. Further, there is the danger of violating the indigenous principle if outsiders impose a specific organizational form of church, regardless of what form that might be.[69]

---

thinking of the differences between the smaller, house church model and the institutional church as he knew it.

66 Guder, *Conversion of the Church,* 199.

67 Guder, *Conversion of the Church,* 198.

68 Jerry A. Rankin, "Rankin File: Difficult to believe?" *The Commission* (May-June 2003), 55.

69 See Guder, *Conversion of the Church,* 146-7. Guder asserts that every community of Christ takes on some tangible structure. At the same time, he believes that this structure should look different from place to place. He suggests various models of the church structure that might emerge in different settings. What is key, according to Guder, is that we realize there is no universal, normative way to organize these communities.

CPM and the SC Paradigm

With the emergence of the CPM phenomenon, the Board recognized the critical role of the strategy coordinator within many of these movements. Bridges reported, "At a mission conference in Asia involving Christians from many countries, a participant shook his head and said, 'Every time I try to track down what's going on in one of these church-planting movements, I find at the end of the string there's a strategy coordinator.'"[70] By 2003, the Board affirmed its commitment to "the empowerment of field-based strategy coordinators who lead teams in the development and implementation of comprehensive strategies to begin and nurture Church Planting Movements."[71] At the same time, the emergence of the CPM phenomenon significantly altered the SC paradigm.

Key Philosophical Shifts in the SC Paradigm

During Stroope's tenure as area director for CSI, the SC paradigm matured yet also faced the danger of stagnation resulting from institutionalization. The "Re-dreaming the Dream" conference held in February 1996 was an effort to maintain the vitality of the paradigm and CSI. Stroope and others within CSI had realized that the paradigm's survival depended on its ability to change, thus the call to re-dream the dream. At about the time of this conference, the CPM phenomenon emerged onto the scene. CPM and the paradigm's ability to adjust and change in response to it helped the paradigm to recapture some of its dynamism.

When the NRM paradigm arrived on the scene of Southern Baptist mission efforts in 1986, it marked the advent of a new trend in missions for the Board. Garrison's 1990 book *The Non-residential Missionary* presented the new paradigm to the public. A little over ten years later, the paradigm would undergo some significant changes, primarily as the result of the CPM phenomenon. In a short document intended to highlight some of the significant changes, Sergeant wrote:

> As I sit down to write this, it is 1999, less than a decade after the introduction of the Non-residential Missionary (NRM) concept to the public. Even though the years have been few, the changes to the concept have been great. There have been spin-offs such as People Specific Advocates and People Group Advocates. There have been name changes, the most common name now being Strategy Coordinator (SC). But, more importantly, some of the basic underlying presuppositions have changed.[72]

[70] Bridges, "ANALYSIS: Strategy Coordinator."

[71] "Board of Trustees Minutes," November 10, 2003.

[72] Curtis Sergeant, *NRM to SC: What's Changed* (Singapore: Global Training Center, 1999) [electronic document], 1.

Sergeant listed four major philosophical shifts in the paradigm that he had identified. First, Sergeant stated that within the NRM paradigm a primary emphasis centred on creating access for Christian workers among an unreached people group; however, the emphasis was now on creating access for the gospel message.[73] Garrison expressed the earlier concept of establishing Christian presence, stating, "To be effective in its goal of evangelism and church planting, each non-residential ministry must identify opportunities to foster a witnessing Christian presence among the population target."[74] According to Sergeant, access by Christian workers does not guarantee gospel witness or necessarily lead to a CPM because often "when people become preoccupied with maintaining their presence, they are not likely to be bold in their witness."[75] Therefore, the issue is assuring a people group's access to the gospel more than personal access by missionaries.

The second shift identified by Sergeant was that the SC should see his or her primary role as catalyzing local believers to complete the evangelization of their own people instead of a channel for outside resources.[76] The significant difference here is the emphasis on local resources as opposed to outside ones. In describing the NRM approach, Garrison stated, "By using every possible Christian contact, rather than a single, limited evangelistic contact, the non-residential missionary is able to catalyze hundreds – and even thousands – of agents in a concerted effort to serve a specific population segment."[77] Garrison further added, "Non-residential missionaries are gospel 'redistribution agents'" pleading "the case of their people before the world court of Christian conscience."[78] For Sergeant, the emphasis had changed, and it was now one of "starting work in such a way that very soon the work will be accelerated and carried to completion by local believers….the resources are in the harvest."[79] Smith calls the discovery that the resources are in the harvest (the local believers) as the principal strength of the SC paradigm in relation to church-planting movements because it recognizes that "all the ESSENTIAL ingredients to see a people group reached reside within that people group."[80]

The shift of emphasis from planting beachhead churches to facilitating a church-planting movement is the third philosophical shift identified by Sergeant.[81] When the NRM paradigm emerged, the emphasis within the Board

[73] Sergeant, *NRM to SC,* 1.
[74] Garrison, *Non-residential Missionary,* 18.
[75] Sergeant, *NRM to SC,* 1.
[76] Sergeant, *NRM to SC,* 1.
[77] Garrison, *Non-residential Missionary,* 15.
[78] Garrison, *Non-residential Missionary,* 43.
[79] Sergeant, *NRM to SC,* 1.
[80] Smith, "Additional Document."
[81] Sergeant, *NRM to SC,* 1. See Glossary for definitions of beachhead church and CPM.

was evangelism that results in churches. Until the emergence of the CPM phenomenon, this goal remained the same. Whether through the NRM role or another role, the Board expected missionaries to plant churches that eventually would be "capable of pursuing Christ independent of foreign efforts."[82] The shift identified by Sergeant took the goal one step further toward catalyzing "church-planting movements with enough momentum that they will saturate their own people group with reproducing churches and become a missionary people themselves, joining in the task of world evangelization."[83] To just be independent of foreign influence and resources was no longer sufficient, but the churches must be reproducing and missionary churches in their own right.

According to Sergeant, "The NRM assumption was that the task was so large that it would take a lifetime before significant breakthroughs would result in an unreached people group."[84] Garrison confirmed this assumption, stating:

> Because the non-residential missionary's task is a dynamic one, there is literally no end to the cycle of studying the situation and resources, devising and implementing new evangelization strategies, monitoring results and refining methods. At the end of each cycle is the beginning of a new, deeper and more extensive array of evangelization efforts.[85]

With the emergence of church-planting movements, the emphasis with the SC paradigm shifted toward developing an exit strategy. Such an exit strategy was built on the belief that as local churches planted among a people group began to reproduce and multiply, the missionary needed to step aside in order to allow those churches to complete the missionary task among their own people. "The assumption," according to Sergeant, "is that they can tackle another target group after getting the work well begun in their first one."[86]

These four shifts, on the surface, may seem to be subtle changes. However, by challenging some of the primary presuppositions of the NRM/SC paradigm, Sergeant and others were plotting a course that would significantly alter the future development of the paradigm over the next few years. The Smiths, who along with Sergeant implemented SC training throughout many areas of the Board for several years after the launching of New Directions, charted some of the significant changes resulting from this philosophical shift. Table 9 shows the comparison between what Smith calls the old paradigm and the new.

While some of these changes were positive, other changes are a result of the reductionism and institutionalization of the CPM phenomenon by the Board.

---

[82] Garrison, *Non-residential Missionary,* 16.

[83] Sergeant, *NRM to SC,* 1.

[84] Sergeant, *NRM to SC,* 1.

[85] Garrison, *Non-residential Missionary,* 19.

[86] Sergeant, *NRM to SC,* 1.

On the one hand, the CPM phenomenon helped the SC paradigm retain its vitality, and helped to propel the Board to alter its missiology in light of the changing realities in the world. At the same time, the reductionism of the CPM phenomenon and the rapid rate at which the Board moved toward institutionalizing it threaten to rob the paradigm of its rediscovered vitality.

One of the most significant changes charted by Smith centres on the change from embracing and encouraging innovation toward learning and implementing proven methods. The NRM/SC paradigm was an innovative paradigm that, although it encountered much resistance and opposition from many within the Board, exerted a strong influence on the Board's missiology. The move away from innovation and toward the implementation of specific methodologies, which had been instrumental in a CPM in a particular setting, is a step toward turning CPM into a mechanical process. Several times in Smith's comparison, he refers to the emphasis on implementing methodologies that have proven to be effective in facilitating church-planting movements. In doing so, Smith asserts, such tools and methods help strategy coordinators "connect the dots" and move toward a CPM.[87]

Garrison, reflecting back on the weaknesses and strengths of the NRM/SC paradigm, acknowledged that an emphasis on innovation created a wide spectrum of possibilities in terms of the evangelization of unreached people groups, yet, on the other hand, "made us vulnerable to experimentation as an end in itself (something that still plagues pre-CPM practitioners)."[88] Stressing the need to learn and implement proven CPM methodologies, Garrison adds, "In the current Church-Planting Movement paradigm, those who are effective practitioners know so much more about what is possible, what works, and what doesn't."[89]

Garrison has recently initiated an effort to create a Best Practices Institute, which will seek "to provide Christ's servants with tested and proven tools, resources and insights that will help stimulate and nurture Church-Planting Movements around the world."[90] The Best Practices Institute that Garrison is

---

87 Smith, "Additional Document."

88 Garrison, "Response to Bruce."

89 Garrison, "Response to Bruce."

90 V. David Garrison, *Board of Directors* (India: by the author, 2005) [electronic document], 1. The concept of "Best Practices" is term often used in the business world to describe the best possible way to do something. In "Best Practices," the concept of benchmarking is common. A benchmark is "something that serves as a standard by which others may be measured or judged" (Merriam-Webster's Collegiate Dictionary, 2004). For more information on the use of "Best Practices" in business, see the website http://bpinsitute.net and *Best Practices in Leadership Development and Organization Change: How the Best Companies Ensure Meaningful Change and Sustainable Leadership*, ed. Louis Carter, David Ulrich, and Marshall Goldsmith (San Francisco: Pfeiffer, 2005).

launching will benchmark only methods that have demonstrated effectiveness in facilitating church-planting movements.[91] Table 9 also demonstrates the benchmarking of methodologies identified as leading to reproducing churches as one of the changes in the SC paradigm. While seeking to learn from the methods and work of others who have been a part of a church-planting movement is important, the Board must be careful not to become overly prescriptive in this effort. A review of the case studies presented in Garrison's 2000 and 2004 publications, respectively, reveals the uniqueness of every church-planting movement described. It is true, that many of the characteristics of a CPM as delineated by Garrison are evident in all of these case studies. At the same time, the methodologies employed by various strategy coordinators, missionaries and others involved in these movements vary from people group to people group and place to place. The Board must be proactive in continuing to encourage innovation while, at the same time, helping strategy coordinators learn from those who have been involved in these movements. If innovation is completely discouraged at the expense of just implementing the methods of others that have proven to be effective in a particular setting, the Board runs the risk of further reducing church-planting movements to a handful of specific methodologies.

Table 9: Strategy Coordinator: old and new paradigm[92]

Old Paradigm	New Paradigm
Innovation: Initially, it was important to try many new things to find out what would work. Innovation was encouraged in order to discover what might work.	**Productivity:** Although still discovering innovative methods, there are now many principles and practices that have proven effective. Emphasis is now on implementing methods that worked before.
Try everything and see what works: Being busy doing many things, whether necessarily effective or not, was encouraged and rewarded.	**Focus on what has worked:** Busyness, per se, no longer recognized as valid. Focus on what is proven effective. Emphasize the critical path to end vision.
Mobilize using a mirror: Emphasis was on mobilizing resources from the missionary's home or near neighbour country/culture.	**Mobilize using a yardstick:** Emphasis is on mobilizing resources closest to the unreached people group that can most effectively have an

[91] V. David Garrison, "Best Practices Institute," electronic letter to South Asia Regional Leadership Team, November 22, 2005; V. David Garrison, "Response to BP Site," electronic letter to South Asia Regional Leadership Team, December 06, 2005. See Garrison, *God Redeeming a Lost World,* 307-30 for a few examples of benchmark methodologies that Garrison mentions in his November 22, 2005, electronic letter, which he seeks to include in his Best Practices Institute.

[92] Adapted from Smith, "Additional Document."

	impact on the group.
Platforms: Assumed that complex platforms would need to be established and maintained in order to establish Christian worker presence.	**Proclamation:** Experience demonstrated that there are no 'closed' countries. Christian witness is possible in any environment. Presence does not equal proclamation. Protecting a platform is secondary to having opportunity and boldness for proclamation.
This is a good idea: Any new idea assumed to be 'good' to try.	**This seems to work all over the world:** Important ideas are those shown to be effective in multiple settings.
Give me ideas: In exploring all possible avenues to find what might work, 'brainstorming' was a high value activity.	**Give me tools:** Having practical tools for implementing what has demonstrated effectiveness is the high value activity that moves toward the end vision.
Research: Information on people groups was limited. Additional information was necessary in order to devise plans that might be effective in reaching them.	**Relationships:** While there is always more to know about a people group, the relevant information is now largely available. In order to have an impact on a people group **WHO** you know is now more important than **WHAT** you know.
Widespread seed sowing: Broadly spreading the Gospel in order to provide 'access' to the message was the goal.	**Getting to church immediately:** Rapidly multiplying churches are now the goal and provide self-sustaining access to the gospel throughout a people group.
Emphasis on principles and theory: An assumption that with principles and theory, the SC would be able to 'connect the dots to plan and implement an appropriate strategy.	**Emphasis on hands on learning and practical skills needed to see church-planting movements:** Proven, effective tools used to help SC personnel 'connect the dots' and to do what is needed to produce church-planting movements.

Smith also identified another one of the changes in the paradigm as a shift away from principles and theory to more of an emphasis on learning the practical skills. Practical skills are as important in mission work and church planting as in other occupations; however, the Board again must strike a balance. The Board is walking down a treacherous path if it simply seeks to reduce church-planting movements to methods.

Escobar refers to this tendency as "managerial missiology."[93] This

[93] Samuel Escobar, "Evangelical missiology: peering into the future at the turn of the century," in *Global Missiology for the 21st Century: The Iguassu Dialogue,* ed. William D. Taylor (Grand Rapids: Baker Academic, 2000), 109. A major proponent of what Escobar calls "managerial missiology" is the church growth movement. This movement

managerial missiology, according to Escobar, has a "pragmatic approach to the task, which deemphasizes theological problems, takes for granted the existence of adequate content, and consequently majors in methods."[94] Such a methodology, he asserts, rests upon a reductionist foundation because it reduces mission to quantitative growth, and "anything that would hinder it has to be eliminated."[95] By reducing church-planting movements to a quantifiable list of characteristics, by making these movements or rapidly multiplying churches as the benchmark for strategy coordinators, and by discouraging innovation for the sake of implementing only those methods that have demonstrated success in nurturing these movements, the Board is slipping into a managerial missiology.

Again, what is important to stress here is not that these methods are wrong or that others should not benefit from learning from many of these 'best practices." However, the issue is the danger of reductionism. The Board needs to heed Guder's warning regarding the danger of reductionism:

> Reductionism is at work when we as human witnesses are no longer aware of our own reductions of the gospel. It is present when we argue a supreme authority or rightness or a finality to our formulations. A reductionist view assigns an authority to a reduction that ends up making it into a distortion.[96]

The Board must be careful in benchmarking specific methodologies that it does not present these methods as guarantees for facilitating a church-planting movement. As Garrison states, "God's work isn't mechanical or magical."[97] It appears paradoxical to benchmark specific methodologies that help strategy coordinators connect the dots in order to facilitate a church-planting movement, while, at the same time, making the disclaimer that connecting the dots will not guarantee a church-planting movement.

While there is danger in the reductionism and institutionalization of church-planting movements, there are some positive changes within the SC paradigm resulting from the CPM phenomenon. Sergeant's analysis of the changes in the SC paradigm and Table 9 highlight a few of these positive changes.

As the new paradigm emerged within the Board, NRM/SC personnel focused on the mobilization of GCC resources with the assumption that most of these resources would come from either the missionary's home culture or a neighbouring culture of the unreached people group. One of the lessons learned

---

has strongly influenced many of the Board's leaders and mission strategists. The Board's benchmarking of specific, proven CPM methodologies further reveals the impact of this movement on the Board's missiology.

[94] Escobar, "Evangelical missiology," 110.

[95] Escobar, "Evangelical missiology," 111.

[96] Guder, *Conversion of the Church,* 101.

[97] Garrison, *God Redeeming a Lost World,* 273.

from the CPM phenomenon is the concept that the resources are in the harvest. In other words, SC personnel discovered that the mobilization of resources closest to or from within the people group itself were the most effective. Added to this was the discovery that the planting of indigenous churches with the ability to multiply resulted in a self-sustaining gospel witness capable of continuing the evangelization of the people group.

Further, as both Smith and Sergeant have revealed, simply having a physical presence of Christians among an unreached people group does not guarantee a proclamation of the gospel message. While NRM/SC personnel demonstrated effectiveness in being able to secure presence within many of the restrictive environments where these unreached peoples resided, what often resulted was an overemphasis on protecting one's presence at the expense of proclaiming the gospel message. However, a number of strategy coordinators discovered responsiveness among some of these unreached peoples. This discovery of responsiveness among unreached peoples generally considered unresponsive, has led to an emphasis on access to the gospel message not just access for missionaries. Proclamation must always accompany presence.

The shift toward developing an exit perspective is a healthy change in the paradigm. By beginning one's work with a clear exit strategy, the belief is that the SC will work in such a way as to facilitate local believers to assume the leadership of their own churches as well as to facilitate the local churches to assume responsibility for the evangelization of their own people group. Willis identified one of the weaknesses of the Board's mission efforts as missionaries' failure to pass on the mission vision and passion to the churches they have planted in their mission fields.[98] The emphasis on an exit perspective is a hopeful shift to remedy this past failure.

The Missing Ingredient: The Holy Spirit

Church-planting movements are genuine. The Board has documented numerous movements. These movements are the result of the Holy Spirit moving throughout a people group. A few strategy coordinators, seeking to find ways to penetrate unreached people groups with the gospel, discovered God's Spirit at work in ways previously unimagined. These few strategy coordinators have also discovered there are things that they can do to either help or hinder these movements. Others can learn from the successes and failures of these strategy coordinators who had firsthand experience with these movements.

However, the Board runs the real risk of quenching the work of the Holy Spirit by reducing church-planting movements to a set of characteristics and

---

[98] Avery T. Willis, Jr., "The Unfinished Task," in *Missiology: An Introduction to the Foundations, History, and Strategies of World Missions,* eds. John Mark Terry, Ebbie Smith and Justice Anderson (Nashville: Broadman and Holman, 1998), 682.

specific methodologies. Burrows laments the fact that, for the most part, missiologists have tended to neglect the person and role of the Holy Spirit in mission.[99] In reviewing much of what Southern Baptists say and write about church-planting movements, the Holy Spirit receives scant attention.[100]

An integral part of the SC paradigm is *missio Dei*, recognizing God as the initiator and the end of mission. Further, the SC paradigm's evangelical roots reveal a firm belief that Jesus is the message of mission. Yet, the third aspect of mission – the Holy Spirit as the implementer of and power behind mission – appears lacking.[101] Shenk reminds us that "God's redemptive mission cannot be understood apart from the role of the Holy Spirit."[102] Moreau, Corwin and McGee assert that the Holy Spirit "is the agent who empowers Christians for

---

[99] William R. Burrows, "A Seventh Paradigm? Catholics and Radical Inculturation," in *Mission in Bold Humility,* eds. Willem Saayman and Klippies Kritzinger (Maryknoll: Orbis, 1996), 128.

[100] In Garrison, *Church Planting Movements,* there is only direct reference to the Holy Spirit and this is in the penultimate paragraph of the book. In Garrison, *God Redeeming a Lost World,* there is still scant attention paid to the role of the Holy Spirit in these church-planting movements, although a few paragraphs do focus on one aspect of the work of the Holy Spirit; i.e., signs and wonders. Noticing this lack of acknowledgement to the work of the Holy Spirit in these movements, I developed an alternative definition, which stressed that a church-planting movement was a "Holy Spirit-controlled process." A review of articles on CPM produced by the Board and various reports of Board leaders further reveals a general tendency to neglect the role of the Holy Spirit in these movements.

[101] In recent years, there has been a call from many within the evangelical community to rediscover a Trinitarian missiology. Leslie Newbigin is one of the most noted Trinitarian missiologists. See Newbigin, *The Open Secret: An Introduction to the Theology of Mission,* revised edition (Grand Rapids: Eerdmans Publishing, 1995). See also Thomas F. Foust and others, eds. *A Scandalous Prophet: The Way of Mission after Newbigin,* (Grand Rapids: Eerdmans Publishing, 2002), 57-91 and *Global Missiology for the 21st Century: The Iguassu Dialogue,* ed. William D. Taylor (Grand Rapids: Baker Academic, 2000, 189-256. For a brief presentation of a Southern Baptist view of the role of the Trinity in mission, see G. William Schweer, "The Missionary Mandate of God's Nature," in *Missiology: An Introduction to the Foundations, History, and Strategies of World Missions,* eds. John Mark Terry, Ebbie Smith and Justice Anderson (Nashville: Broadman and Holman, 1998), 97-113.

[102] Wilbert R. Shenk, *Changing Frontiers of Mission,* American Society of Missiology Studies, no. 28 (Maryknoll: Orbis Books, 1999), 14. See also Alan Roxburgh, "Rethinking Trinitarian Missiology," in *Global Missiology for the 21st Century: The Iguassu Dialogue,* ed. William D. Taylor (Grand Rapids: Baker Academic, 2000), 179-88; and Ajith Fernando, "The Holy Spirit: The Divine Implementer of Mission," in *Global Missiology for the 21st Century: The Iguassu Dialogue,* ed. William D. Taylor (Grand Rapids: Baker Academic, 2000), 223-38.

mission and makes mission work possible for the church."[103] Schweer points out that the New Testament shows "how vital the activities of the Holy Spirit are in missionary expansion."[104] The following statement by Kuitse summarizes the relationship between Father, Son and Holy Spirit in mission:

> The good news is embodied in one person, living at a certain time and in a certain place. The good news about God's loving concern for the world is good news for all people at all times and places. Therefore, the good news has to reach to others and be told to others living in other times and places. It is the Spirit who, via mission, brings the good news embodied in the one to the many. It is the Spirit who, via mission, crosses boundaries of time and place to let people in other nations and cultures share in the good news. The Spirit keeps the memory of Christ and the dream of God's reign, revealed in Christ, alive at different times and at different places in the world.[105]

The Board's interpretation of the SC paradigm and church-planting movements reveals a bias in its missiology toward pragmatism. Escobar views such a bias as leading to a "reductionist theological foundation."[106] The Board's seeming neglect of the role of the Holy Spirit reveals that its theological foundation of mission suffers from this reductionism. The Board needs to adequately address this issue and strike a balance between the pragmatic methodologies and the spiritual dimension of mission. To do otherwise may lead the SC paradigm to lose its dynamism.

One explanation for this neglect of the role of the Holy Spirit in mission perhaps stems from the Board of Trustees' and other Southern Baptist leaders' concern over charismatic practices emerging within churches planted in these church-planting movements. The issue of whether or not to include signs and wonders in the Board's 2000 publication on church-planting movements indicates one concern about a negative reaction by some Southern Baptists. Eitel raised the issue of charismatic practices, particularly in the area of spiritual warfare, as one area the Board needed to address.[107] At the February 2004 Board meeting, a trustee made the following motion:

---

[103] A. Scott Moreau, Gary R. Corwin and Gary B. McGee, *Introducing World Missions: A Biblical, Historical, and Practical Survey* (Grand Rapids: Baker Academic, 2004), 82.
[104] Schweer, "The Missionary Mandate," 108.
[105] Roelf S. Kuitse, "Holy Spirit: Source of Messianic Mission," in *The Transfiguration of Mission: Biblical Theological and & Historical Foundations,* Institute of Mennonite Studies Missionary Studies, No. 12, ed. Wilbert R. Shenk (Scottdale: Herald Press, 1993), 113.
[106] Escobar, "Evangelical missiology," 111.
[107] Eitel, "Vision Assessment," October 2003, 7; Eitel, "Reply to Rankin," November 6, 2003, 4. See also Keith E. Eitel, *Points of Discussion: IMB Trustee Meeting,* (Wake Forest: by the author, February 2004) [electronic document], 4-5.

> I move that the Board of Trustees direct the Overseas Committee to perform routine audits of new IMB church plants and submit an annual report to the Board of Trustees. The purpose of these audits is to determine the doctrinal alignment with the BF&M 2000 and the extent of charismatic practices in these new churches.[108]

The Board needs to address the concerns by some Southern Baptists regarding charismatic practices. Much of the concern about 'signs and wonders' or spiritual warfare derives from the excesses perceived in those who espouse power evangelism and assert that 'signs and wonders' are a requirement for a genuine Christian experience.[109] However, the excesses should not deter us from acknowledging the reality that the Holy Spirit continues to work through 'signs and wonders' in many places of our world today.[110]

While there are excesses in some charismatic practices, the Board should also recognize the work of the Holy Spirit is not limited to signs and wonders

---

108 "Board of Trustees Minutes," (Richmond: Southern Baptist International Mission Board, Accession Number 2790, February 2, 2004). The BF&M 2000 is the *Baptist Faith and Message 2000.* See Jerry A. Rankin, "Text of the Letter to IMB Missionaries," (Richmond: Southern Baptist International Mission Board, January 31, 2002); available from https://solomon.imb.org; stories database; Mark Kelly, "President Asks Missionaries to Sign BF&M Affirmation," (Richmond: Southern Baptist International Mission Board, January 31, 2002); available from https://solomon.imb.org; stories database. Rankin asked all IMB missionaries appointed before 2000 to sing the revised Baptist Faith and Message (original 1963) as an indication of their willingness to work in ways consistent with the denomination's beliefs.

109 See C. Peter Wagner, *Warfare Prayer: How to Seek God's Power and Protection in the Battle to Build His Kingdom* (Ventura: Regal Books, 1992); C. Peter Wagner, *Breaking Strongholds in Your City: How to Use Spiritual Mapping to Make Your Prayers More Strategic, Effective and Targeted* (Ventura: Regal Books, 1993); C. Peter Wagner, *Acts of the Holy Spirit* (Ventura: Regal Books, 1994); *Spiritual Power and Missions: Raising the Issues,* ed. Edward Rommen (Pasadena: William Carey Library Publishers, 1995); and John Wimber and Keith Springer, *Power Evangelism* (North Pomfret, VT: Trafalgar Square Publishers, 2000).

110 See Carlton, *Acts 29,* 234. In a discussion about signs and wonders, I warn about two common extreme attitudes toward signs and wonders. First, a number of Christian hold that these are proof of a genuine Christian experience and the absence of signs and wonders signifies and absence of the Holy Spirit at work. Second, a number of Christians argue that signs and wonders are no longer valid in the spread of the gospel and simply dismiss these as having belonged solely to the era of the New Testament church. I believe both positions fall short. Signs and wonders do not always have to be present nor can we simply relegate them to the era of the New Testament church. The can and often do, in many cultures, accompany the proclamation of the gospel, and they confirm the truth of the gospel message and God's Word.

or spiritual warfare. The Holy Spirit's role in mission is much broader. Indeed, the Holy Spirit's role is non-negotiable. Theologians would never give credence to a theology devoid of the Holy Spirit; therefore, neither can missiologists ignore the central role of the Holy Spirit in mission.

Erickson asserts that the doctrine of the Trinity is the one doctrine that distinguishes Christianity from the other religions of the world.[111] He further asserts, "If we have a subordinationist view of the Trinity, the Holy Spirit may in practice be treated with less than the full respect given the other members of the Trinity."[112] If this is true in theology, then it is also true in missiology.

The Holy Spirit is the agent of the new birth (John 3: 8). One cannot enter the God's kingdom unless he or she is born of the Spirit, and only the Holy Spirit's work in a person's life enables him or her to declare that Jesus is the Lord (I Cor. 12: 3). The Holy Spirit is the one who convicts the world of sin, righteousness and judgment (John 16: 7-11). The Holy Spirit bears witness to and glorifies Jesus Christ (John 15: 26; 16: 14). For those who choose to follow Jesus Christ, the Holy Spirit is the helper and one who teaches all truth (John 14: 16-7; 16: 13). The things, which the Holy Spirit teaches will confirm and conform to rather than contradict the teachings of Jesus (John 14: 26).

The anointing by the Holy Spirit marks the beginning of Jesus' earthly ministry (Matt. 3: 16; Mark 1: 10; Luke 3: 22; 4: 16-9). After his resurrection, Jesus appears to His disciples and commissions them to be His witnesses to the world (Matt. 28: 16-20; John 20: 21-22). Just as Jesus began His earthly ministry with the anointing of the Holy Spirit, so also the disciples must receive the Holy Spirit before they can effectively carry out their mission (John 20: 22; Acts 1: 8).

In the book of Acts, the Holy Spirit launches and sustains the church in its mission (Acts 2: 1-47; 8: 29-40; 13: 1-3; 16: 6-10; 19: 21). The role of the Holy Spirit also is central to the body life of the church (Acts 2: 38-47). The Holy Spirit enables God's people to be bold in their witness (Acts 4: 8, 31; 18: 5) and to experience joy and peace in the face of persecution (Acts 7: 55; 13: 42-52). The Holy Spirit's role is central in choosing those to serve as leaders within the church (Acts 6: 1-7; 11: 24; 20: 28). The growth of the church, both quantitatively and qualitatively, is the result of the Holy Spirit (Acts 2: 14-41; 6:1-7; Eph. 4: 7-15). It is evident throughout the New Testament that the Holy Spirit is the implementer and power behind mission.

A key characteristic of church-planting movements as identified by the Board is the recognition that God's Word is the ultimate authority. God's Word is clear that one of the critical roles of the Holy Spirit is to help followers of Christ understand God's truth (John 14:26). A consequence of neglecting the

---

[111] Millard J. Erickson, *God in Three Persons: A Contemporary Interpretation of the Trinity* (Grand Rapids: Baker Books, 1995), 15.
[112] Erickson, *God in Three Persons*, 26.

person and work of the Holy Spirit in these church-planting movements will be that missionaries may fail to teach new disciples to trust the Holy Spirit to guide them in understanding the truth of God's word. By neglecting the Holy Spirit's role, missionaries may put more confidence in their discipleship methods. This also may, unintentionally, create a dependence on the missionary as the source of authority rather than studying and interpreting God's word under the guidance of the Holy Spirit.[113] With the shift in the SC paradigm toward an exit perspective, as pointed out by Sergeant, it is even more critical that the Board's missiology not overlook this role of the Holy Spirit in these movements. Allen, analyzing the work of Paul, concluded that the secret to Paul's success was his reliance upon the Holy Spirit to guide new Christians.[114] Without a solid theological foundation that recognizes the important role of the Holy Spirit in mission, strategy coordinators and other missionaries may find themselves guilty of the accusations Allen levelled against missionaries nearly one hundred years ago:

> In everything we have taught our converts to turn to us, to accept our guidance. We have asked nothing of them but obedience. We have educated our converts to put us in the place of Christ. We believe that it is the Holy Spirit of Christ which inspires and guides us: we cannot believe that the same Holy Spirit will guide and inspire them. We believe that the Holy Spirit has taught us the true conceptions of morality, doctrine, ritual: we cannot believe that the same Spirit will teach them…
>
> …The Holy Ghost is given to Christians that He may guide them, and that they may learn His power to guide them, not that they may be stupidly obedient to the voice of authority….
>
> …If we have no faith in the power of the Holy Spirit in them, they will not learn to have faith in the power of the Holy Spirit in themselves.[115]

A healthy, Biblical understanding of the Holy Spirit's role in mission is essential. In its excitement to join God as He works in these church-planting movements, the Board has elevated pragmatic methodologies at the expense of maintaining a solid, pneumatological foundation in its missiology. As a result, the SC paradigm may lose it vitality, a vitality that pushed and pulled the IMB into a new arena of mission. The Board must not sacrifice the mysterious dimension of the Holy Spirit's work in mission or in these church-planting movements on the altar of pragmatism. Otherwise, this new missiological

[113] Roland Allen, *Missionary Methods: St. Paul's or Ours,* American edition (London: World Dominion Press, 1962. Reprint. Grand Rapids: Eerdmans Publishing, 1998), 143-6 (page citations are to the reprint edition).

[114] Allen, *Missionary Methods*, 152.

[115] Allen, *Missionary Methods,* 143-5, 152.

paradigm, which the Board has embraced for the 21st century, will lose its effectiveness and hinder the Board's impact on global evangelization.

Conclusion

With the launching of New Directions in 1997, which embraced the SC paradigm as the Board's primary paradigm for the 21st century, the SC paradigm faced the danger of institutionalization. The risk in this process was the paradigm's loss of vitality. The emergence of the CPM phenomenon at about the same time as New Directions injected a new energy into the SC paradigm. As the Board began to identify various explosive movements around the world, it sought to position itself to pour its energies and resources toward facilitating and nurturing such movements wherever its missionaries served. Extensive research and study took place to define and describe these movements so that Board missionaries might be able to evaluate their efforts and make the necessary course changes in their work to align themselves with what the Board perceived God was doing in these church-planting movements. The emergence of these movements not only breathed new life into the SC paradigm, but also led to significant changes in some of its original presuppositions on which it was developed. The changes in these presuppositions led to some practical changes in the strategy coordinator role.

However, the Board's efforts to define and describe these church-planting movements resulted in a reductionist understanding of these movements. Further, a shift in the emphasis of the SC paradigm away from innovation toward learning and implementing proven, effective methodologies employed by missionaries in these church-planting movements, led to a bias toward pragmatic approaches. The Board moved toward prescribing methodologies that it believed, if implemented, would lead strategy coordinators and other missionaries toward facilitating church-planting movements. Although the Board did not claim these methodologies would guarantee a CPM, it discouraged innovation in favour of methods that it perceived demonstrated effectiveness. This partiality toward pragmatism further resulted in a reductionist missiology, one that neglected the crucial role of the Holy Spirit in mission and in these church-planting movements. A rediscovery of the Holy Spirit's role in mission is vital, else the SC paradigm faces calcification and church-planting movements become a mechanized method of carrying out God's mission.

In 1996, Stroope, recognizing the SC paradigm's survival depended on its ability to change, called for a "Re-dreaming the Dream" conference. A decade later, the survival of the paradigm is at stake. An environment of innovation and a healthy, Biblical understanding of the Holy Spirit in mission perhaps are two keys that will enable the paradigm to survive. If not, perhaps a new paradigm will arise on the scene.

CHAPTER 6

Concluding Observations

The major objective of this research was to demonstrate the extensive impact of the non-residential missionary (NRM)/strategy coordinator (SC) mission paradigm on the International Mission Board (IMB) during the past twenty years. Since there exists no previous research on this new missiological paradigm, the present effort sought to provide a historical picture of its development along with an analysis of its key elements. Using Bosch's post-modern paradigm nomenclature as an interpretive grid, this research posited the NRM/SC paradigm as a post-modern evangelical paradigm, with significant points of convergence with and divergence from Bosch. Further, by examining the development of this paradigm through Guder's lenses of reductionism and institutionalization, this research sought to demonstrate how both threaten this young missiological paradigm. New Directions brought about the institutionalization of the paradigm. The church-planting movement (CPM) phenomenon brought some significant philosophical changes to the paradigm and helped it retain much of its vitality in the face of this institutionalization. However, the reductionism prevalent in the Board's understanding and description of church-planting movements once again threatens the paradigm's effectiveness and existence. The Board must confront these issues if it wants to continue to exert a significant impact on global evangelization in the 21st century.

Those who are knowledgeable of the Southern Baptists' global mission enterprise are aware of the key missiological shifts within the IMB over the past few decades. A few of these key shifts cited in this research are (1) an emphasis on ethno linguistic people groups rather than geo-political countries; (2) an increasing emphasis on missionary deployment to unreached (World A or Last Frontier) peoples as opposed to traditional mission fields; (3) an emphasis on wider cooperation with the Great Commission Christian (GCC) community as opposed to segregation from other evangelical groups; (4) an emphasis on church-planting instead of denominational building activities; and (5) an emphasis on facilitating church-planting movements rather than simply evangelism that results in churches. The extensive examination of the historical development of the NRM/SC paradigm helps to provide Southern Baptists and other evangelical Christians with a more thorough understanding of the primary influence behind these missiological shifts. Understanding the historical context and the various influences that have shaped this new missiological paradigm provides significant information needed to evaluate more adequately this paradigm's contribution and relevance to the global mission effort.

The NRM/SC paradigm emerged in a time of transition, especially in the West, from modernity to post-modernity. In the latter part of the 20th century, there was strong criticism of the evangelical modern mission movement. Critics decried what they believed was an extreme reliance on a quantitative approach to mission, a misguided sense of triumphalism and a tendency to rely upon what Escobar has called "managerial missiology." The modern evangelical mission movement exerted a significant influence on the Board's missiology out of which the NRM/SC paradigm emerged. While the NRM/SC paradigm retains some of these modernity elements, it is also a post-modern evangelical paradigm in progress. By positing this paradigm as such, this research has sought to demonstrate the immense challenge the paradigm faces as it seeks to forge a different way of doing mission in a post-modern world. The paradigm must honestly evaluate the past and distance itself from those aspects that are no longer relevant. At the same time, it also must seek to integrate key components necessary to develop a comprehensive missiology for the 21st century.

The key distinctives of New Directions (now Strategic Directions for the 21st Century) demonstrates the pervasive influence of this new paradigm on the Board's missiology. At the same time, New Directions was a step toward institutionalizing the paradigm, a step that easily could have stripped the new paradigm of its vivacity. The paradigm's ability to respond quickly to change enabled it to retain much of its dynamism in the midst of institutionalization. The institutionalizing of the paradigm led to reductionism as the Board sought to translate it across the entire organization. The Board's desire to control what it perceived was a paradigm out of control, coupled with reducing the paradigm to a set of methodologies, resulted in reductionism. This research challenges mission organizations to consider fostering an environment that allows dichotomous paradigms to co-exist in order to avoid calcification. Although the co-existence of differing paradigms creates friction and tension, such an environment often serves to fuel innovation. The Board's desire to take the vision of global evangelization seriously led it to launch the NRM/SC paradigm. Such innovation must continue to be encouraged in the global mission effort.

With the emergence of the CPM phenomenon, the Board quickly sought to embrace it as the new wave of mission for the 21st century and believed it to be an important key in completing global evangelization. The Board identified the NRM/SC paradigm as a major contribution to and a driving force behind these church-planting movements. As the Board sought to understand and describe these movements, it faced, once again, the challenge of reductionism. One of the consequences of this reductionism is the neglect of the Holy Spirit in the Board's missiology. As this research has sought to reveal, an over-emphasis on pragmatic methods at the expense of the spiritual in mission produces a theologically deficient missiology. As people who uphold the authority of God's Word as absolute, Southern Baptists must ensure that their missiology is firmly rooted in His Word. A missiology firmly grounded in God's Word will not overlook the critical role of the Holy Spirit in mission.

This research hopefully raises some questions and stimulates a desire for additional research related to this study, but outside the scope of this initial effort. This study has traced the historical development of this new missiological paradigm within the IMB; however, there is a need for further research that compares the development of this paradigm with other similar paradigm shifts in the broader evangelical community. In the latter part of the 20th century, there were developments in the global evangelical community such as the AD2000 movement and the Adopt-A-People movement. Further research may reveal the depth of the interrelationship between the NRM/SC paradigm and these other evangelical movements. This research has demonstrated the influence of various persons and events in the global evangelical community that influenced the development of this paradigm within the Board. Further research may reveal the reciprocating influence of this paradigm on some of the latter 20th century evangelical efforts toward global evangelization.

Some Southern Baptists, displeased with the conservative resurgence in the Southern Baptist Convention (SBC), formed the Cooperative Baptist Fellowship as an alternative to the SBC. After resigning from the Board in the early 1990s, Parks became the executive director of CBF international mission effort. This research has noted the significant influence of Parks on the development of the NRM/SC paradigm. When Parks joined the CBF, he took with him the NRM/SC paradigm, which became an integral part of this new agency's missiology. A comparison of the subsequent development of the paradigm within CBF and the IMB needs further study.

One significant missiological shift resulting from the NRM/SC paradigm was the Board's increasingly deeper involvement and partnership with other GCC agencies. These partnerships have developed within the ministry of specific strategy coordinators as well as organization-to-organization partnerships initiated by the Board Further, these partnerships have raised a number of questions and concerns from some within the Southern Baptist Convention, most of which focus on the theological and ecclesiological issues surrounding these partnerships. There is a need for more extensive research regarding the impact of these wider GCC relationships on the Board.

This trend toward wider involvement with GCC agencies coincided with the trend towards the internationalization of mission. This internationalization of mission was the result of the changing landscape of Christianity around the world. During the latter part of the 20th century, the majority of evangelical Christians shifted from the West to the South and the East. The NRM/SC paradigm emerged within this changing environment. Further research on the relationship between this trend and the NRM/SC paradigm would prove invaluable to the Board's continual development of an effective and appropriate missiology for the 21st century.

The increase of Southern Baptist churches seeking involvement that is more personal in the global evangelization effort is another missiological shift resulting from the influence of this paradigm. This research has highlighted some of the efforts of the Board to respond to these churches. The impact this trend has on Southern Baptist churches and the historical relationship between the Board and its constituent churches warrants further study.

The most significant missiological shift in the past few years has resulted from the church-planting movement phenomenon. Important changes in the new paradigm resulted as the Board embraced church-planting movements as its primary mission emphasis. Most noticeable in these movements is the emergence of the house church. With these house churches emerges a different ecclesiology, one that challenges the conventional thinking of many Southern Baptists. The ecclesiological issues that have emerged in these church-planting movements need additional study.

This research has highlighted the Board's over-emphasis on pragmatic methodologies in relation to church-planting movements. While Garrison has made an invaluable contribution to the evangelical community with his effort to define and describe church-planting movements, there is a need for an in-depth Biblical and theological evaluation of these movements. A comprehensive missiology that has as its aim the facilitating of church-planting movements is in need of a solid, Biblical underpinning, which such a study can provide.

The Final Word

Kierkegaard once wrote, "Many have gone astray through not understanding how to continue a good beginning."[1] This new missiological paradigm for Southern Baptists is not complete, but it is a good beginning. The challenge before Southern Baptists and its IMB is to move forward with this new beginning, allowing God to continue to mould and shape the new paradigm, as He deems necessary. May the following words of Kierkegaard serve to inspire Southern Baptists as they seek to be a part of God's mission to the world:

> I will work on with energy and not waste time looking back, not like the man who was caught in quicksand and began calculating how far down he had already sunk, forgetting all the while he was sinking deeper. I will hurry along the path I

[1] Charles E. Moore, ed. *Provocations: Spiritual Writings of Kierkegaard* (Maryknoll: Orbis Books, 2002), 246.

have discovered, not looking back as did Lot's wife, but remembering that it is a hill up which we have to struggle.[2]

[2] Moore, *Provocations,* 245.

APPENDIX A

THE NONRESIDENTIAL MISSIONARY AND STRATEGY COORDINATOR MISSION PARADIGM

CHRONOLOGY OF PERTINENT EVENTS [1]

1910		Edinburgh Conference was held. This conference focused exclusively on unoccupied fields (geographic terms as opposed to ethnographic terms).
1934		W. Cameron Townsend opens Camp Wycliffe in Arkansas designed to train young people in basic linguistics and Bible translation methods. This is the birth of Wycliffe Bible Translators.
1941		L.G. Brierly (WEC) begins research on the remaining unevangelized peoples (RUP)
1952		Dr. Paul E. Freed founds a missionary organization that led to radio broadcasting two years later. This organization eventually became known as Trans World Radio, which by the end of the century broadcast the Gospel in more than 110 languages.
1955		Donald McGavran develops the concept of people movements based on his ministry among the Satnami people of India. This was the birth of the Church Growth Movement, which led to the development of the homogenous unit principle.
1955		Brother Andrew, founder of Open Doors, makes first trip behind the Iron Curtain to take Bibles to persecuted Christians. Open Doors asserts, "We go where others do not go, and do what others do not do."
1960		Chicago meeting sponsored by the Interdenominational Foreign Mission Association (IFMA) brings together thousands of missionaries, pastors and lay people, calling on Christian young people to speedily occupy the remaining unevangelized fields.
1966		Missions Advanced Research and Communication (MARC) develops the modern day concept of people groups.
1972	June	Luther Copeland, Southern Baptist missionary and outgoing President of the U.S. Association of Professors of Mission (APM) proposes a conference to be held along the lines of the 1910 Edinburgh Conference.

1972	December	R. Pierce Beaver organizes the Consultation on Frontier Peoples in Chicago, Illinois.
1974	July	International Conference on World Evangelization (ICOWE) meets in Lausanne, Switzerland. Ralph Winter introduces the concept of 'hidden peoples' to the world evangelical community. ICOWE announces that research has identified 16,750 unreached people groups.
1974		MARC publishes the first *Unreached Peoples Directory.*
1976	June	Southern Baptist Convention adopts Bold Mission Thrust stating the overall goal of 'every person in the world having the opportunity to hear the gospel of Christ in the next 25 years.'
1978		Patrick Johnstone publishes *Operation World.*
1979		J. Christy Wilson, Jr. publishes *Today's Tentmakers: Self-Support – An Alternative Model for Worldwide Witness* in which he seeks to show that it is possible for Christians to gain access to closed countries if one is willing to forego the traditional approach of going openly as a missionary.
1979	April	R. Keith Parks elected Executive Director of the Foreign Mission Board (FMB of the Southern Baptist Convention, effective 01 January 1980.
1980	June	Consultation on World Evangelization in Pattaya attempts to develop strategies for evangelizing the unreached peoples.
1980	September	Ted Ward from Michigan State University addresses the Board of Trustees emphasizing possible new directions for Southern Baptist missions in light of changing world conditions.
1980	November	World Consultation on Frontier Mission in Edinburgh announces the vision of "A Church for Every People by the Year 2000." Edinburgh conference focuses specifically on unreached areas and peoples.
1981	February March	Winston Crawley, Vice-President for Planning (FMB) introduces the people group and 'hidden peoples' concepts to the Board of Trustees in back-to-back reports.
1981	March	R. Keith Parks appoints Catherine Walker as 'Special Assistant to the President for Intercessory Prayer.' This is the first time in history that the FMB treats prayer as a key missionary strategy and a formal office of prayer established within the FMB structure.
1982		David B. Barrett publishes *World Christian Encyclopaedia.*
1985	April	FMB votes to establish Cooperative Services International (CSI) to lead Southern Baptists in responding to opportunities in China.
1985	April	David B. Barrett contracts with the FMB to base his World Evangelization Research Center at the FMB office in Richmond, VA. Barrett's research led to the development of the concepts of

		World A, World B and World C in an attempt to classify the world's people groups in terms of their evangelization.
1985	June	R. Keith Parks and David Barrett convene the Global Evangelization Consultation in Ridgecrest, NC. Representatives of the FMB and Baptist partners representing 21 nations meet together to discuss partnership in fulfilling the Great Commission.
1986	December	Bill Smith, while conducting research for his doctorate degree, visits the World Evangelization Research Center in Richmond. Smith becomes aware of a major unreached people group in Asia and begins to develop strategies to reach this people group.
1987	March	Global Strategy Group (GSG) formed at the FMB.
1987	September	Dr. Parks and other FMB leaders meet with major mission groups in Dallas, Texas to discuss partnership on a global evangelization strategy.
1987	November	A definition for the NRM presented to the GSG for consideration.
1987		Bill Smith officially becomes the first Non-residential Missionary (NRM) within the FMB, residing in Bangkok and targeting a major unreached people group in a neighbouring country.
1987		R. Keith Parks publishes *World in View* in which he details a global mission vision for the FMB and Southern Baptists.
1987		43 Southern Baptist-related colleges and universities form the Cooperative Services International Education Consortium (CSI-EC) to coordinate the exchange of professors and students and to establish satellite higher education programs in World A countries.
1988	February	Mike and Kay Stroope assigned as the second NRM couple, focusing on a major unreached people group in the Middle East.
1988	March	Lewis Myers presents to the GSG a paper entitled "Ministry to Restricted Peoples," defining the NRM as personnel with a full-time assignment to evangelize an unevangelized population segment and who resides and works from a location outside the assignment.
1988	May	NRM program domiciled in CSI with a program director overseeing its development and day-to-day operations.
1988	October	David Garrison named as the NRM program director. Three new NRM couples assigned bringing the total to 5.
1989	January	At the Global Consultation on World Evangelization in Singapore, 314 leaders of denominations and missions-oriented organizations from 50 countries adopt the 'Great Commission Manifesto,' noting that it was possible to take the gospel to all peoples by the year 2000.
1989	June	13 NRMs assigned, targeting more than 170 million people in 11

		countries.
1990	January	FMB releases its vision for the end of the 20th Century in "What's Next? Nine Needs for the 90's."
1990	May	FMB separates CSI and the NRM program.
1990	May	R. Keith Parks issues a plea to Southern Baptists to rise above the theological controversy gripping the denomination and to focus on missions, arguing that the controversy has diluted the denomination's focus on missions. Tension between Parks and conservative members of the board of trustees intensifies.
1990	December	FMB reports 28 NRMs, targeting 284 million people.
1990		David Garrison publishes *The Non-residential Missionary: A New Strategy and the People it Serves* in which he describes this emerging missions paradigm adopted by the FMB.
1991	October	*The Commission* magazine publishes article, "Shaping New Strategies, Adjusting FMB Vision in Light of World A."
1991	December	FMB reports 40 NRMs, targeting 350 million of the world's least evangelized peoples.
1992	June	Board of Trustees approved CSI to become the fifth strategic region functioning with one administrative area.
1992	August	FMB merges CSI and the NRM program again. CSI becomes its own administrative area within the FMB with Mike Stroope chosen to be the Area Director. The new CSI has responsibility for targeting World A peoples without regard to specific geographical boundaries.
1992	October	R. Keith Parks resigns as President of the FMB, citing major philosophical differences regarding missions between the board of trustees and him as one of the key reasons.
1993	January	FMB reports 432 career missionaries out of 3890 (11.1%) targeting World A peoples. FMB missionaries are working among 80 of the world's known 212 megapeoples (people groups with over 1 million in population).
1993	June	Jerry Rankin elected as the 10th President of the FMB, affirming to lead the FMB to multiply efforts to reach World A while returning to a more diversified, field-oriented approach to missions' strategy.
1993	October	FMB announces that 41% of its highest priority personnel requests for the coming year (30 out of 73) are for workers in World A.
1994	January	FMB reports 497 career missionaries (13% of its missionary force) working in World A and targeting 85 out of 212 megapeoples.
1994	December	FMB trustees adopt new vision statement, stating the FMB would "lead Southern Baptists…to bring all peoples of the world to

		saving faith in Jesus Christ."
1995	July	CSI, under the leadership of Mike Stroope, develops the vision and principles that will guide its work.
1995	September	FMB launches "On Mission with God to the Last Frontier," targeting 2,466 people groups considered to have no or very limited access to the gospel.
1995	September	FMB announces that in the past ten years, the FMB has moved from having 1% to 13.5% of its resources and missionaries in World A.
1995	May	Avery Willis, Vice-President of the FMB, apologizes to participants of the Global Conference on World Evangelization in Seoul. Willis apologizes for the fact that Southern Baptists previously had acted as if they alone would complete global evangelization, and he affirms the commitment of the FMB to work together with other evangelical agencies to get the gospel to every people group in the world. Shortly afterwards, the FMB begins to openly share its research database with other evangelical agencies who were devoted to global evangelization.
1996	March	FMB announces that 15% of new church starts reported by Southern Baptist missionaries in previous year were in World A. CSI ranked third of all regions in new church starts.
1997	April	Trustees approve name change from Foreign Mission Board to International Mission Board (IMB). Trustees also approve major restructuring of the board, leading to the dissolution of CSI. The concept of church-planting movements becomes part of overall strategy of the mission board. Overseas administration divided into 15 regions. Changes approved as "New Directions for the 21st Century."
1997	April	With the dissolution of CSI under "New Directions," Mike Stroope resigns and forms separate ministry called "All Peoples." Several other missionaries also resign to join Stroope in this effort.
1997	June	David Garrison named vice-president for strategy coordination and mobilization. Five out of 15 new regional leaders elected from the ranks of CSI.
1998	January	Rankin announces Vision 2001, which states the goals of 1000 IMB missionaries in China and India (35% of world's population) and 1000 other IMB missionaries assigned to other unreached people groups in World A.
1998	February	IMB partnership efforts with other Great Commission Christians expands as executive leaders of the largest evangelical missions organizations meet in Richmond, Virginia, at the invitation of the IMB.

1998		IMB Overseas Leadership team adopts new vision statement: "We will facilitate the lost coming to saving faith in Jesus Christ by beginning and nurturing church-planting movements among all peoples."
1999	January	IMB publishes *Something New Under the Sun: New Directions at the International Mission Board* seeking to explain the details of New Directions to Southern Baptist missionaries and churches.
1999	January	IMB launches "Unfinished Task," which states as its objective the acceleration of the effort to take the gospel to the remaining people groups in the world who have yet to hear the gospel.
1999	January	Lewis Myers and Jim Slack publish *To the Edge: A Planning Process for People Group Specific Strategy Development.* This manual designed for training IMB missionaries throughout the world with same type of training used by CSI.
1999		Jerry Rankin publishes *Mobilizing for Missions in the New Millennium: A Great Commission Vision for Southern Baptists in the 21st Century.*
2000	January	In India, R. Bruce Carlton, in cooperation with S.D. Ponraj, launches effort to specifically train local church planters/ missionaries in the principles of Strategy Coordination and church-planting movements. This is the first effort specifically to provide Strategy Coordinator training for local workers rather than just Western missionaries.
2000		David Garrison publishes booklet *Church Planting Movements.* This small booklet begins to popularize church-planting movements within the IMB missionary force, Southern Baptist churches and wider evangelical community.
2000		Keith Eitel publishes *Paradigm Wars: The Southern Baptist International Mission Board Faces the Third Millennium.*
2000		IMB releases video on church-planting movements entitled *Like a Mighty Wave*. Video, like Garrison's booklet, begins to popularize church-planting movements within evangelical community.
2001	December	Results of the IMB's Global Analysis Project (GAP) released, showing there were 2,161 people groups (1.65 billion people) and 400 cities (population over 100,000) with no significant Christian witness.
2001		IMB announces that, for the first time in history, missionary count exceeds 5000.
2003	May	IMB announces it will have to cut its budget and limit missionary appointments because of financial crisis.
2003	May	R. Bruce Carlton *Acts 29: Practical Training in Facilitating Church-Planting Movements Among the Neglected Harvest*

		Fields. Within one year, material is translated and published in 14 different languages.
2003	August	IMB Regional Leaders meet for Global Summit. The board's Global Research Department presents data showing explosive growth in church planting in World A while at the same time slow growth in traditional areas. At the same time, regional leaders confronted the reality that personnel and resources allocated to World A were significantly less than traditional areas.
2003	November	IMB leaders from around the world gather at Windshape Retreat Center in Georgia. During this retreat Rankin relates to board leadership the need to allocate personnel and resources more to World A in light of the imbalance brought to light by the board's global research department and the explosive growth in church planting in World A.
2003	November	IMB announces that its missionary personnel are engaging 1371 different people groups. IMB also states that there are 7 confirmed church-planting movements with another 42 church-planting movements reported.
2004		David Garrison publishes *Church-Planting Movements: How God is Redeeming a Lost World.*

---

[1]This chronology is compiled primarily from H.C. Shreck and D.B. Barrett, eds. *Unreached Peoples: Clarifying the Task,* (Monrovia, CA: MARC, 1987); Ralph D. Winter, "Thy Kingdom Come: The Story of a Movement," (Pasadena: US Center for World Mission, 1995). Available from http://www.dawnministries.org/resources/downloads/download_files/thy_kingdom_come.pdf; Lewis Myers and Jim Slack, *To The Edge: A Planning Process for People Group Specific Strategy Development,* (Richmond, VA: International Mission Board of the Southern Baptist Convention, 1998); "Board Meeting Minutes," International Mission Board, 1980-2004; "Global Strategy Group Minutes," International Mission Board, 1987-1997; and *The Commission,* (Richmond, VA: International Mission Board of the Southern Baptist Convention,1980-2004).

APPENDIX B

BOLD NEW THRUSTS IN FOREIGN MISSIONS 1976-2000[1]

1. Great overarching objective: To preach the gospel to all the people in the world.

2. One hundred percent increase in missionary staff – more than 5,000 by A.D. 2000.

3. Missionaries at work in at least 125 countries as God may lead.

4. Accelerated tempo of volunteer lay involvement overseas – up to 3,000 per year needed now, and up to 10,000 per year by A.D. 2000.

5. Greatly expanded efforts in evangelism – major thrusts in urban areas and among students and other young people.

6. Tenfold multiplication of overseas churches – with concomitant increases in baptisms and church membership.

7. Extraordinary efforts in leadership training – through strengthened seminaries, Theological Education by Extension, and lay leadership training.

8. Vastly increased use of radio, television, and publications on mission fields, and penetration by way of mass media of areas not presently open to missionary activities.

9. Accentuated attention to human need – through health care, disease prevention, benevolent and social ministries.

10. Vigorous, appropriate, and prompt responses to world hunger and disasters.

---

[1] Adopted by Foreign Mission Board, January 13, 1976. The above highlights from Baker J. Cauthen and Frank K. Means, *Advance to Bold Mission Thrust,* 319-20.

APPENDIX C

TWELVE DIMENSIONS AND 84 CHARACTERISTICS OF NONRESIDENTIAL MISSIONARIES[1]

Don't be put off by this catalogue below! It's not a definition of a supermissionary of superhuman abilities. Regard it as you would a new city road map or a new telephone directory, or a new college textbook. It's a careful definition of, or guide to, a new concept: the non-residential missionary. He or she is simply a committed Christian worker or couple who want to serve an unevangelized population segment in a restricted-access part of the world. This therefore is a list of emphases or aspects or steps or stages or activities which should characterize him or them. Any ordinary missionary or couple, from any country, of any nationality, are capable of filling this bill. He doesn't have to engage in all possible evangelistic activities himself – merely check that somebody does. It is in fact a list of a number of steps he or she should take, or aspects of mission that he should embrace.

The list of emphases or aspects is divided into 12 major categories or dimensions (in boldface capital type on the left). The list then gives in its second column 84 characteristics or descriptors (descriptive nouns or verbs or adjectives describing who the missionary is or what he does). Each is then expanded and explained in the one-sentence comment that follows.

While most of the 12 major dimensions below describe his life's ministry over the years to AD2000 and beyond, all of them could be begun and well under way within 12 months of him first hearing the call. The research and survey side could easily be completed within 6 months, though it would be updated continuously thereafter.

The non-residential missionary can be described here as:

Ref	**DIMENSION** *Characteristic*	One-line comment or explanation
	CALLED	
1	called	He or she is **called** to follow Christ across today's world.
2	missionary	He is a **missionary** working with the Christian world mission.
3	foreign	Most of the time he crosses political frontiers as an alien or **foreigner**.
4	cross-cultural	His ministry is **cross-cultural**, from his own culture to a different culture.
5	evangelizer	His primary role is as **evangelizer**, among unevangelized populations.
6	global	**Globally** oriented, he combs the world for other Great Commission co-operators.
7	professional	He and his spouse are **professional** foreign missionaries.
8	career	Being a missionary is his **career**, possibly or probably for life.
9	monovocational	though he may have secular skills, mission or ministry is his **overarching vocation.**
10	full-time	He undertakes it as a **full-time** job, not a part-time interest.
11	legal	In whichever country he visits, he **obeys the laws** concerning overt evangelism.
12	non-political	He is **apolitical** and secure from future state hostility, evictions or bannings.
13	non-traditional	As traditional residential mission is impossible, he becomes **non-traditional.**
14	non-residential	Unable to reside in his target segment, he becomes **non-residential**
15	mobile	Resident with his family 70% of the time, he remains **mobile** and flexible.
	APPOINTED	
16	recruited	He is **recruited** by a foreign mission board or agency or church or support body.
17	selected	They test his vocation and qualifications and then **select** him for service.

18 trained	In missionary learning centres, he becomes **trained** in missions and missiology.
19 appointed	He is **appointed** by his board as one of their recognized missionaries.
20 sent	He is employed and **sent** by his board or sending body out on mission.
21 supported	He is subsequently **supported** by his board regularly (money, aid, prayer, travel).

MATCHED-UP

22 targeting	He holds discussions to locate a **target** population (people, city, or country).
23 matched-up	His talents and vocation are now **matched up** with possible segments.
24 focused	He finally **focuses** in on one single unevangelized population segment.
25 concentrated	It becomes a **concentrated** evangelizing ministry avoiding diversions.
26 commissioned	His board agrees to engage this segment and **commissions** him to his new ministry.

RESEARCHING

27 language-learning	He learns the **language** (market fluency) and thereby wins credibility.
28 studying	He master his segment; **studies,** maps, books, bibliographies, reports, tapes.
29 consulting	He compiles a list of **consultants** and centres expert on his segment.
30 researching	He **researches** (makes new discoveries about) his target population.
31 specializing	He takes vernacular newspapers and journals, and joins **specialist** societies.

NETWORKING

32 surveying	He **surveys** the entire spectrum of Great Commission activities within his segment.
33 recognizing	He **recognizes**, and aligns himself with, all involved Great Commission Christians.
34 cooperating	He actively **cooperates** with them, and gets them to cooperate with each other.
35 networking	He documents the existing **network**, become a major node, makes it a team.
36 team-player	He forges a **Great Commission team** out of all working for his segment.
37 informing	He develops a wide-ranging **information** network and keeps the team informed.

38 catalyzing	Where necessary, as a **catalyser** he urges new work and new approaches.
39 contextualizing	He helps the network honour the **global context** of all segments and their interests.
STRATEGIZING	
40 biblical	He studies and emulates **biblical** strategic roles (Apostle Paul, et alii).
41 discerning	He analyses and **discerns** bridges and barriers to the gospel in his segment.
42 strategizing	He works out, privately and through the network, and over all **strategy.**
43 coordinating	He **coordinates** any other approaches or ministries when necessary.
44 integrating	He supports holistic ministry by helping to **integrate** evangelism and social concern.
45 communicating	Even when isolated, he **communicates** continually via phone, modem, electronic mail.
46 translating	He circulates strategic concepts **translated** into the language.
47 prioritizing	He assists the network to **prioritize** its Great Commission activities.
48 telecommunicating	If he has become a laptop computer user, he **telecommunicates** discreetly.
49 databasing	He utilizes multilingual infobases and **databases**, keeps up to date.
50 updated	He receives monthly computerized **updates** on his segment: literature, data, contacts.
51 reporting	He **reports** monthly to his agency on one short standard form or computer screen.
52 updating	He provides fuller **updating** status material, as available, regularly to his base.
53 monitoring	He tracks and **monitors** his segment's unevangelized status continually.
54 calendaring	He **calendars** (keeps track of future dates) and ensures items occur on schedule.
INTERCEDING	
55 praying	He gets the network **praying** that the AD2000 overarching objective may be met.
56 prayer-mobilizing	He **mobilizes prayer partners** in any country where this is possible.
57 interceding	He develops a ministry of informed **intercession** by homes churches and agencies.

EVANGELIZING

58 evangelizing	He main task is **evangelizing**, in its 200 or so distinct dimensions and methods.
59 goal-oriented	His **goal** is that everyone in his segment become evangelized by AD 2000.
60 responsible	He accepts **responsibility** to see to it that the whole network achieves this goal.
61 future-oriented	He orients his ministry to both AD 2000, and **'AD 2000 and Beyond'.**
62 teaching	His main **teaching** is, informally, on how the network can achieve this goal.

MINISTERING

63 ministering	He continually draws up new **ministry options** and gets the team implementing them.
64 megaministering	He plans for **megaministry** approaches to his segment.
65 proclaiming	He sees to it that by all methods a continuous **proclamation** of Christ goes on.
66 seed-sowing	He goal is: to see adequate scripture distribution, **broadcasting**, literature, etc.
67 disciple-making	His goal is: at least 100 new **disciples made** in this segment by AD 2000.
68 church-planting	His goal is: 4 or 5 new beachhead churches **planted** and leaders trained by AD 2000.
69 indigenizing	He encourages emergence of new **indigenous** expressions of Christianity in his segment.

IMPLEMENTING

70 visiting	He **visits** his target as a tourist or for secular events (conferences, etc).
71 entrepreneurial	Creative and versatile, he exploits **opportunities** as and when they occur.
72 facilitating	As a **facilitator**, he actively assists others to get their roles performed.
73 locating	He advises on possible **location** of tentmakers or others resident in the segment.
74 mobilizing	As a **mobilizer,** he locates new resources, finds additional personnel.
75 implementing	As an **implementer**, he ensures all agreed steps actually get implemented.
76 conflict-avoiding	He **avoids conflict** between his segment's interests and outside Christian work.

ADVOCATING

77 relating	He maintains **good relations** with secular, religious and Christian authorities.
78 advocating	He serves as an **advocate,** anywhere, for his segment and their evangelization.

79 lobbying	When necessary, he **lobbies** energetically on behalf of his segment.
80 low-key	Aware of the dangers of publicity, he keeps a **low profile.**
81 sensitizing	He alerts and **sensitizes** the network to needs for confidentiality and security.
TRAINING	
82 equipping	He sees to it that indigenous leadership emerges **equipped** for ministry.
83 training	He assists with **training** seminars for new non-residential missionaries anywhere.
84 recruiting	He keeps alert to **recruit** non-residential missionaries for segments elsewhere.

---

[1] David B. Barrett and James W. Reapsome. *Seven Hundred Plans to Evangelize the World: The rise of a global evangelization movement,* AD2000 Series (Birmingham: New Hope, 1988), 36-7.

APPENDIX D

POLICY: DEPLOYMENT OF MISSIONARY PERSONNEL IN RESPONSE TO GLOBAL PRIORITIES

(May 1990)[1]

1. Philosophy of Global Deployment

   The Foreign Mission Board seeks to respond to global needs in a timely fashion in order to accomplish Bold Mission Thrust. It will be necessary on occasion, therefore, for veteran missionaries to deploy into new strategic assignments. Occasions which would warrant such inter-regional strategic deployment would include:

   1) Entering new countries

   2) Engagement with new unreached people groups or large cities

   3) Initiation of a new emphasis, strategy or the opening of a new opportunity

   4) Unusual opportunities or responsiveness in evangelism

   5) Indication of a limited time frame for entry or development in a country

   All Foreign Mission Board missionary personnel shall be considered as a global pool for the purpose of meeting such needs on a timely basis. The leadership of the Holy Spirit individually and corporately shall be primary. Missionaries who are being considered for such assignments must affirm their willingness to enter the process.

2. Guidelines for Deployment

   1) The strategic deployment concept, including guidelines, shall be communicated to all personnel.

2) Occasions and priorities for inter-regional strategic deployment shall be identified by the Global Strategy Group and communicated first to area directors/NRM Director. Missionaries shall be deployed only into positions which have been identified as strategic priorities by the G.S.G.

3) Job requests shall be channelled through the annual process when possible but shall not be confined to this process.

4) Area directors shall have three months in which to recommend personnel to meet the identified needs.

5) Thos needs that remain unmet after three months shall be listed in INTERCOM, along with a brief description of the need and any specific requirements/limitations for that position.

6) Missionaries who feel led to inquire about such positions shall do so through their area director/NRM Director, who will refer them to the appropriate office.

7) When needs are unmet after a period of six months, the Regional Vice Presidents shall request the nomination of candidate by area directors/NRM director using criteria such as the following:

    1. Missions having missionaries in addition to or outside of their base staffing plan

    2. Missions with strong national conventions.

    3. Missions with large numbers of missionaries.

    4. Missions in countries with sizable evangelical Christian communities.

    5. Missions with specific plans for reduction in staff.

    6. Missions with visa restrictions.

7. Missionaries who are being deployed in response to a strategic global priority shall be transferred according to existing policy.

8. These strategic priorities worldwide shall constitute a continuing list of possible opportunities/need for deployment. The list shall be updated every six months or as required.

---

[1] *Cooperative Services International Non-residential Missionary Review* (Richmond: Southern Baptist International Mission Board, January 1992), 119-20.

APPENDIX E

TEN GUIDING PRINCIPLES OF CSI

1. DESTINATION IS THE POINT AND YOU ARE THE KEY!

Plans, program and technology are not our foremost consideration but only means to the end. An indigenous church-planting movement among every people must be the point of all we do. You (your competence and character) are the key in reaching the destination. Thus, we must do all we can to adequately support, train and guide you.

2. WE MUST CONTINUALLY CHANGE.

Our willingness to challenge and change the way we do things has been one of our strengths. Unwillingness to challenge what has become status quo or conventional wisdom in CSI will mean stagnation. Thus, we must continually check our course, making minor adjustments and major changes.

3. ORGANIZATIONAL CONFORMITY FOR THE SAKE OF CONFORMITY IS DEATH.

Our Lord has created something unique and distinctive in CSI for the sake of the nations. To sacrifice this on the altar of organizational expediency or uniformity is wrong. We are part of the organizational family, and yet we do not have to look or act exactly like our brothers and sisters. Our motivation must not be conformity to organizational standards, procedures and policies for the sake of conformity. Rather, our motives must be driven by what it will take to reach the nations.

4. THE WAY FORWARD FOR CSI MUST BE THROUGH HUMILITY AND SERVICE.

This which we believe about the nations and to be the very heart of God will not be grasped by others through arrogance or power of persuasion, but only through humility and service to those around us and the rest of our organization. The politics of power and earth are not the way of our Lord, so they should not be our way either. We must continually remember that we are participants in World A only at our Lord's gracious invitation.

5. WE ALL LIVE UNDER AUTHORITY AND ARE ACCOUNTABLE.

We live together under the covenant to bless the nations. In this relationship, we mentor, correct, teach and support each other. Thus, all of us are accountable to someone in a corporate-like structure where individuals are empowered for appropriate decision-making and leadership. The context in which we work and the stewardship of resources demand that we operate in the most efficient, effective manner possible.

6. THE GREATER OUR DIVERSITY, THE GREATER OUR STRENGTH.

A levelling of everyone to the lowest common denominator is not our aim. Everyone must not look and act the same. Equity is not our way of operating. Each of you will be treated differently. The aim is the maximizing of everyone's unique gifts and personality so that the destination is reached.

7. COMMUNICATION MUST BE WIDE AND SECURE.

We must redouble our efforts and use the latest means in order to communicate effectively and securely with each other and our constituency.

8. THE EDGE IS WHERE WE BELONG.

As individuals and as a group, we dare not draw back from the edge of World A. We are people who are gifted for and called to the edge; thus, with passion and intent we must continue to enter new people groups and cities rather than seeking only to consolidate the gains we have made.

9. WE WILL DO WHATEVER IT TAKES TO GET TO THE DESTINATION.

This does not mean that the end justifies every means. Rather, it means that we do what our Lord has asked of us, believing that He intends for His church to exist among all peoples before He returns. To get to this destination, we must move beyond restrictive thinking, work with GCC brothers and sisters, and believe He is working in every situation.

10. THE ORGANIZATION IS NOT YOUR GOD.

Your call is from the One who called Abraham to be a blessing to the nations. Your dependency must rest in Him alone. Your power does not lie in the organization's resources or name but in the One who created all things. If our worship and allegiance is not focused singularly on the One who made all peoples and on His Son, then we disqualify ourselves from this race.

APPENDIX F

IMB RELATIONSHIPS
LEVELS, GOALS & GUIDELINES[1]

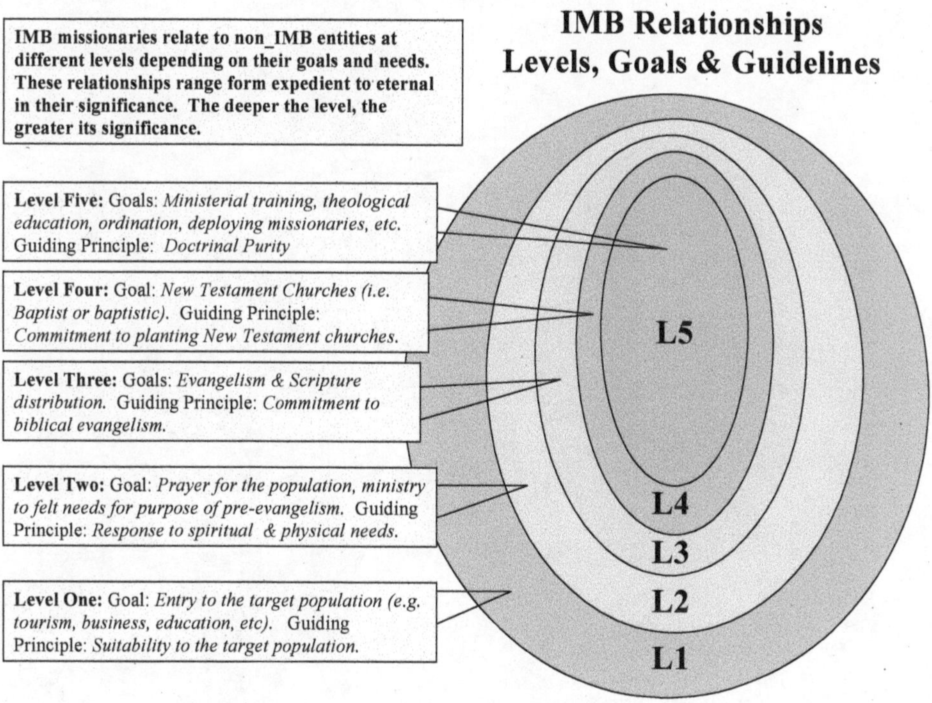

APPENDIX G

CPM ASSESSMENT TOOL

CPM INDICATORS

A Self Administered Assessment Tool

After reading the CPM book, viewing the CPM PowerPoint presentation, and/or attending a CPM workshop, analyze your own people group assignment, then complete the following CPM indicators Self Assessment Tool to get a clear representation of your progress toward a CPM.

1. Prayer
2. Abundant Gospel Sowing
3. Intentional Church Planting
4. Scriptural Authority
5. Local Leadership
6. Lay Leadership
7. Cell/House Churches
8. Churches Planting Churches
9. Rapid Reproduction
10. Healthy Churches
11. Worship in Heart Language
12. Communal Evangelism
13. Rapid Involvement of Converts
14. Passions and Fearlessness
15. Christianity with a Price
16. Leadership Crisis/Spiritual Void
17. OJT for Church Leadership
18. Decentralized Authority
19. Low Profile for Outsiders
20. Missionaries Suffer
21. Extra Biblical Requirements
22. Cultural Identity Lost
23. Poor Examples of Christianity
24. Non-Reproducible Church Models
25. Subsidies Creating Dependence
26. Extra-Biblical Leadership Requirements
27. Trying to Keep within One Denomination
28. Linear Sequential Patterns
29. Prescriptive Strategies

TEN UNIVERSAL ELEMENTS (1-10) On a scale of one to ten (one being the lowest and ten the highest) rate the evidence of each of these ten universal elements of a CPM in your assigned people group or city.

TEN COMMON FACTORS (11-20) On a scale of one to ten (one being the lowest and ten the highest) rate the evidence of each of these ten common factors of a CPM in your assigned people group or city.

NINE OBSTACLES (21-29) On a scale of one to ten (Ten being the lowest and one the highest) rate the evidence of each of these nine obstacles to a CPM in your assigned people group or city.

Consult the chart below to get a visual interpretation of your CPM strengths and weaknesses….

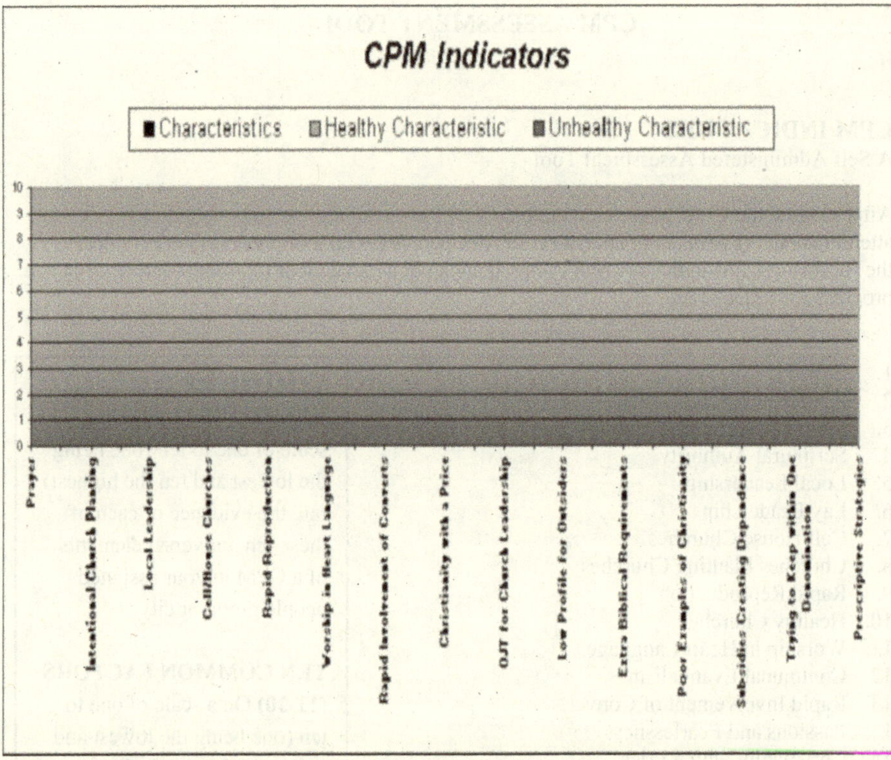

APPENDIX H

Church Planting Movement Assessment Guide[1]

This guide outlines the essential components of a CPM assessment and report. The assessment team should use this guide in crafting its approach to ensure that each of the key items is addressed.

The purpose of the assessment is fourfold:

1. To accurately describe the history, nature, and extent of the movement;
2. To describe and evaluate the faith and practice of churches within the movement;
3. To identify effective strategies and practices that may benefit other work; and,
4. To suggest interventions needed to address current issues or to avert future ones.

Research Methodology

The assessment team should employ quantitative, qualitative, or mixed research methodologies appropriate to the population segment under consideration and to the information sources available. The assessment team should consult with the Regional Research Coordinator and/or Global Research Department regarding the strengths and weaknesses of various approaches. Appendix A outlines possible approaches the assessment team may employ.

The final report of the assessment team must include a description of the methodology employed, the rationale underlying that choice, and a brief discussion of the strengths and weaknesses of the approach.

Information Sources

The assessment team should carefully consider the reliability of the many and varied information sources it utilizes in the course of its work. The final report must include a brief discussion of sources used by the team and an evaluation of their reliability.

Security Issues

The assessment team must thoroughly discuss its plans with regional leadership before conducting the assessment to ensure that the team's presence, organizational identity, and activities do not jeopardize the movement, other work, or field personnel and their partners.

The final report must address the security risk of the report itself and establish parameters regarding its distribution and use.

Part I: Description of Population Segment

The assessment team can gather much of this information prior to conducting its field research Sources include the CPPI database, the Ethnologue, the regional research coordinator, and field personnel.

I. Name of People Group or other population segment (alternative names)

II. Location(s)

III. Population

IV. Language(s)

V. Religion(s)

VI. History of Christian Work

Part II: Description of Informants

Regardless of the particular research methodology employed, local informants (i.e. believers within the movement) are invaluable to the work of the assessment team. The team will want to collect some basic information regarding each informant and link this to the information provided by that informant. This will enable the team to compare and contrast information provided by individuals sharing certain characteristics (e.g. did men and women answer questions the same way, how do responses of leaders differ from those of members, did members of church in the northern part of the province answer questions the same way as those from the southern part, etc.).

I. Gender

II. Age

III. Residence (e.g. province, village, etc.)

IV. Highest educational level attained

V. Language(s) spoken

VI. How long has the informant been a Christian?

VII. Does the informant have a leadership role in the church? If so, what?

VIII. Other relevant demographic information regarding the informant

Part III: History, Nature, and Extent of the Movement

IX. Describe the history of the movement. Include key individuals, groups, and events.

X. Nature of the Movement: Is this a CPM?

A church planting movement is a sustained, rapid multiplication of churches planting churches within a given population segment The following items are essential for determining whether or not a church planting movement is underway.

A. *Sustainability*

A key factor that separates church planting movements from short-lived increases in church plants (such as those resulting from an evangelistic crusade or church planting campaigns) is sustainability. Once begun, church planting movements are not reliant on significant outside initiative, assistance, or resources. The following items are critical for answering the question of sustainability.

1. **Evangelism, discipleship, and church planting DNA**

   Church planting movements are dependent upon the evangelism, discipleship, and church planting efforts of church members.

a) Who in the church is doing the evangelism, discipleship, and church planting? What percentage of church membership is engaged in evangelism? Discipling others? Church planting?

b) How soon after coming to faith are individuals sharing their faith and discipling others? Planting churches?

c) Who provides training and mentoring in the process of evangelism, discipleship, and church planting? What is the frequency and duration of such training and mentoring?

d) What is the content, format (formal vs. informal, individual/small group/conference, etc.), and location of such training and mentoring?

2. Selection and training of church leadership

a) Who is receiving leadership training within churches?

b) Are churches choosing their own leadership? How?

c) Are churches identifying multiple leaders in each church?

d) What roles do leaders play? What things can only be done by leaders?

e) How are leaders trained? Who teaches them?

f) What is the content , format, and location of such training?

3. Indigeneity

a) Are churches finding places to meet without outside funding?

b) Is leadership coming from within the local church?

c) Is the local church handling its own celebration of the Lord's Supper and baptism?

d) Are members in the church self-feeding from God's Word? How do church members study God's Word?

e) Is the worship and ministry language of the church compatible with that of the community?

f) What are the sources, transmission, and uses of outside funding?

g) Are the churches producing their own music?

h) What languages are used in the worship and ministry of the church?

i) Are the churches finding ways to take the gospel to others?

B. Rapid Multiplication

By definition, church planting movements involve rapid multiplication. How rapid is "rapid?" In a church planting movement, the majority of churches reproduce within twelve months. Demographic information collected above may reveal that only particular segments of the larger people group are experiencing a CPM.

1. What percentage of churches are reproducing each year?

2. How long does it take for new churches to reproduce?

3. What percentage of new churches are reproducing within twelve months?

XI. Extent of the Movement

An important part of the work of the assessment team is to determine the extent of the movement. This may present one of the greatest challenges to the team. The nature of the research methodology employed as well as that of the information available to the team will greatly affect the reliability of this determination. Some possibilities include: a) a census of churches in the movement; b) a sufficiently-large random sample of churches in the movement; c) written records or reports regarding growth of the movement; d) estimates by leaders and/or members. The team should always aim to make the most accurate estimate possible given the constraints of the situation in which it is conducting its assessment.

Appendix B provides definitions of many terms used in this assessment. Carefully note distinctions between various categories (e.g. the difference between "churches" and "outreach groups").

A. Total churches: This year? One year Ago? Five years ago? Ten years ago? Average Annual Growth Rates?

B. Total number of new churches planted: This year? Last year?

C. Total membership: This year? Five years ago? Ten year is ago? Average Annual Growth Rates?

D. Total number of baptisms: This year? Last year?

E. Total number of outreach groups: This year? One year Ago? Five years ago? Ten years ago? Average Annual Growth Rates?

F. Total number of new outreach groups started: This year? Last year?

G. Total number of missionaries sent from this group to another people group within the same country: This year? Last year? Five years ago?

H. Total number of missionaries sent from this group to a people group in another country: This year? Last year? Five years ago?

I. What is the geographic distribution of the movement? Are there any places or segments of the group where the movement is not spreading? Why?

J. Note any ethnic, linguistic, cultural, or other significant boundaries the movement has crossed.

Part IV: Faith and Practice

XII. How do believers define "church"?

XIII. Describe the practices of the churches in terms of their five basic purposes. You may have partially addressed some of these items above:

A. Worship

B. Ministry

C. Evangelism

D. Fellowship

E. Discipleship –What percentage of church membership receives personal discipleship training?

XIV. Describe the availability and use of Scripture. What percentage of church membership participates in the Bible-teaching ministries of the church?

XV. Describe the role and prevalence of prayer in churches.

XVI. Describe the nature and extent of persecution, if present. How are believers prepared for such persecution?

XVII. Are churches durable or ephemeral? What percentage of new churches survive one year? Two years? Three years or more?

XVIII. Describe the nature and extent of charismatic practices, if any.

XIX. Describe the nature and extent of any syncretistic elements within the movement?

XX. Do churches have any documents that outline their beliefs?

XXI. Is the faith and practice of the churches consistent with that of Baptists? Note any areas of concern and the extent of such variant faith and practice.

Part V: Lessons Learned: Effective Strategies and Practices

XXII. What were the key elements that contributed to the growth of this movement?

XXIII. What challenges has the movement encountered thus far and how has it addressed them?

Part VI: Issues and Intervention

XXIV. What are the strengths of the movement? Its weaknesses?

XXV. What is the future of the movement?

XXVI. What should we do now to strengthen the movement?

---

[1] Taken from the CPM Assessment Guide developed by the Global Research Department of the International Mission Board (revision dated March 11, 2004).

Glossary

Beachhead Church. The initial churches planted among a people group or population segment previously considered unreached or unevangelized.

Church-planting movement (CPM). "A Holy Spirit-controlled process of rapid, multiple reproduction of indigenous churches among a specific people group so that every individual within that people group has the opportunity to hear and respond to the Good News of Jesus Christ."[1]

Evangelized persons. "Individuals who have had adequate opportunity or opportunities to hear the gospel and respond to it."[2]

Great Commission Christian (GCC). "A Bible-believing, evangelical follower of the Lord Jesus Christ desiring to carry out His command to make disciples among every tribe, nation and tongue in the world."[3]

Megacity. An urban area, metropolis or city whose population is one million or more.

Megapeople. A people group whose population is one million or more.

Mission. The entire scope of God's salvific plan and intention among the nations (*Missio Dei).*

Missions. Sending forth representatives of the church who focus on carrying out the task of world evangelization through the planting and nurturing of churches among the non-Christian world.

Non-residential missionary (NRM). "A full-time, professional career foreign missionary who is matched up with a single unevangelized population segment for purposes of concentrating on priorities of initial evangelization and eliminating gaps and inadvertent duplications with

---

[1] R. Bruce Carlton, *Acts 29: Practical Training in Facilitating Church-Planting Movements Among the Neglected Harvest Fields* (Singapore, by the author, 2003), 18.

[2] David B. Barrett and Todd M. Johnson, *Our Globe And How To Reach It,* 122.

[3] R. Bruce Carlton, *Project Thessalonica: Acts 29 Training for Churches* (Singapore, by the author, 2004), 10.

other agencies."[4] The non-residential missionary lives outside of the area where the target people live. The overarching objective of a non-residential missionary is seeing that all persons in the unevangelized population segment are evangelized.

People group. A human population group that claims affinity via a common language, a shared ethnicity and a common culture. In terms of evangelization, this term describes the largest possible grouping of people within which the gospel is able to spread without facing significant social barriers.

Reached. "Having heard the gospel, understanding it and having had opportunity to respond by joining an indigenous church or fellowship of one's own culture."[5]

Restricted-access country. "A country whose government or regime restricts access by foreign missionaries wishing to reside, foreign Christians wishing to visit, or foreign Christian literature, or broadcasting, or other Christian ministry or influences."[6]

Strategy coordinator (SC). A missionary who targets a single, neglected people group, city or cluster of peoples groups in a defined area, collaborates with many Great Commission Christians, and takes responsibility for developing and implementing a comprehensive master plan aimed at facilitating an indigenous church-planting movement. Such a missionary may or may not live among the target people. For Southern Baptists, this term replaced the title non-residential missionary in 1992.

10/40 Window. The term among evangelical Christians to denote an imaginary rectangular-shaped window, whose height is 10 degrees north latitude to 40 degrees north latitude, and whose width stretches from West Africa to Asia. Over 2 billion people reside in this window that contains over 60 countries. The overwhelming majority of unreached peoples reside within this window.

Tentmaker. Cross-cultural Christian workers who have a secular identity/vocation while, at the same time, intentionally seeking to witness

---

[4] V. David Garrison, *The Non-residential Missionary: A New Strategy and the People It Serves* (Monrovia, CA: MARC, 1990), 13.

[5] Barrett and Reapsome, 125.

[6] Barrett and Reapsome, 125.

and make disciples. Typically, tentmakers serve in restricted-access countries or among unreached people groups.

Unevangelized persons. Individuals that have not yet had adequate opportunity or opportunities to hear and respond to the gospel.

Unreached people group (UPG). A people group that lacks an indigenous church or community of Christians with the resources to carry out the evangelization of the remainder of the people group without having cross-cultural or outside assistance.

Viable indigenous church. Within a people group, a community of followers of Jesus Christ who have adequate membership and resources needed to evangelize their own people group without needing any outside or cross-cultural assistance.

World A. A people group or population segment that is less than 50% evangelized. These people groups often are referred to as unreached or unevangelized.

World B. A people group or population segment that is more than 50% evangelized, but less than 60% church members or less than 60% who have decided to follow Christ.

World C. Often referred to as the Christian world or people who call themselves Christian. World C people are those greater than 95% evangelized and whose church membership exceeds 60%.

Selected Bibliography

Allen, Roland. *Missionary Methods: St. Paul's or Ours.* American edition. London: World Dominion Press, Reprint. Grand Rapids: William B. Eerdmans, 1998.

________. *The Spontaneous Expansion of the Church.* American edition. Grand Rapids: William B. Eerdmans, 1962. Reprint. Eugene, OR: Wipf and Stock, 1997.

Baldridge, Gary. *Keith Parks: Breaking Barriers & Opening Frontiers.* Macon: Smyth & Helwys Publishing, Inc., 1999.

The Baptist Faith and Message. Nashville: Southern Baptist Convention, 2005.

Barnett, Mike. "Innovation in Mission Operations: Creative-Access Platforms." In *The Changing Face of World Missions: Engaging Contemporary Issues and Trends,* eds. Michael Pocock, Gailyn Van Rheenen and Douglas McConnell, Encountering Mission Series, ed. A. Scott Moreau, 209-44. Grand Rapids: Baker Academic, 2005.

Barrett, David B. *World Christian Encyclopaedia: A Comparative Survey of Churches and Religions in the Modern World AD 1900-2000.* New York: Oxford University Press, 1982.

________. *Towards a Global Strategy for World Evangelization.* Richmond: Southern Baptist Foreign Mission Board, Accession Number 625, May 24, 1983.

________. "Silver and Gold Have I None: Church of the Poor or Church of the Rich?" *International Bulletin* 7, No. 4 (October 1983): 146-51.

________. "Five Statistical Eras of Global Mission, "*Missiology* 12, No. 1 (January 1984), 21-39.

________. *Evangelize! A Historical Survey of the Concept.* AD2000 Series. Birmingham: New Hope, 1987.

Barrett, David B., George T. Kurian, and Todd M. Johnson. *World Christian Encyclopaedia: A Comparative Survey of Churches and Religions in the Modern World.* 2nd edition. New York: Oxford University Press, 2001.

Barrett, David B. and James W. Reapsome. *Seven Hundred Plans to Evangelize the World: The Rise of a Global Evangelization Movement,* AD Series. Birmingham: New Hope, 1988.

Barrett, David B. and Todd M. Johnson. *Our Globe and How To Reach It: Seeing the World Evangelized by AD2000 and Beyond.* AD2000 Series. Birmingham: New Hope, 1990.

"Board Appoints its first NRMs." *The Commission* (August 1989), 71.

"Board of Trustees Minutes." Richmond: Southern Baptist Foreign Mission Board, Accession Number 1659, July 16, 1964.

________. Richmond: Southern Baptist Foreign Mission Board, Accession Number 1835, April 12, 1966.

________. Richmond: Southern Baptist Foreign Mission Board, Accession Number 1502, September 08, 1966.

________. Richmond: Southern Baptist Foreign Mission Board, Accession Number 1314, March 10, 1981.

________. Richmond: Southern Baptist Foreign Mission Board, Accession Number 1511, February 08, 1982.
________. Richmond: Southern Baptist Foreign Mission Board, Accession Number 679, September 14, 1982.
________. Richmond: Southern Baptist Foreign Mission Board Accession Number 625, May 24, 1983.
________. Glorieta, NM: Southern Baptist Foreign Mission Board, Accession Number 618, August 08, 1983.
________. Richmond: Southern Baptist Foreign Mission Board, Accession Number 598, February 11, 1985.
________. Nashville: Southern Baptist Foreign Mission Board, Accession Number 589, April 15, 1985.
________. Ridgecrest, NC: Southern Baptist Foreign Mission Board, Accession Number 575, June 24, 1986.
________. Richmond: Southern Baptist Foreign Mission Board, Accession Number 447, February 09, 1987.
________. Glorieta, NM: Southern Baptist Foreign Mission Board, Accession Number 573, August 08, 1987.
________. Richmond: Southern Baptist Foreign Mission Board, Accession Number 444, December 07, 1987.
________. Richmond: Southern Baptist Foreign Mission Board, Accession Number 1362, February 08, 1988.
________. Richmond: Southern Baptist Foreign Mission Board, Accession Number 528, October 10, 1988.
________. Richmond: Southern Baptist Foreign Mission Board, Accession Number 531, February 13, 1989.
________. Little Rock: Southern Baptist Foreign Mission Board, Accession Number 436, April 09, 1989.
________. Ridgecrest, NC: Southern Baptist Foreign Mission Board, Accession Number 733, June 24, 1990.
________. Glorieta, NM: Southern Baptist Foreign Mission Board, Accession Number 543, July 21, 1990.
________. Richmond: Southern Baptist Foreign Mission Board, Accession Number 654, August 12, 1991.
________. Clemson, SC: Southern Baptist Foreign Mission Board, Accession Number 1029, April 06, 1992.
________. El Paso: Southern Baptist Foreign Mission Board, Accession Number 1033, June 22, 1992.
________. Richmond: Southern Baptist Foreign Mission Board, Accession Number 1113, August 17, 1992.
________. Richmond: Southern Baptist Foreign Mission Board, Accession Number 1358, October 10, 1993.
________. Richmond: Southern Baptist Foreign Mission Board, Accession Number 1395, December 03, 1993.
________. Richmond: Southern Baptist Foreign Mission Board, Accession Number 1639, October 10, 1994.
________. Richmond: Southern Baptist Foreign Mission Board, Accession Number 1677, December 112, 1994.

________. Richmond: Southern Baptist Foreign Mission Board, Accession Number 1961, October 09, 1995.

________. Knoxville: Southern Baptist Foreign Mission Board, Accession Number 2162, February 12, 1996.

________. Richmond: Southern Baptist Foreign Mission Board, Accession Number 2464, October 06, 1996.

________. Little Rock: Southern Baptist International Mission Board, Accession Number 2530, April 07, 1997.

________. Richmond: Southern Baptist International Mission Board Accession Number 2556, June 02, 1997.

________. Fort Lauderdale, FL: Southern Baptist International Mission Board, Accession Number 2656, November 18, 1998.

________. Richmond: Southern Baptist International Mission Board, Accession Number 2685, May 18, 2000.

________. Framingham, MA: Southern Baptist International Mission Board, Accession Number 2376, May 06, 2003.

________. Lexington: Southern Baptist International Mission Board, Accession Number 2788, November 10, 2003.

________. Richmond: Southern Baptist International Mission Board Accession Number 2790, February 02, 2004.

________. Charlotte, NC: Southern Baptist International Mission Board, Accession Number 2810, March 14, 2005.

________. Midland, TX: Southern Baptist International Mission Board, Accession Number 2812, May 19, 2005.

Bosch, David J. "Evangelism: An Holistic Approach." *Journal of Theology for Southern Africa* 36 (September 1981): 43-63.

________. "The Structure of Mission: An Exposition of Matthew 28:16-20." In *Exploring Church Growth* ed. Wilbert R. Shenk, 218-48. Grand Rapids: William B. Eerdmans, 1983.

________."Mission in the 1990s: Three Views." *International Bulletin,* 14, No. 4 (October 1990: 149-52).

________. *Transforming Mission: Paradigm Shifts in Theology of Mission,* American Society of Missiology Series, No. 16. Maryknoll: Orbis Books, 1991.

Bridges, Erich. "New Kid on the Block: the 'Non-residential Missionary.'" *The Commission* (August 1988), 45.

________. "Missionaries See Results in Unevangelized 'World A.'" Richmond: Southern Baptist Foreign Mission Board, May 10, 1993; available from https://solomon.imb.org; Stories database (accessed September 28, 2004).

________. "Rankin Writes Missionaries, Calls Election 'a Miracle.'" Richmond: Southern Baptist Foreign Mission Board, June 25, 1993; available from https://solomon.imb.org; Stories database (accessed September 15, 2004).

________. "367 New Churches Prove 'Last Frontier' Reachable." Richmond: Southern Baptist Foreign Mission Board, March 14, 1996; available from https://solomon.imb.org; Stories database (accessed September 15, 2004).

________. "Mobilization: The World Connection." Richmond: Southern Baptist International Mission Board, July 01, 1999; available from https://solomon.imb.org; Stories database (accessed September 28, 2004).

________. "ANALYSIS: Strategy Coordinator Role sets off Missions Revolution."

Richmond: Southern Baptist International Mission Board, September 28, 1999; available from http://solomon.imb.org; Stories database (accessed September 15, 2004).

________. "RapAdvance: How Rapid?" Richmond: Southern Baptist International Mission Board, October 01, 1999; available from https://solomon.imb.org; Stories database (accessed January 22, 2005).

Brother Andrew with John and Elizabeth Sherrill. *God's Smuggler*. Old Tappan, NJ: Fleming H. Revell Company, 1967.

Bruce, Joe W. *Report to the Board: Middle America and Canada.* Ridgecrest, NC: Southern Baptist Foreign Mission Board, Accession Number 1922, August 17, 1995.

______. *Report to the Board: Middle America and Canada.* Atlanta: Southern Baptist Foreign Mission Board, Accession Number 2438, August 13, 1996.

Bryan, Charles W. *Report to the Board: Office of Overseas Operations.* Richmond: Southern Baptist Foreign Mission Board, Accession Number 989, October 13, 1982.

______. *Report to the Board: Office of Overseas Operations*. Richmond: Southern Baptist Foreign Mission Board, Accession Number 1335, February 08, 1983.

Burrows, William R. "A Seventh Paradigm? Catholics and Radical Inculturation." In *Mission in Bold Humility: David Bosch's Work Considered,* eds. Willem Saayman and Klippies Kritzinger, 121-38. Maryknoll: Orbis Books, 1996).

"Busy in World A." *The Commission* (October-November 1993), 3.

Carlton, R. Bruce. *Rapid Advance of South Asia Team Scorecard.* Singapore: Rapid Advance of South Asia, 2000. [electronic document]; available from the author.

______."Towards a New Understanding of Missions: A Challenge to the Conventional Missions Thinking of Our Day." In *Strategic Coordination in Mission: Training Manual for the Nehemiah Institute for Strategic Coordination,* eds. S. D. Ponraj and R. Bruce Carlton, 8-12. Chennai: Mission Education Books, 2001.

______."Notes from the November 2003 Global Regional Leadership Team Forum." Rome, GA: Southern Baptist International Mission Board, 2003. [electronic document]; available from the Author.

______. *Acts 29: Practical Training in Facilitating Church-Planting Movements Among The Neglected Harvest Fields.* Singapore: by the author, 2003.

______. *Project Thessalonica: Acts 29 Training for Churches.* Singapore: by the author, 2004.

Cauthen, Baker J. and Frank K. Means. *Advance to Bold Mission Thrust: A History of Southern Baptist Foreign Missions, 1845-1980*. Richmond: Southern Baptist Foreign Mission Board, 1981.

Coggins, Wade T. "God at Work Around the World." *Missiology* 12, No. 1 (January 1984): 75-9.

"Compassion Net." Richmond: Southern Baptist International Mission Board, 2005; available at http://imb.org/CompassionNet.

Cooperative Services International Non-residential Missionary Program Executive Overview. Preview Committee Edition. Richmond: Southern Baptist Foreign Mission Board, January 08, 1992.

Cooperative Services International Non-residential Missionary Program Review. Preview Committee Edition. Richmond: Southern Baptist Foreign Mission Board, January 1992.

Cooperative Services International Statistical Review 1992-1995. Richmond: Southern Baptist Foreign Mission Board, February 02, 1996.

Crawley, Winston. *Report to the Board: Vice-President for Planning.* Richmond: Southern Baptist Foreign Mission Board, Accession Number 751, October 13, 1980.

________. "Horizons: 'Hidden Peoples.'" *The Commission* (February-March 1981), 78.

________. *Report to the Board: Vice-President for Planning.* Richmond: Southern Baptist Foreign Mission Board, Accession Number 1368, February 10, 1981.

________. *Report to the Board: Vice-President for Planning.* Richmond: Southern Baptist Foreign Mission Board, Accession Number 1314, March 10, 1981.

________. "Horizons: Gates to Closed Places Could Swing Open." *The Commission* (September 1983), 65.

________. "Horizons: Which Ones Are Closed?" *The Commission* (August 1984), 7.

________. *Global Mission A Story to Tell: An Interpretation of Southern Baptist Foreign Missions.* Nashville: Broadman Press, 1985.

De Wet, Chris. "The Church Growth Movement." *Missionalia* 14, No. 2 (August 1986): 85-99.

Eitel, Keith E. *Paradigm Wars: The Southern Baptist International Mission Board Faces the Third Millennium.* Waynesboro: Paternoster Publishing, 2000.

________. "Vision Assessment: The International Mission Board of the Southern Baptist Convention." Electronic mail letter to Jerry Rankin, October 2003.

________. "Reply to Rankin." Electronic mail letter to Jerry Rankin, November 06, 2003.

Erickson, Millard J. *God in Three Persons: A Contemporary Interpretation of the Trinity.* Grand Rapids: Baker Books, 1995

Escobar, Samuel. "Evangelical missiology: peering into the future at the turn of the century." In *Global Missiology for the21st Century The Iguassu Dialogue,* ed. William D. Taylor, 101-22. Grand Rapids: Baker Academic, 2000.

Estep, William R. *Whole Gospel Whole World: The Foreign Mission Board of the Southern Baptist Convention 1845-1995.* Nashville: Broadman Press, 1994.

Faulkner, John H. *Report to the Board: Eastern and Southern Africa.* Knoxville: Southern Baptist Foreign Mission Board, Accession Number 2162, February 13, 1996.

"Findings of the Commission Edinburgh 1910," in *Classics of Christian Missions,* ed. Francis M. DuBose, 329-37. Nashville: Broadman Press, 1979

Fudge,. Bill. *Report to the Board.* Sacramento: Southern Baptist International Mission Board, Accession Number 2676, November 19, 1999.

Garrison, V. David. *The Non-residential Missionary: A New Strategy and the People it Serves.* Innovations in Mission, ed. Bryant L. Myers. Monrovia: MARC, 1990.

________. "An Unexpected New Strategy." *International Journal of Frontier Missions* 7, No. 4 (October 1990), 107-15.

________. *Church Planting Movement Profile.* Richmond: Southern Baptist International Mission Board, 1999, [electronic document].

________. *Church Planting Movements.* Richmond: Southern Baptist International Mission Board, 2000.

________. *Global Analysis Project Report.* Shreveport, LA: Southern Baptist International Mission Board, Accession Number 2698, March 08, 2001.

________. *Church Planting Movements: How God is Redeeming a Lost World.* Midlothian, VA: WIGTake Resources, 2004.

________. "Response to Bruce." Electronic mail letter to Bruce Carlton, December 21, 2004.

_______. *Board of Directors.* India: by the author, 2005, [electronic document].

_______. "Response to Your Questions about the SC Paradigm vs. Church Growth." Electronic mail letter to Bruce Carlton, September 14, 2005.

_______. "Response: Healthy Churches." Electronic mail letter to Bruce Carlton, November 09, 2005.

_______. "Best Practices Institute." Electronic mail letter to the South Asia Regional Leadership Team, November 22, 2005.

_______."Response to BP Site." Electronic mail letter to South Asia Regional Leadership Team, December 06, 2005.

Gay, Larry. *Report to the Board.* Sacramento: Southern Baptist International Mission Board, Accession Number 2676, November 15, 1999.

_______. *Report to the Board.* Shreveport, LA: Southern Baptist International Mission Board, Accession Number 2698, March 08, 2001.

"Global Strategy Group Minutes." Richmond: Southern Baptist Foreign Mission Board, Accession Number 350, May 12, 1987.

_______. Richmond: Southern Baptist Foreign Mission Board, Accession Number 393, June 29, 1987.

_______. Richmond: Southern Baptist Foreign Mission Board, Accession Number 356, September 08, 1987.

_______. Richmond: Southern Baptist Foreign Mission Board, Accession Number 395, November 24, 1987.

_______. Richmond: Southern Baptist Foreign Mission Board, Accession Number 378, March 06, 1989.

_______. Richmond: Southern Baptist Foreign Mission Board, Accession Number 379, April 04, 1989.

_______. Richmond: Southern Baptist Foreign Mission Board, Accession Number 381, October 03, 1989.

_______. Richmond: Southern Baptist Foreign Mission Board, Accession Number 832, April 24, 1990.

_______. Richmond: Southern Baptist Foreign Mission Board, Accession Number 369, October 16, 1990.

_______. Richmond: Southern Baptist Foreign Mission Board, Accession Number 655, November 16, 1990.

_______. Richmond: Southern Baptist Foreign Mission Board, Accession Number 574, March 04, 1991.

_______. Richmond: Southern Baptist Foreign Mission Board, Accession Number 824, July 24, 1991.

_______. Richmond: Southern Baptist Foreign Mission Board, Accession Number 826, October 03, 1991.

_______. Richmond: Southern Baptist Foreign Mission Board, Accession Number 955, April 14, 1992.

_______. Richmond: Southern Baptist Foreign Mission Board, Accession Number 1034, May 05, 1992.

_______. Richmond: Southern Baptist Foreign Mission Board, Accession Number 1277, May 03, 1993.

Goff, William E. *Report to the Board: Spanish South America.* Richmond: Southern Baptist Foreign Mission Board, Accession Number 1677, December 13, 1994.

Guder, Darrell L. *The Continuing Conversion of the Church.* The Gospel and Our Culture Series, ed. Craig van Gelder. Grand Rapids: William B. Eerdmans, 2000.

Hadaway, Robin. "Balancing the Biblical Perspectives: A Missiological Analysis," *Journal of Evangelism and Missions* 2 (Spring 2003): 103-14.

Harvey, Mark. "Missionaries Needed: Non-residential Missionaries." *The Commission* (August 1990), 71.

Hiebert, Paul G. "Barrett and Beyond." *Missiology* 12, No. 1 (January 1984): 64-73.

Jennings, Jason and Laurence Haughton. *It's not the Big that Eat the Small...It's the Fast that Eat the Slow: How to Use Speed as a Competitive Tool in Business.* New York: Harper Collins Publisher, 2000.

Kammerdiener, Don R. *Linking Strategy and Administration.* Glorieta: Southern Baptist Foreign Mission Board, Accession Number 543, July 21, 1990.

________. *Report to the Board: Executive Vice-President.* Richmond: Southern Baptist Foreign Mission Board, Accession Number 570, February 11, 1991.

Kelly, Mark. "New Directions." Richmond: Southern Baptist International Mission Board, June 01, 1997; available from https://solomon.imb.org; Stories database (accessed September 28, 2004).

________. "Mission Leaders Discuss Ways to Speed Outreach." Richmond: Southern Baptist International Mission Board, July 01, 1999; available from https://solomon.imb.org; Stories database (accessed September 15, 2004).

________. "Lost World Needs More, not Fewer Missionaries." Richmond: Southern Baptist International Mission Board, August 13, 2003; available from https://solomon.imb.org; Stories database (accessed September 28, 2004).

________. "IMB trustees evaluate strategy shift, adopt $258.9m budget, respond to criticism." Richmond: Southern Baptist International Mission Board, November 18, 2003; available from https://solomon.imb.org; Stories database (accessed September 28, 2004).

Kuitse, Roelf S. "Holy Spirit: Source of Messianic Mission." In *The Transfiguration of Mission: Biblical Theological & Historical Foundations.* Institute of Mennonite Studies Missionary Studies, 12, ed. Wilbert R. Shenk, 106-29. Scottdale, PA: Herald Press, 1993).

Like a Mighty Wav: Church Planting Movements. Produced by the Southern Baptist International Mission Board, 12 minutes, 2001, videocassette.

Martin, Don. "Evangelical Groups Seek and End Run to End Times." Richmond: Southern Baptist Foreign Mission Board, May 31, 1995; available from https://solomon.imb.org; Stories database (accessed September 28, 2004).

Mays, Patrick. "After Christendom, What? Renewal and Discovery of Church and Mission in the West." *Missiology* 27, No. 2 (April 1999): 245-58.

Meador, Clyde. *Report to the Board: Southern Asia and the Pacific.* Ft. Worth: Southern Baptist Foreign Mission Board, Accession Number 1513, April 27, 1994.

Mission and Evangelism – History. Geneva: World Council of Churches, n.d.; available from http://www.wcc-coe.org/wcc/what/mission/hist-e.html; Internet (accessed November 22, 2004).

McConnell, Douglas and J. Ted Esler. "The Impact of New Technologies: Life in the Virtual World and Beyond." In *The Changing Face of world Missions: Engaging Contemporary Issues and Trends,* eds. Michael Pocock, Gailyn Van Rheenen and Douglas McConnell, Encountering Mission Series, ed. A. Scott Moreau, 299-320. Grand Rapids: Baker Academic, 2005.

McGavran, Donald A. "The Dimensions of World Evangelization." In *Let the Earth Hear His Voice: International Congress on World Evangelization Lausanne, Switzerland,* ed. J. D. Douglas, 94- Minneapolis: World Wide Publications, 1975.

________. *Understanding Church Growth.* 3rd edition. Revised and edited by C. Peter Wagner. Grand Rapids: William B. Eerdmans, 1990.

Moffett, Samuel Hugh. "The Filaments of a World Mission." *Missiology* 12, No. 1 (January 1984): 69-74.

Moore, Charles E., ed. *Provocations: Spiritual Writings of Kierkegaard.* Maryknoll: Orbis Books, 2002.

Moreau, A. Scott, Gary R. Corwin, and Gary B. McGee. *Introducing World Missions: A Biblical, Historical, and Practical Survey.* Grand Rapids: Baker Academic, 2004.

Myers, Lewis I., Jr. *Netweaving As A Shaping Concept.* Richmond: Southern Baptist Foreign Mission Board, Accession Number 444, December 07, 1987.

________. *Report to the Board: Cooperative Services International.* Glorieta: Southern Baptist Foreign Mission Board, Accession Number 530, July 16, 1988.

________. *The World of Gaps.* Richmond: Southern Baptist Foreign Mission Board, Accession Number 528, October 10, 1988.

________. *Report to the Board: Cooperative Services International.* Richmond: Southern Baptist Foreign Mission Board, Accession Number 539, December 11, 1989.

________. *And Yet There is More.* Richmond: Southern Baptist Foreign Mission Board, Accession Number 542, June 08, 1990.

________. "New Horizons: Seed Time and Harvest." Richmond: Southern Baptist Foreign Mission Board, January 01, 1991; available from https://solomon.imb.org; Stories database (accessed September 28, 2004).

________. *Two Roads, One Destination.* Richmond: Southern Baptist Foreign Mission Board, Accession Number 570, February 11, 1991.

________. *Report to the Board.* Richmond: Southern Baptist Foreign Mission Board, Accession Number 1395, December 06, 1993.

________. *Roads Less Traveled.* Orlando: Southern Baptist Foreign Mission Board, Accession Number 1560, June 10, 1994.

Myers, Lewis I., Jr. and Jim Slack. *To The Edge: A Planning Process for People Group Specific Strategy Development.* Richmond: Southern Baptist Foreign Mission Board, 1999.

Neill, Stephen. "A World Christian Encyclopaedia." *Missiology,* 12, No.1 (January 1984): 5-19.

O'Brien, William R. "'World A': Unbegun task?" *The Commission* (October-November 1990), 70.

Parks, R. Keith. *Report to the Board.* Richmond: Southern Baptist Foreign Mission Board, Accession Number 736, January 7, 1980.

________. "The Future of Missions: Change." *The Commission* (October 1980), 2.

________. *Report to the Board.* Richmond: Southern Baptist Foreign Mission Board, Accession Number 751, October 13, 1980.

________. *Foreign Missions – The Next Thrust.* Indianapolis: Southern Baptist Foreign Mission Board, Accession Number 871, April 11, 1983.

________. *Report to the Board.* Biloxi, MS: Southern Baptist Foreign Mission Board, Accession Number 597, April 09, 1984.

________. *Shaping Change in Foreign Missions.* Richmond: Southern Baptist Foreign

Mission Board, Accession Number 636, October 07, 1985.
_______. *Transforming a Vision into Reality.* Richmond: Southern Baptist Foreign Mission Board, Accession Number, 584, February 10, 1986.
_______. *God-Given Visions Transform.* Richmond: Southern Baptist Foreign Mission Board,Accession Number 588, September 8, 1986.
_______. *Charting a Course – By Candlelight.* Richmond: Southern Baptist Foreign Mission Board, Accession Number 587, December 08, 1986.
_______. *World in View,* AD2000 Series. Birmingham: New Hope, 1987.
_______. *Will the Recommendations from the Transition Committee Change Our Foreign Mission Effort?* Richmond: Southern Baptist Foreign Mission Board, Accession Number 447, February 09, 1987.
_______. "World in View: Networking What It Is and Isn't." *The Commission* (January 1988), 6.
_______. *The State of Southern Baptist World Mission Efforts.* Richmond: Southern Baptist Foreign Mission Board, Accession Number 622, December 12, 1988.
_______. *The Information Age and World Missions Are Made For Each Other.* Richmond: Southern Baptist Foreign Mission Board, Accession Number 571, December 10, 1990.
_______. *Controlling Principles in Southern Baptist Foreign Missions.* Clemson, SC: Southern Baptist Foreign Mission Board, Accession Number 1029, April 06, 1992.
_______. Interview by Philip O. Hopkins, April 04, 2000. Transcript Southeastern SBC Historical Missiology Oral History Collection, Southeastern Baptist Theological Seminary, Wake Forest, SC.
"People Teams." Richmond: Southern Baptist International Mission Board, 2005; available at http://PeopleTeams.org
Phillips, Bill. *Report to the Board: West Africa.* Richmond: Southern Baptist Foreign Mission Board, Accession Number 1677, December 12, 1994.
_______. *Report to the Board: West Africa.* Richmond: Southern Baptist Foreign Mission Board, Accession Number 1961, October 09, 1995.
_______. *Report to the Board.* Ft. Lauderdale, FL: Southern Baptist International Mission Board, Accession Number 2656, November 18, 1998.
Piper, John. *Let the Nations Be Glad! The Supremacy of God in Missions.* Grand Rapids: Baker Books, 1993.
"Prayer*plus* Partnership." Richmond: Southern Baptist International Mission Board, 2005; available at http://imb.org/CompassionNet/prayerplus.asp.
Rankin, Jerry A. *Report to the Board.* Ft. Worth: Southern Baptist Foreign Mission Board, Accession Number 1513, April 25, 1994.
_______. *Report to the Board.* Alexandria, VA: Southern Baptist Foreign Mission Board, Accession Number 1607, August 15, 1994.
_______. "From the Rankin File: A Kingdom Task." *The Commission* (January-February 1995), 103.
_______. *Report to the Board.* Wake Forest, NC: Southern Baptist Foreign Mission Board, Accession Number 1743, February 13, 1995.
_______. "Compelled by a Vision." *The Commission* (March-April 1995), 103.
_______. *Report to the Board.* Cape Girardeau, MO: Southern Baptist Foreign Mission Board, Accession Number 2338, April 18, 1996.
_______. *Report to the Board.* Winston-Salem, NC: Southern Baptist Foreign Mission Board, Accession Number 2509, February 10, 1997.

________. "What's in a Name?" *The Commission* (June 1997): 53.

________. "From the Rankin File: Help that Hurts." *The Commission* (August 19970, 53.

________. "The Present Situation in Missions." In *Missiology: An Introduction to the Foundations, History, and Strategies of World Missions,* eds. John Mark Terry, Ebbie Smith and Justice Anderson, 30-50. Nashville: Broadman and Holman, 1998.

________. "From the Rankin File: Vision 2001." *The Commission* (January 1998), 53.

________. " From the Rankin File: Great Commission Partners." *The Commission* (March 1998), 53.

________. *Mobilizing for Missions in the New Millennium.* Richmond: Southern Baptist International Mission Board, 1999.

________. "From the Rankin File: Into all the World." *The Commission* (April 1999), 29.

________. "From the Rankin File: Organizing for Global Impact." *The Commission* (September 1999), 53.

________. "Missions in the New Millennium – A Conversation with Jerry Rankin." Richmond: Southern Baptist International Mission Board, January 01, 2000; available from https://solomon.imb.org; Stories database (accessed September 28, 2004).

________. "The 21st Century World May Look Dismal, but the Future of Missions is Bright." Richmond: Southern Baptist International Mission Board, May 10, 2001; available from https://solomon.imb.org; Stories database (accessed September 26, 2004).

________. *Report to the Board.* Richmond: Southern Baptist International Mission Board, Accession Number 2699, May 21, 2001.

________. *Report to the Board.* Knoxville: Southern Baptist International Mission Board, Accession Number 2732, March 13, 2003.

________. "From the Rankin File: Difficult to believe?" *The Commission* (May-June 2003), 55.

Records of World Congress on Evangelism Collection 14. Wheaton: Billy Graham Center Archives, 2004; available from http://www.wheaton.edu/bgc/archives/GUIDES/014.htm; Internet (accessed November 22, 2004).

Redreaming the Dream. Chiang Mai, Thailand: Cooperative Services International, February 1996.

Saayman, Willem A. "The Case of South Africa: Practice, Context, and Ideology." In *Exploring Church Growth,* ed. Wilbert R. Shenk, 132-43. Grand Rapids: William B. Eerdmans, 1983.

________.*Unity and Mission: A study of the concept of unity in ecumenical discussions since 1961and its influence on the world mission of the church.* Pretoria: University of South Africa, 1984.

________. "The Church Growth Movement: An Appropriate Challenge? A Response to Chris De Wet." *Missionalia* 14, No. 2 (August 1986): 100-2.

Schweer, G. William. "The Missionary Mandate of God's Nature." In *Missiology: An Introduction To the Foundations, History, and Strategies of World Mission,* eds. John Mark Terry, Ebbie Smith and Justice Anderson, 97-113. Nashville: Broadman and Holman, 1998.

Sergeant, Curtis. *NRM to SC: What's Changed.* Singapore: Global Training Center, 1999, [electronic document].

________. "Response: Questions about CPM Profile." Electronic mail letter to Bruce Carlton, November 09, 2005.

Sergeant, Curtis, William Smith and Susan Smith. *Characteristics of a CPM.* Richmond: Southern Baptist International Mission Board, 1999, [electronic document].

Shenk, Wilbert R. *Changing Frontiers of Mission.* American Society of Missiology Studies, No. 28. Maryknoll: Orbis Books, 1999.

Sherrill, Jon D. "Jerry Rankin: Ideology of a Postmodern Paradigm," *Faith and Mission* 16, No. 1 (Fall 1998).

Shreck, Harley C. and David Barrett, eds. *Unreached Peoples: Clarifying the Task.* Lausanne Unreached People Series, eds. Edward R. Dayton and Samuel Wilson. Monrovia: MARC, 1987.

Skelton, Martha. "Reflecting on a Missions Career." Richmond: Southern Baptist Foreign Mission Board, October 01, 1992; available from https://solomon.imb.org; Stories database (accessed December 13, 2004).

Smith, Ebbie. "Contemporary Theology of Religions." In *Missiology: An Introduction to the Foundations, History, and Strategies of World Missions,* eds. John Mark Terry, Ebbie Smith and Justice Anderson, 416-33. Nashville: Broadman and Holman, 1988.

Smith, William "Additional Document." Electronic mail letter to Bruce Carlton, November 26, 2004.

________. "Thoughts for Bruce." Electronic mail letter to Bruce Carlton, November 28, 2004.

________. "Response to Bruce." Electronic mail letter to Bruce Carlton, November 30, 2004.

________. Interview by author, January 07, 2005. Singapore. Written transcript. Available from the author.

________. "Response to Your Questions about the SC Paradigm vs. Church Growth." Electronic mail letter to Bruce Carlton, September 14, 2005.

Something New Under the Sun: New Directions at the International Mission Board. Richmond: Southern Baptist International Mission Board, January 1999).

Sorrell, Ken. "SC Survey." Electronic mail letter to Bruce Carlton, March 29, 2005.

"The Southern Baptists Restructure to Reach the Unreached Peoples: An Interview with Jerry Rankin, IMB President and Avery Willis, Senior Vice President for Overseas Operations." *Mission Frontiers Online* (July-October 1997); available from http://www.missionfrontiers.org/1997/0710/jo976.htm (accessed November 20, 2004).

Speidel, Mary E. "Personalizing Missions is Focus of FMB Conference." Richmond: Southern Baptist Foreign Mission Board, October 19, 1995; available from https://solomon.imb.org; Stories database (accessed September 28, 2004).

________. "Churches in Touch with God Can Reach a Lost World." Richmond: Southern Baptist International Mission Board, June 09, 1999; available from https://solomon.imb.org; Stories database (accessed September 15, 2004).

Stanley, Bob."Parks Proposes Major Changes to Carry out Global Strategy." Richmond: Southern Baptist Foreign Mission Board, December 10, 1986; available from https://solomon.imb.org; Stories database (accessed September 26, 2004).

Stanley, Brian. "Twentieth-Century World Christianity: A Perspective from the History of Missions." In *Christianity Reborn: The Global Expansion of Evangelicalism in the*

Twentieth Century, ed. Donald M. Lewis. Studies in the History of Christian Mission, eds. R. E. Frykenberg and Brian Stanley, 52-83. Grand Rapids: William B. Eerdmans, 2004.

Status of Global Evangelization. Richmond: Southern Baptist International Mission Board, July 2004.

Steele, Steve and Jim Montgomery. "'Table 71' Creates Most Significant Missiological Advance Since 1974." *Mission Frontiers* (November-December 2002): 9-12.

Stowe, David N. "A New Perspective on the World Christian Mission." *Missiology,* 12, No. 1 (January 1984): 49-54.

Strategic Directions-21 Evaluation Report of the International Mission Board. Richmond: Southern Baptist Foreign Mission Board, September 30, 2003.

Stroope, Michael W. *Cooperative Services International 1992/1993 Statistical Report: Area Director's Narrative Summary.* Richmond: Southern Baptist Foreign Mission Board, September 1993.

________. *Report to the Board: Cooperative Services International.* Richmond: Southern Baptist Foreign Mission Board, Accession Number 1395, December 08, 1993.

________. *Cooperative Services International 1993/1994 Statistical Report: Area Director's Narrative Summary.* Richmond: Southern Baptist Foreign Mission Board, September 1994.

________. *Perspective and Prospects: A Proposal for Avery Willis.* Richmond: Southern Baptist Foreign Mission Board, March 02, 1995.

________. *Report to the Board.* Huntsville, AL: Southern Baptist Foreign Mission Board, Accession Number 1787, April 27, 1995.

________. *CSI Guiding Principles.* London: Cooperative Services International, July 1995.

________. *One Day...Is Today!* Richmond: Southern Baptist Foreign Mission Board, Accession Number 1961, October 10, 1995.

________. *Report to the Board.* Cape Girardeau, MO: Southern Baptist Foreign Mission Board, Accession Number 2338, April 18, 1996.

________. *Taking the Edge All Peoples Nothing Less.* Richmond: Southern Baptist Foreign Mission Board, Accession Number 2464, October 08, 1996.

________. Interview by Keith E. Eitel, February 25, 1998. Transcript Southeastern SBC Historical Missiology Oral History Collection, Southeastern Baptist Theological Seminary, Wake Forest, SC.

________. Interview by author, July 07, 2005. Lexington. Written transcript. Available from the author.

Sweet, Leonard. *Post-Modern Pilgrims.* Nashville: Broadman and Holman, 2000.

Templin, Phil. *Report to the Board.* Louisville, KY: Southern Baptist International Mission Board, Accession Number 2635, September 14, 1998.

The Urbana Heritage: A Brief History of Urbana Conventions. Urbana: Intervarsity, n.d.; available from http://www.urbana.org/_articles.cfm?RecordId+60; Internet (accessed November 22, 2004).

Vision, Objectives, Goals and Principles. London: Cooperative Services International, 1995.

Webb, Leland. "Re-targeting the Planet." Richmond: Southern Baptist Foreign Mission Board, September 01, 1990; available from https://solomon.imb.org; Stories database (accessed September 15, 2004).

Williard, David. "Shaping New Strategies: Adjusting FMB vision in light of World A." *The Commission* (October-November 1991), 38-45.

_______. "Evangelized?" *The Commission* (October-November 1991), 58.

_______. "Shaping New Strategies: Praying Forth the Harvest." *The Commission* (January 1992), 58-63.

_______. "Erecting Foundations in World A." Richmond: Southern Baptist Foreign Mission Board, October 01, 1991; available from https://solomon.imb.org; Stories database (accessed September 28, 2004).

_______. "Q's and A's on World A." Richmond: Southern Baptist Foreign Mission Board, October 01, 1991; available from https://solomon.imb.org; Stories database (accessed September 15, 2004).

_______. "Shaping New Strategies: FMB Reinstates Journeyman Tradition." Richmond: Southern Baptist Foreign Mission Board, April 01, 1993; available from https://solomon.imb.org; Stories database (accessed September 28, 2004).

_______. "World A: Out of the Shadows to Stay." Richmond: Southern Baptist Foreign Mission Board, January 01, 1994; available from https://solomon.imb.org; Stories database (accessed September 28, 2004).

_______. "World A: What it is; How to get there." Richmond: Southern Baptist Foreign Mission Board, January 01, 1994; available from https://solomon.imb.org; Stories database (accessed September 28, 2004).

Willis, Avery T., Jr. *Report to the Board.* Richmond: Southern Baptist Foreign Mission Board, Accession Number 1677, December 12, 1994.

_______. *Report to the Board.* Ridgecrest, NC: Southern Baptist Foreign Mission Board, Accession Number 1922, August 14, 1995.

_______. *Report to the Board.* Memphis: Southern Baptist Foreign Mission Board, Accession Number 2093, December 11, 1995.

_______. *Report to the Board.* Atlanta: Southern Baptist Foreign Mission Board, Accession Number 2438, August 13, 1996.

_______. "The Unfinished Task." In *Missiology: An Introduction to the Foundations, History, and Strategies of World Missions,* eds. John Mark Terry, Ebbie Smith and Justice Anderson, 668-84. Nashville: Broadman and Holman, 1998.

_______. *Report to the Board.* Del City, OK: Southern Baptist International Mission Board, Accession Number 2616, March 19, 1998)

_______. *Report to the Board.* Portland: Southern Baptist International Mission Board, Accession Number 2696, November 06, 2000.

Wilson, J. Christy, Jr. *Today's Tentmakers: Self-support- An Alternative Model for Worldwide Witness.* Wheaton: Tyndale House Publishers, 1979.

Winter, Ralph. "The Highest Priority: Cross-Cultural Evangelism. "In *Let the Earth Hear His Voice: International Congress on World Evangelization Lausanne, Switzerland,* ed. J. D. Douglas, 213- Minneapolis: World Wide Publications, 1975.

_______. "Penetrating New Frontiers." In *Unreached Peoples '79,* eds. C. Peter Wagner and Edward R. Dayton, 37-77. Elgin, IL: David C. Cook Publishing, 1979.

_______. "The New Macedonia: A Revolutionary New Era in Mission Begins." In *Perspectives on the World Christian Movement,* eds. Ralph Winter and Stephen Hawthorne, 301-5. Pasadena: William Carey Library, 1981).

_______. *Thy Kingdom Come: The Story of a Movement.* Pasadena: U.S. Center for World Mission, May 1995; available from http://dawnministries.org/resources/

downloads/download_files/thy_kingdom_come.pdf; Internet (accessed November 21, 2004).

"The Xtreme Team." Richmond: Southern Baptist International Mission Board, 2004; available at http://www.thextremeteam.org.

Yammarori, Ted. *God's New Envoys: A Bold Strategy for Penetrating Closed Countries.* Sisters, OR: Multnomah Press, 1987.

Index

REGNUM EDINBURGH 2010 SERIES
Series Listing

David A. Kerr, Kenneth R. Ross (eds.)
Edinburgh 2010: Mission Then and Now
2009 / 978-1-870345-73-6 / xiv + 343pp (paperback)
2009 / 978-1-870345-76-7 / xiv + 343pp (hardback)

No one can hope to fully understand the modern Christian missionary movement without engaging substantially with the World Missionary Conference, held at Edinburgh in 1910. As the centenary of the Conference approaches, the time is ripe to examine its meaning in light of the past century and the questions facing Christian witness today. This book is the first to systematically examine the eight Commissions which reported to Edinburgh 1910 and gave the conference much of its substance and enduring value. It will deepen and extend the reflection being stimulated by the upcoming centenary and will kindle the missionary imagination for 2010 and beyond.

Daryl M. Balia, Kirsteen Kim (eds.)
Edinburgh 2010: Witnessing to Christ Today
2010 / 978-1-870345-77-4 / xiv +301pp (approx)

This volume, the second in the Edinburgh 2010 series, includes reports of the nine main study groups working on different themes for the celebration of the centenary of the World Missionary Conference, Edinburgh 1910. Their collaborative work brings together perspectives that are as inclusive as possible of contemporary world Christianity and helps readers to grasp what it means in different contexts to be 'witnessing to Christ today'.

REGNUM STUDIES IN GLOBAL CHRISTIANITY
(Previously GLOBAL THEOLOGICAL VOICES series)
Series Listing

David Emmanuuel Singh (ed.)
Jesus and the Cross
Reflections of Christians from Islamic Contexts
2008 / 978-1-870345-65-1 / x + 226pp

The Cross reminds us that the sins of the world are not borne through the exercise of power but through Jesus Christ's submission to the will of the Father. The papers in this volume are organised in three parts: scriptural, contextual and theological. The central question being addressed is: how do Christians living in contexts, where Islam is a majority or minority religion, experience, express or think of the Cross? This is, therefore, an exercise in listening. As the contexts from where these engagements arise are varied, the papers in drawing scriptural, contextual and theological reflections offer a cross-section of Christian thinking about Jesus and the Cross.

Sung-wook Hong
Naming God in Korea
The Case of Protestant Christianity
2008 / 978-1-870345-66-8 / xiv + 170pp

Since Christianity was introduced to Korea more than a century ago, one of the most controversial issue has been the Korean term for the Christian 'God'. This issue is not merely about naming the Christian God in Korean language, but it relates to the question of theological contextualization—the relationship between the gospel and culture—and the question of Korean Christian identity. This book examines the theological contextualization of the concept of 'God' in the contemporary Korean context and applies the translatability of Christianity to that context. It also demonstrates the nature of the gospel in relation to cultures, i.e., the universality of the gospel expressed in all human cultures.

Hubert van Beek (ed.)
Revisioning Christian Unity
The Global Christian Forum
2009 / 978-1-870345-74-3 / xx + 288pp

This book contains the records of the Global Christian Forum gathering held in Limuru near Nairobi, Kenya, on 6 – 9 November 2007 as well as the papers presented at that historic event. Also included are a summary of the Global Christian Forum process from its inception until the 2007 gathering and the reports of the evaluation of the process that was carried out in 2008.

Paul Hang-Sik Cho

Eschatology and Ecology

The Case of the Protestant Church in Korea

2010 / 978-1-870345-75-0/

This book raises the question of why Korean people, and Korean Protestant Christians in particular, pay so little attention (in theory or practice) to ecological issues. The author argues that there is an important connection (or elective affinity) between this lack of attention and the other-worldly eschatology that is so dominant within Korean Protestant Christianity. Dispensational premillennialism, originally imported by American missionaries, resonated with traditional religious beliefs in Korea and soon came to dominate much of Korean Protestantism. This book argues that this, of all forms of millennialism, is the most damaging to ecological concerns.

REGNUM STUDIES IN MISSION
Series Listing

Kwame Bediako

Theology and Identity

The Impact of Culture upon Christian Thought in the Second Century and in Modern Africa

1992 / 1-870345-10-X / xviii + 508pp

The author examines the question of Christian identity in the context of the Graeco–Roman culture of the early Roman Empire. He then addresses the modern African predicament of quests for identity and integration.

Christopher Sugden

Seeking the Asian Face of Jesus

The Practice and Theology of Christian Social Witness in Indonesia and India 1974–1996

1997 / 1-870345-26-6 / xx + 496pp

This study focuses on contemporary holistic mission with the poor in India and Indonesia combined with the call to transformation of all life in Christ with micro-credit enterprise schemes. 'The literature on contextual theology now has a new standard to rise to' – Lamin Sanneh (Yale University, USA).

Hwa Yung

Mangoes or Bananas?

The Quest for an Authentic Asian Christian Theology

1997 / 1-870345-25-8 / xii + 274pp

Asian Christian thought remains largely captive to Greek dualism and Enlightenment rationalism because of the overwhelming dominance of Western culture. Authentic contextual Christian theologies will emerge within Asian Christianity with a dual recovery of confidence in culture and the gospel.

Keith E. Eitel

Paradigm Wars

1999 / 1-870345-12-6 / x + 140pp

The Southern Baptist International Mission Board Faces the Third Millennium

The International Mission Board of the Southern Baptist Convention is the largest denominational mission agency in North America. This volume chronicles the historic and contemporary forces that led to the IMB's recent extensive reorganization, providing the most comprehensive case study to date of a historic mission agency restructuring to continue its mission purpose into the twenty-first century more effectively.

Samuel Jayakumar

Dalit Consciousness and Christian Conversion

Historical Resources for a Contemporary Debate

1999 / 81-7214-497-0 / xxiv + 434pp

(Published jointly with ISPCK)

The main focus of this historical study is social change and transformation among the Dalit Christian communities in India. Historiography tests the evidence in the light of the conclusions of the modern Dalit liberation theologians.

Vinay Samuel and Christopher Sugden (eds.)

Mission as Transformation

A Theology of the Whole Gospel

1999/ 0870345133/522pp

This book brings together in one volume twenty five years of biblical reflection on mission practice with the poor from around the world. The approach of holistic mission, which integrates proclamation, evangelism, church planting and social transformation seamlessly as a whole, has been adopted since 1983 by most evangelical development agencies, most indigenous mission agencies and many Pentecostal churches. This volume helps anyone understand how evangelicals, struggling to unite evangelism and social action, found their way in the last twenty five years to the biblical view of mission in which God calls all human beings to love God and their neighbour; never creating a separation between the two.

Christopher Sugden

Gospel, Culture and Transformation

2000 / 1-870345-32-0 / viii + 152pp

A Reprint, with a New Introduction, of Part Two of Seeking the Asian Face of Jesus

Gospel, Culture and Transformation explores the practice of mission especially in relation to transforming cultures and communities. - 'Transformation is to enable God's vision of society to be actualised in all relationships: social, economic and spiritual, so that God's will may be reflected in human society and his love experienced by all communities, especially the poor.'

Bernhard Ott

Beyond Fragmentation: Integrating Mission and Theological Education

A Critical Assessment of some Recent Developments in Evangelical Theological Education

2001 / 1-870345-14-2 / xxviii + 382pp

Beyond Fragmentation is an enquiry into the development of Mission Studies in evangelical theological education in Germany and German-speaking Switzerland between 1960 and 1995. The author undertakes a detailed examination of the paradigm shifts which have taken place in recent years in both the theology of mission and the understanding of theological education.

Gideon Githiga

The Church as the Bulwark against Authoritarianism

Development of Church and State Relations in Kenya, with Particular Reference to the Years after Political Independence 1963-1992

2002 / 1-870345-38-X / xviii + 218pp

'All who care for love, peace and unity in Kenyan society will want to read this careful history by Bishop Githiga of how Kenyan Christians, drawing on the Bible, have sought to share the love of God, bring his peace and build up the unity of the nation, often in the face of great difficulties and opposition.' Canon Dr Chris Sugden, Oxford Centre for Mission Studies.

Myung Sung-Hoon, Hong Young-Gi (eds.)

Charis and Charisma

David Yonggi Cho and the Growth of Yoido Full Gospel Church

2003 / 1-870345-45-2 / xxii + 218pp

This book discusses the factors responsible for the growth of the world's largest church. It expounds the role of the Holy Spirit, the leadership, prayer, preaching, cell groups and creativity in promoting church growth. It focuses on God's grace (charis) and inspiring leadership (charisma) as the two essential factors and the book's purpose is to present a model for church growth worldwide.

Samuel Jayakumar

Mission Reader

Historical Models for Wholistic Mission in the Indian Context

2003 / 1-870345-42-8 / x + 250pp

(Published jointly with ISPCK)

This book is written from an evangelical point of view revalidating and reaffirming the Christian commitment to wholistic mission. The roots of the 'wholistic mission' combining 'evangelism and social concerns' are to be located in the history and tradition of Christian evangelism in the past; and the civilizing purpose of evangelism is compatible with modernity as an instrument in nation building.

Bob Robinson

Christians Meeting Hindus

An Analysis and Theological Critique of the Hindu-Christian Encounter in India

2004 / 1-870345-39-8 / xviii + 392pp

This book focuses on the Hindu-Christian encounter, especially the intentional meeting called dialogue, mainly during the last four decades of the twentieth century, and specifically in India itself.

Gene Early

Leadership Expectations

How Executive Expectations are Created and Used in a Non-Profit Setting

2005 / 1-870345-30-4 / xxiv + 276pp

The author creates an Expectation Enactment Analysis to study the role of the Chancellor of the University of the Nations-Kona, Hawaii. This study is grounded in the field of managerial work, jobs, and behaviour and draws on symbolic interactionism, role theory, role identity theory and enactment theory. The result is a conceptual framework for developing an understanding of managerial roles.

Tharcisse Gatwa

The Churches and Ethnic Ideology in the Rwandan Crises 1900-1994

2005 / 1-870345-24-X / approx 300pp

Since the early years of the twentieth century Christianity has become a new factor in Rwandan society. This book investigates the role Christian churches played in the formulation and development of the racial ideology that culminated in the 1994 genocide.

Julie Ma

Mission Possible

Biblical Strategies for Reaching the Lost

2005 / 1-870345-37-1 / xvi + 142pp

This is a missiology book for the church which liberates missiology from the specialists for the benefit of every believer. It also serves as a textbook that is simple and friendly, and yet solid in biblical interpretation. This book links the biblical teaching to the actual and contemporary missiological settings with examples, making the Bible come alive to the reader.

Allan Anderson, Edmond Tang (eds.)

Asian and Pentecostal

The Charismatic Face of Christianity in Asia

2005 / 1-870345-43-6 / xiv + 596pp

(Published jointly with APTS Press)

This book provides a thematic discussion and pioneering case studies on the history and development of Pentecostal and Charismatic churches in the countries of South Asia, South East Asia and East Asia.

I. Mark Beaumont

Christology in Dialogue with Muslims

A Critical Analysis of Christian Presentations of Christ for Muslims from the Ninth and Twentieth Centuries

2005 / 1-870345-46-0 / xxvi + 228pp

This book analyses Christian presentations of Christ for Muslims in the most creative periods of Christian-Muslim dialogue, the first half of the ninth century and the second half of the twentieth century. In these two periods, Christians made serious attempts to present their faith in Christ in terms that take into account Muslim perceptions of him, with a view to bridging the gap between Muslim and Christian convictions.

Thomas Czövek,

Three Seasons of Charismatic Leadership

A Literary-Critical and Theological Interpretation of the Narrative of Saul, David and Solomon

2006 / 978-1-870345484 / 272pp

This book investigates the charismatic leadership of Saul, David and Solomon. It suggests that charismatic leaders emerge in crisis situations in order to resolve the crisis by the charisma granted by God. Czovek argues that Saul proved himself as a charismatic leader as long as he acted resolutely and independently from his mentor Samuel. In the author's eyes, Saul's failure to establish himself as a charismatic leader is caused by his inability to step out from Samuel's shadow.

Jemima Atieno Oluoch

The Christian Political Theology of Dr. John Henry Okullu

2006 / 1-870345-51-7 / xx + 137pp

This book reconstructs the Christian political theology of Bishop John Henry Okullu, DD, through establishing what motivated him and the biblical basis for his socio-political activities. It also attempts to reconstruct the socio-political environment that nurtured Dr Okullu's prophetic ministry.

Richard Burgess

Nigeria's Christian Revolution

The Civil War Revival and Its Pentecostal Progeny (1967-2006)

2008 / 978-1-870345-63-7 / xxii + 347pp

This book describes the revival that occurred among the Igbo people of Eastern Nigeria and the new Pentecostal churches it generated, and documents the changes that have occurred as the movement has responded to global flows and local demands. As such, it explores the nature of revivalist and Pentecostal experience, but does so against the backdrop of local socio-political and economic developments, such as decolonisation and civil war, as well as broader processes, such as modernisation and globalisation.

David Emmanuel Singh & Bernard C Farr (eds.)
Christianity and Cultures
Shaping Christian Thinking in Context
2008 / 978-1-870345-69-9 / x + 260pp

This volume marks an important milestone, the 25th anniversary of the Oxford Centre for Mission Studies (OCMS). The papers here have been exclusively sourced from Transformation, a quarterly journal of OCMS, and seek to provide a tripartite view of Christianity's engagement with cultures by focusing on the question: how is Christian thinking being formed or reformed through its interaction with the varied contexts it encounters? The subject matters include different strands of theological-missiological thinking, socio-political engagements and forms of family relationships in interaction with the host cultures.

Tormod Engelsviken, Ernst Harbakk, Rolv Olsen, Thor Strandenæs (eds.)
Mission to the World
Communicating the Gospel in the 21st Century:
Essays in Honour of Knud Jørgensen
2008 / 978-1-870345-64-4 / 472pp

Knud Jørgensen is Director of Areopagos and Associate Professor of Missiology at MF Norwegian School of Theology. This book reflects on the main areas of Jørgensen's commitment to mission. At the same time it focuses on the main frontier of mission, the world, the content of mission, the Gospel, the fact that the Gospel has to be communicated, and the context of contemporary mission in the 21st century.

Al Tizon
Transformation after Lausanne
Radical Evangelical Mission in Global-Local Perspective
2008 / 978-1-870345-68-2 / xx + 281pp

After Lausanne '74, a worldwide network of radical evangelical mission theologians and practitioners use the notion of "Mission as Transformation" to integrate evangelism and social concern together, thus lifting theological voices from the Two Thirds World to places of prominence. This book documents the definitive gatherings, theological tensions, and social forces within and without evangelicalism that led up to Mission as Transformation. And it does so through a global-local grid that points the way toward greater holistic mission in the 21st century.

Bambang Budijanto

Values and Participation

Development in Rural Indonesia

2009 / 978-1-870345-70-5 / x + 237pp

Socio-religious values and socio-economic development are inter-dependant, inter-related and are constantly changing in the context of macro political structures, economic policy, religious organizations and globalization; and micro influences such as local affinities, identity, politics, leadership and beliefs. The three Lopait communities in Central Java, Indonesia provide an excellent model of the rich and complex negotiations and interactions among all the above factors. The book argues that the comprehensive approach in understanding the socio-religious values of each local community is essential to accurately describing their respective identity which will help institutions and agencies, both governmental and non-governmental, to relate to these communities with dignity and respect.

Young-hoon Lee

The Holy Spirit Movement in Korea

Its Historical and Theological Development

2009 / 978-1-870345-67-5 / x + 174pp

This book traces the historical and theological development of the Holy Spirit Movement in Korea through six successive periods (from 1900 to the present time). These periods are characterized by repentance and revival (1900-20), persecution and suffering under Japanese occupation (1920-40), confusion and division (1940-60), explosive revival in which the Pentecostal movement played a major role in the rapid growth of Korean churches (1960-80), the movement reaching out to all denominations (1980-2000), and the new context demanding the Holy Spirit movement to open new horizons in its mission engagement (2000-). The volume also discusses the relationship between this movement and other religions such as shamanism, and looks forward to further engagement with issues of concern in wider society.

Alan R. Johnson

Leadership in a Slum

A Bangkok Case Study

2009 / 978-1-870345-71-2 xx + 238pp

This book looks at leadership in the social context of a slum in Bangkok from an angle different from traditional studies which measure well educated Thais on leadership scales derived in the West. Using both systematic data collection and participant observation, it develops a culturally preferred model as well as a set of models based in Thai concepts that reflect on-the-ground realities. This work challenges the dominance of the patron-client rubric for understanding all forms of Thai leadership and offers a view for understanding leadership rooted in local social systems, contrary to approaches that assume the universal applicability of leadership research findings across all cultural settings. It concludes by looking at the implications of the anthropological approach for those who are involved in leadership training in Thai settings and beyond.

Titre Ande

Leadership and Authority

Bula Matari and Life - Community Ecclesiology in Congo

2010 / 978-1-870345-72-9 xvii + 189pp

This book proposes that Christian theology in Africa can make significant developments if a critical understanding of the socio-political context in contemporary Africa is taken seriously. The Christian leadership in post-colonial Africa has cloned its understanding and use of authority on the Bula Matari model, which was issued from the brutality of colonialism and political absolutism in post-colonial Africa. This model has caused many problems in churches, including dysfunction, conflicts, divisions and a lack of prophetic ministry. Titre proposes a Life-Community ecclesiology for liberating authority, where leadership is a function, not a status, and 'apostolic succession' belongs to all the people of God.

Frank Kwesi Adams

Odwira and the Gospel

A Study of the Asante Odwira Festival and its Significance for Christianity in Ghana

2010/978-1-870345-59-0

The study of the Odwira festival is the key to the understanding of Asante religious and political life in Ghana. The book explores the nature of the Odwira festival longitudinally - in pre-colonial, colonial and post-independence Ghana - and examines the Odwira ideology and its implications for understanding the Asante self-identity. The book also discusses how some elements of faith portrayed in the Odwira festival could provide a framework for Christianity to engage with Asante culture at a greater depth. Theological themes in Asante belief that have emerged from this study include the theology of sacrament, ecclesiology, eschatology, Christology and a complex concept of time. The author argues that Asante cultural identity lies at the heart of the process by which the Asante Christian faith is carried forward.

Bruce Carlton

Strategy Coordinator

Changing the Course of Southern Baptist Missions

2010/ 978-1-870345-78-1 *xvii + 268pp*

In 1976, the Southern Baptist Convention adopted its Bold New Thrusts in Foreign Missions with the overarching goal of sharing the gospel with every person in the world by the year 2000. The formation of Cooperative Services International (CSI) in 1985 and the assigning of the first non-residential missionary (NRM) in 1987 demonstrated the Foreign Mission Board's (now International Mission Board) commitment to take the gospel message to countries that restricted traditional missionary presence and to people groups identified as having little or no access to the gospel. Carlton traces the historical development along with an analysis of the key components of the paradigm and its significant impact on Southern Baptists' missiology.

OTHER REGNUM TITLES

Vinay Samuel, Chris Sugden (eds.)
The Church in Response to Human Need
1987 / 1870345045 / xii+268pp

Philip Sampson, Vinay Samuel, Chris Sugden (eds.)
Faith and Modernity
Essays in modernity and post-modernity
1994 / 1870345177 / 352pp

Klaus Fiedler
The Story of Faith Missions
1994 / 0745926878 / 428pp

Douglas Peterson
Not by Might nor by Power
A Pentecostal Theology of Social Concern in Latin America
1996 / 1870345207 / xvi+260pp

David Gitari
In Season and Out of Season
Sermons to a Nation
1996 / 1870345118 / 155pp

David. W. Virtue
A Vision of Hope
The Story of Samuel Habib
1996 / 1870345169 / xiv+137pp

Everett A Wilson
Strategy of the Spirit
J.Philip Hogan and the Growth of the Assemblies of God Worldwide, 1960 - 1990
1997/1870345231/214

Murray Dempster, Byron Klaus, Douglas Petersen (eds.)
The Globalization of Pentecostalism
A Religion Made to Travel
1999 / 1870345290 / xvii+406pp

Peter Johnson, Chris Sugden (eds.)
Markets, Fair Trade and the Kingdom of God
Essays to Celebrate Traidcraft's 21st Birthday
2001 / 1870345193 / xii+155pp

Deryke Belshaw, Robert Calderisi, Chris Sugden (eds.)
Faith in Development
Partnership Between the World Bank and the Churches of Africa
2001 / 978-0821348482 / *246pp*

Robert Hillman, Coral Chamberlain, Linda Harding
Healing & Wholeness
Reflections on the Healing Ministry
2002 / 978-1- 870345-35- 4 / xvii+283pp

David Bussau, Russell Mask
Christian Microenterprise Development
An Introduction
2003 / 1870345282 / xiii+142pp

David Singh
Sainthood and Revelatory Discourse
An Examination of the Basis for the Authority of Bayan in Mahdawi Islam
2003 / 8172147285 / xxiv+485pp

For the up-to-date listing of the Regnum books see www.ocms.ac.uk/regnum

regnum

Regnum Books International

Regnum is an Imprint of The Oxford Centre for Mission Studies
St. Philip and St. James Church
Woodstock Road
Oxford, OX2 6HR
Web: www.ocms.ac.uk/regnum